Demetrios Matheou is a London-based journalist and writer. He is the film critic for the *Sunday Herald* in Scotland, and also writes about film for the *Independent on Sunday*, the *Guardian*, *Observer* and *Sight & Sound*. He contributed the eponymous entry of Faber's *Ten Bad Dates with De Niro*.

# The Faber Book of
# New South American Cinema

## DEMETRIOS MATHEOU

*faber and faber*

First published in 2010
by Faber and Faber Limited
Bloomsbury House
74–77 Great Russell Street
London WC1B 3DA

Typeset by Faber and Faber
Printed in the UK by CPI Mackays, Chatham ME5 8TD

A CIP record for this book
is available from the British Library

ISBN 978–0–571–23179–9

2 4 6 8 10 9 7 5 3 1

for Sylvia

# Contents

# Introduction

This book is very much concerned with 'personal' film-making – with directors who tell stories true to their experience, unencumbered by genre or tradition, often working in adversity and sometimes with their own money, yet always filming from the heart. So it seems apt to start on a personal note, and say how I found myself on this particular journey – one inspired by a road movie and which required my very own road trip, literal and metaphorical, around a continent.

The seed was planted not in South America, but Central America. In 1995 I was about to redirect my journalistic compass from architecture to cinema, but wanted first to do some gallivanting. Thus I found myself in Guatemala City, staying with a reporter friend who was covering that volatile period in the country's history. This was a time when the battle between the government and guerrillas was raging with some ferocity, while in the towns and cities foreigners were kidnapped on a regular basis – sometimes for political reasons, sometimes financial, often a combination of the two. My intrepid friend discovered this for herself: having cornered the controversial editor of a right-wing newspaper for an interview – in a jacuzzi – she subsequently found a photo of her car, number plates clearly visible, published in his newspaper under the headline, 'Who is the mystery blonde?' It was a tip-off to any self-motivating kidnapper that a price would be paid for her abduction. She bought a new car. And she eventually returned to a quieter life in London, where, serendipitously, she offered me my first film column.

Before I left Guatemala City for the interior, my friend gave me a copy of *The Motorcycle Diaries*, Ernesto Guevara's memoir of his first, formative trip around South America. I read it on my travels through a country that 'Che' had also visited: it shared many of the iniquities of those countries in the south, and his experience of it contributed to the forging of his political consciousness. And as I journeyed up to the villages of Guatemala's Western Highlands, high on a plateau, and encountered the indigenous Indians who lived there, in some of the most abject poverty I'd seen, Guevara's accounts of his experiences in Argentina, Chile and Peru struck an obvious chord. The people he described in his diaries had also been abused and betrayed by European colonists: they too had been dispossessed.

*The Motorcycle Diaries* had only recently been published, the manuscript having been found several years after the revolutionary's death. My copy was a gorgeous hardback, containing photographs of Guevara, his friend Alberto Granado and their accident-prone bike, The Mighty One – pictures that evoked their spirit of adventure and growing awareness of the world in which they lived. I almost lost that copy in Belize, when I ignored my gut instinct and accepted an invitation from a couple of impossibly smiley strangers to accompany them on an island jaunt in their rickety canoe, which promptly sank like a stone, twenty metres from the shore: as I swam back, my new friends shrugging underwater, it was with one arm aloft, determinedly keeping 'Che' dry.

Fast forward to 2001. I was interviewing the Brazilian director Walter Salles. Salles had been at the forefront of Brazil's *retomada da produção*, the rebirth of the country's cinema in the mid-nineties, after a period in which it had been crushed by a hostile government. When Salles' *Central do Brasil* (*Central Station*) won the Golden Bear in Berlin in 1998, it alerted international audiences that Brazilian cinema had come back to life.

While talking to Salles, ostensibly about his new film *Abril despedaçado* (*Behind the Sun*, 2001), hearing of his next project sparked my curiosity (and multiplied my admiration): he was planning to adapt *The Motorcycle Diaries* for the screen. Salles

Rediscovering Brazil: Walter Salles' *Central Station* (1998)

spoke briefly of his intention to take the exact journey made by Guevara and Granado: from Buenos Aires, across Argentina to Chile, then Peru. I did not waste a second, declaring my allegiance to the spirit of the diaries and requesting that I accompany them on their trip. Salles asked me if I spoke Portuguese. No. Spanish? Well, not exactly. Considering my inability to converse with what he intended to be a Latin American crew, and perhaps considering the ill-living hack opposite him as unable to endure the hardships he knew lay ahead, he politely declined. So I was left to wait eagerly in the wings for the finished film – but in any case, it seemed inevitable that our paths would cross again.

And so it proved. In 2005 I was discussing possible projects with Walter Donohue at Faber, and mentioned Salles, when he immediately returned, 'How about South America?' By that time the case for there being a Latin American revival – described as the *buena onda*, the good wave – had been indelibly made by a quartet of critical and box-office successes: *Central Station*, the Mexican pair *Amores perros* (by Alejandro González Iñárritu, 2000) and *Y tu mamá también* (Alfonso Cuarón, 2001), and *Cidade de Deus* (*City of God*, 2002), by Salles' fellow Brazilian

Fernando Meirelles. There had also been a sudden surge of work by gifted Argentine directors, including Pablo Trapero, Lucrecia Martel and Daniel Burman, film-makers bristling with originality and verve, with Fabián Bielinsky's dazzling conman movie *Nueve reinas* (*Nine Queens*, 2000) proving one of the most successful international art-house hits of its year. And in 2004 *Diarios de motocicleta* (*The Motorcycle Diaries*), the truly continental, Latin American film Salles had envisaged, had been released to universal acclaim.

Argentine trailblazer: Fabián Bielinsky's *Nine Queens* (2000)

These films were performing on a number of levels: at home they were attracting excellent audiences, rejuvenating interest in quality local films; they were winning awards at home and abroad; and they were making an impression, especially the Brazilian and Mexican films, on overseas audiences.

Nevertheless, my first reaction was muted. For a start, it seemed like awfully hard work. More than that, I was unsure if there was a substantive reason – beyond the 'wave' identified, like all such waves, by film festivals and journalists – for bringing together a continent's work. Ask a French, German or English director to take part in a book on 'European cinema' and you'd probably get short shrift. Admittedly there had been, in the sixties and seventies, a New Latin American Cinema movement bonded by left-wing political agendas and shared cinematic forms (only to be snuffed out by the dictatorships that stained the continent). But what, if anything, did the contemporary filmmakers in these countries have in common, beyond a land mass and, with the exception of the Brazilians, a language?

But Donohue hadn't pulled the idea out of a hat, and he suggested I have a chat with Salles – 'See if he will make you think differently.' Could the two Walters be conspiring together, I wondered? Donohue seemed to know that Salles and I had a destination in common within weeks: the Karlovy Vary film festival in the Czech Republic. I gave the director a call and arranged to meet, at the grandiose, chocolate-boxy Hotel Pup: thousands of miles and a cultural quantum leap from the *Pampas*, the *sertão*, the Amazon or the Andes – but one brief conversation there would point me towards South America.

So why a book on South American cinema? First, one should draw attention to the fact that I do not deal with work from Cuba, Central America or Mexico, just this very continent-specific part of the Latin renaissance. There is a mundane reason for this – Faber published a book on Mexican cinema in 2007 – but also a profound one, which goes to the heart of the project.

Brazil is not the only South American country to have enjoyed a cinematic renaissance since the mid-nineties. Argentina, the other historically major film producer on the continent, also returned to life at the same time, leading to what is now known as the *nuevo cine argentino*, New Argentine Cinema. A very young generation of Chilean directors, many working in digital, has since begun to make its presence felt. And Uruguay, Peru, Colombia and Venezuela are among those, at the time of writing, in the midst of reconstructing their film industries.

Crucially, their collective re-emergence goes hand in hand with the emergence from years of adversity of the countries themselves. South Americans, and therefore South American filmmakers, are united by patterns of experience: first colonialism, whose mark in terms of inequitable societies across the continent is still visible; latterly, for most, bloody and repressive military dictatorships, followed by inept and corrupt civilian governments, and economic crisis. Cinema has been buffeted between these negative forces, its voice censored, sometimes its productivity halted altogether.

Brazil's experience is complicated. During twenty-one years of military dictatorship, between 1964 and 1985, the state imposed censorship on cinematic output, yet also supported a vast level of production, even ensuring local exhibition (a rarity anywhere outside Hollywood and Bollywood). Of course, having an all-powerful, state-run film body was another means of control, and the overall quality in this period may be summed up by the popular *pornchinchadas*, or soft-porn musicals. Yet a few directors managed to make excellent films (some containing sly, leftish critiques of the regime), including Brazil's most successful ever film, Bruno Barreto's *Dona Flor e seus dois maridos* (*Dona Flor and Her Two Husbands*, 1976) and Hector Babenco's seminal *Pixote* (1981). In contrast, within a few years of democracy the country was in economic tatters and the government, with startling and targeted antipathy, withdrew all state support from Brazilian films, leading Babenco to declare in 1991 that 'Brazilian cinema is dead'.

Similarly, in Argentina, relief at the end of the *guerra sucia*, the Dirty War (1976–83), was short-lived, as the country entered a long and devastating period of neo-liberalism, then recession, leading to the biggest economic crisis in its history. And the film industry suffered accordingly. Over the Andes, in Chile, Augusto Pinochet's highly repressive regime (1973–90) numbered filmmakers among its three thousand dead, with others, among them Raoul Ruiz, going into exile. With film schools occupied by the military, there's no wonder that in 1990 Chilean cinema was effectively starting from scratch.

As one looks around the continent, there are variations on this theme: fear followed by disappointment, censorship by impoverishment, cinemas closing everywhere, all the while Hollywood insinuating itself into those that remained. Today we can see that a different kind of wave – of democracies, some left-leaning, all independent of the West and its economic models – has washed over South America, accompanied by gradual economic stability. This has effectively given the current generation of filmmakers two things their predecessors didn't have: freedom, and possibility. At the same time, the trials endured from the seventies to the turn of the new millennium – emotional, psychological, financial, artistic, and for some involving the most terrible personal loss – continue to inform the continent's cinema, while the ongoing social injustices and readjustments offer an endless stream of material.

As Salles told *Screen International* in 2004, at the release of *The Motorcycle Diaries*:

The new wave is not random. I think it has to do with the re-democratisation process that occurred on our continent. If you think that twenty-five years ago we could hardly express ourselves. Brazil was living in a military dictatorship, so was Argentina. How could you have a strong national cinema if you could not express yourself? Well now we can.

And why is this cinema so interesting? Because I don't think we are countries whose identities have been fully crystallised yet. Our films somehow capture these societies in movement, they capture these societies as they are finding themselves.

If the state was responsible for cinema's decline, the state also, in part, began its repair. New governments in Brazil and Argentina led the way in the mid-nineties by introducing film laws: Brazil's involving tax shelters that encouraged private investment in local films, Argentina's to bolster its eroded system of state subsidies. Argentina also saw a proliferation of state-run film schools that were to be a breeding ground for New Argentine

Cinema. Other countries followed suit to varying degrees – notably, of late, Colombia and Venezuela, with the latter making perhaps the most grandiose declaration of intent, president Hugo Chávez himself encouraging the establishment of a state-owned film studio.

But while various forms of state assistance have undoubtedly helped to boost the continent's cinematic output, such systems do not tend to favour new, young and adventurous directors. And I would argue that in the first ten years of this South American film revival – most notable, thus far, in Brazil, Argentina and Chile – much of the most personal and dynamic cinema, not least the films with the quality and resonance to reach out to international audiences, has been a result of the determination and pragmatism of the film-makers themselves.

There are different manifestations of this self-empowerment. In Brazil, the directors Walter Salles, Fernando Meirelles and Andrucha Waddington, having established strong careers in the eighties and early nineties through, variously, television, documentary, commercials and music videos, met the *retomada* with independent production companies ready to make films (see 'Letter from Rio'), astutely utilising the fledgling film laws and, once *Central Station* had woken people up, overseas investment.

At the other end of the spectrum, Pablo Trapero in Argentina and Andrés Wood in Chile both made their first features with little experience behind them, and without state assistance – shooting with friends, borrowing equipment, everyone effectively film-making for free. They were leaping into the unknown. And the results were formative: Trapero's *Mundo grúa* (*Crane World*, 1999) is now regarded as a classic of New Argentine Cinema, while Wood's modest *Historias de fútbol* (*Football Stories*, 1997) gained him invaluable experience for his second film, *Machuca* (2004), one of the signature features of the Chilean revival.

Where directors in other parts of the world might sit impatiently waiting for lottery funding, or their $40-million studio production deal – because, hey, they can't possibly do it for a dollar less – this book relates countless tales of South American directors doing whatever they have to do to turn the cameras: whether it is Lisandro Alonso shooting his marvellous debut *La libertad* (*Freedom*, 2001) on the family farm or – amazingly, given the scale of it – Meirelles dipping into his own pocket to get *City of God* on the road. When Argentina's banks closed their doors, on the eve of his second film, Pablo Trapero and his friends did a quick round of the ATMs, and started filming with the cash in their pockets. One is reminded of an apocryphal anecdote of Babenco's, in which he claimed that one of his early films drew the unwelcome attention of the death squads. What did he do? 'We made them co-producers of the movie.'

If Babenco ironically sums up the pragmatism that always stands Latin film-makers in good stead, Josué Méndez, a very young Peruvian director who completed his second film, *Dioses*, in 2008, epitomises the heart. 'It takes so much time to make films, so much effort, that you can only make them if there's an urgency that goes beyond reason,' he says. There is certainly something in the blood here.

I am romanticising, to a degree. And there have been other incredibly important factors in this recent flowering of South American cinema. Robert Redford's Sundance Institute has been influential, with initiatives including script workshops and, with the Japanese Broadcasting Corporation, the Sundance/NHK International Film-makers Award, whose recipients have included some of the key movies of the past decade, from *Central Station* in 1998, to Martel's *La ciénaga* (*The Swamp*, 2001) and the Uruguayan *Whisky* (2004). The Hubert Bals Fund, which is associated with the Rotterdam Film Festival and has been funding films from developing countries since 1988, has favoured Argentine films in particular, and is a home from home for Lisandro Alonso. Since 1997 Ibermedia, a multi-million-dollar film fund for Spain, Portugal and Latin America, has contributed to the budgets of dozens of films.

Recognition from the A-list festivals, not just in awarding

prizes, but through selecting films in the first place, has also helped to raise the international sales potential of the continent's films. Nevertheless, film-makers taking control of their fate – many as producer-directors, all with a highly tuned awareness of overseas grants and the need for co-production strategies – will be a central theme of the interviews reproduced here, as will be the willingness to collaborate. In Brazil there is a positively heart-warming network of collaboration and patronage: with his company VideoFilmes in Rio de Janeiro, Salles has helped to launch the careers of a number of directors, notably Katia Lund, Karim Ainouz and Sérgio Machado, who in return have formed an integral part of his own circle of advisers and collaborators; Fernando Meirelles, from his O2 Filmes power base in São Paulo, has nurtured cinematographer César Charlone (a Uruguayan who in 2007 directed his first film, *El baño del Papa*, in his own country, produced by Meirelles), writer Bráulio Mantovani, director Cao Hamburger and editor Daniel Rezende, among others. In Argentina, Trapero and Daniel Burman – the two young tyros of New Argentine Cinema – also have their own production companies, with which they now support the careers of others. Whenever I ask a South American director to recommend someone they admire, they always reply, tellingly, not with one name, but a list.

Moreover, the networks are increasingly continental, and varied. Both Salles and Andrés Wood – a Brazilian and a Chilean – have produced Trapero's films in Argentina. The Uruguayan actor Daniel Hendler regularly crosses the border to Argentina to appear as Burman's screen alter ego, while the Uruguayan director Manuel Nieto Zas works as an assistant director for Lisandro Alonso. When Salles was on the road with my totem movie, *The Motorcycle Diaries*, he liaised with production companies in Argentina, Peru and Chile.

There remain many galling problems and obstacles: the struggle against the dominant Hollywood fare for local distribution, leading to a perennial paucity of market share, and therefore difficulty in recouping one's budget; poor local economies, along with the loss of thousands of cinemas (the most ubiquitous new use being as evangelical churches), affecting cinema attendances overall. Frequently, too, there has been an appallingly low level of distribution across the continent – in what one might have assumed, with the possible exception of Portuguese-speaking Brazil, were natural markets. Again, exhibitors often prefer to block-book a Hollywood blockbuster across their screens: the film at the top of the Argentine box office in 2007 was *The Simpsons Movie*, followed by *Shrek the Third*, *Pirates of the Caribbean 3*, *Harry Potter and the Order of the Phoenix* and *Spiderman 3*, with *Spiderman* snatching top spot in Brazil.

It's a very strange state of affairs when the most successful Brazilian and Argentine films make more money in European cinemas than they do in those of their neighbouring countries; and when, say, a Chilean director will admit to having discovered the work of his Argentine and Brazilian peers not in Santiago, but in European festivals, or through pirated DVDs and illegal downloads. That is why the criss-crossing liaisons are so important, both practically (only films with co-production partners from different countries can apply for Ibermedia funding, for example) and personally. As Trapero says:

For me, doing co-productions is not just a way of searching for money, but of finding a way to exchange ideas. Although Chile is different to Argentina, Argentina is different to Brazil, we have more things in common than people might think, living their lives in Buenos Aires or Santiago. Films help us see what is happening elsewhere on our continent, and help to develop our thinking in terms of what it means, today, to be Latin American. In my case, I trust the strength here. It's a young continent, and I love the energy that you can feel.

Burman, who was one of the local producers assisting Walter Salles on *The Motorcycle Diaries*, shares this view. 'That was one of the most important experiences in my life,' he recalls. 'Walter has a pan-regional vision of cinema and an incredibly stimulating way of going about the process of filming. And I agree with him: even though it is very difficult to establish stronger cinematographic links among Latin American countries, due to the current circumstances, it is, without a doubt, the future of our cinema.'

What of the films themselves? The work featured here is not bound together by formal aesthetic or political agendas, but by timing and circumstance: of countries emerging from heinous periods in their history, and directors desperate to start making movies again, with extraordinary material on their doorsteps. This book reflects this common ground, and an auteur cinema not prompted, but informed by social conscience, resulting in remarkably diverse film-making.

As Salles suggested, curiosity about identity – personal, national, continental – courses through the work. While some of these countries could have been accused in the past of being culturally Eurocentric (Buenos Aires is, after all, the 'Paris of the South'), the gaze is now more determinedly inward. The directors covered here are driven by the desire to look at their countries in the here and now: to take their stories from life on the streets and the pages of the newspapers, to consider what it means to be Argentine, Brazilian, Chilean, Uruguayan, Peruvian, with a keen desire to show, more often than not, a quotidian reality, and to consider where their countrymen and women find themselves – socially and economically – after so many years of strife.

The Brazilian film critic José Carlos Avellar, when telling me of the revolutionary cinema that swept across Latin America in the sixties and early seventies, says, 'It was very simple: we didn't want to see films, we wanted to see daily life, and daily life would show us how to make films.' While recent film-makers are more cinephile than that (they are primarily thinking about making movies, not statements), one could still argue the truth of this observation today. The gaze on daily life is ever-present, whether manifesting itself in the variations on neo-realism of

Walter Salles and Pablo Trapero, the poetic expressionism of Karim Ainouz or the rigorous minimalism of Lisandro Alonso, in the baroque flamboyance of Lucrecia Martel or the experimental playfulness of the Chileans Alicia Scherson and Matías Bize. The constant is the local, and the integrity of their perception and recreation of reality.

And yet, although the worlds on offer are particular, the stories are often universal. A middle-aged man struggling to find employment (Trapero's *Mundo grúa*), a boy searching for his father (*Central Station*) and a young man trying to forget his (Burman's *Lost Embrace*), a young woman lonely yet curious in the big city (Scherson's *Play*): in these films we are transported to Buenos Aires, Patagonia, Rio de Janeiro and Santiago, by stories which, at the same time and unerringly, strike a chord within anyone watching them.

Other common factors that will be explored in these interviews are the frequent use of non-actors (a legacy of the neo-realist influence on the continent in the fifties and sixties) and the pronounced dialogue between documentary and fiction – particularly in Brazil, where documentary-makers seem to have formed cinema's front line (or, perhaps more accurately, scouting party), scooping up the country's vital source material, as it happens, before passing the baton to fiction. Associated with this trend, in Brazil we can see how numerous directors continue in a long tradition that started in its silent era of 'mapping' the country on film, from the jungles to the arid *sertão* of the north-east, to the *favela*, or city slum.

Mention of what has almost become a sub-genre in its own right, the *favela* film, raises the question of the nature and degree of social engagement in this period. As many of the directors themselves attest, they are not replicating the militancy of the New Latin American Cinema, in which the likes of the Cinema Novo directors of Brazil and the proponents of Third Cinema in Argentina – fuelled by the Cuban revolution, concerned with issues of neo-colonialism and national identity, intent on finding forms that would speak of and to the people – were bonded by a desire to change the world. Since the transition to democracy, cinema has generally moved away from political films to personal, more introspective ones; or, to borrow a phrase from the film critic B. Ruby Rich, from the revolutionary to the revelatory.

However, one must remember also that to reveal – to turn a mirror on a society, within the auditorium – can be a political act, highlighting social problems and prompting debate. If the Cuban revolution provided fervour and subject matter for the films of the sixties and seventies, then the conditions I've mentioned – the trauma after years of dictatorship, economic hardship and continuing social stratification – add substance to today's cinema. As will become apparent in these interviews, a number of directors care passionately about what is happening in their countries. What distinguishes them from those of the past (with the unavoidable exception of José Padilha, the Brazilian director of the *favela* film and instant *cause célèbre*, *Tropa de Elite*) is their avowed desire to avoid the soapbox. Many of the films we see here are at once personal and political, but they are not didactic.

Those that deal with the dictatorships underline this point, for their handling of the subject rarely involves a full-frontal assault, whether it be guilt-tripping, hand-wringing, stone-throwing or tears. Andrés Wood's *Machuca* smartly views the Pinochet coup through the eyes of a child, while fellow Chilean Pablo Larraín's *Tony Manero* (2008) daringly deals with the subsequent repression as a backdrop to a story about a disco-dancing psychopath. In Brazil, Cao Hamburger's *O ano em que meus pais saíram de férias* (*The Year My Parents Went on Vacation*, 2006) sweetens the pill with soccer and a child's comic coming-of-age; in Argentina, Albertina Carri's extraordinary *Los rubios* (*The Blondes*, 2003) is not just a reflection on the disappearance of her own parents, but a redefinition of the creative possibilities of documentary. Lucrecia Martel's critiques of her home town's provincial bourgeoisie, while not even committing themselves to a definitive period, subtly tease out connections between the moral malaise on screen and malfeasance under the *junta*. These interconnected 'waves' of new South American cinema are marked throughout by intelligence and restraint, as well as humanity, good humour and a striving from directors to find a cinematic language as compelling as their stories.

I will be focusing on a decade of film-making, from 1998 to 2008 (with one exception, Salles' crucial *Foreign Land*, dating from 1996). Taking a leaf out of Guevara's and Salles' journeys of discovery – and because it's tempting to see this cinema renaissance as having started with the *buena onda*, which then slowly enveloped South America – the book will take an anticlockwise foray around part of the continent, as I speak to film-makers and critics in Brazil, Argentina, Uruguay, Chile and Peru.

In case this is not already obvious, I should state now that I am mostly not concerned with the countries' commercially oriented cinema, which on this continent is often derived from and produced by television, or apes Hollywood genre tropes, and which invariably performs better at the domestic box office than independent art-house or auteur cinema. That said, what is striking about many of the films mentioned here is that they have appealed both to local and international audiences.

The primary aim has been to allow directors (among them a notable number of women, compared to other regions) to tell us about themselves and their work. For me, their personal stories are as important as the films. None of these individuals could be called a 'director for hire': almost every film is a personal film. And therefore the personal and the cinematographic are inextricably linked.

A few things that the book is not, or does not do. Though it follows a route, it is not a strict 'country-by country' guide: I prefer to tackle individual directors, or collections of films, though two chapters (born of articles for the film magazine *Sight & Sound*) offer reports on the history and state of play in the two principal film-producing countries, Brazil and Argentina.

The book is not comprehensive, nor could it be, so rich is the new cinema from this part of the world. And it does not deal with the films that the continent's most prominent directors, Salles and Meirelles, have made outside their country, for the obvious reason that my focus is on work made in and of South America.

It also, sadly, stops short of Colombia and Venezuela. Despite burgeoning film production in those countries, I have not considered them for one simple, practical reason: with the exception of the Venezuelan kidnap thriller *Secuestro express* (2005), movies from these countries have yet to 'break out' internationally, which means that no films I could mention would be familiar to readers outside those countries, nor for the most part available.

Likewise Bolivia. The producer Donald Ranvaud, an instrumental figure in the Brazilian breakthrough of this period (with credits on, among others, *Central Station* and *City of God*) and with a good nose for emerging talent, has recently been working in Bolivia and is adamant that a young generation of directors in that small country, working like the Chileans on micro-budgeted digital features, will have plenty to offer. It is just a matter of time. And just as *The Motorcycle Diaries* leaves Guevara still to complete his South American discovery, so this book will, I hope, leave curiosity about the future.

When I speak to my friends in London about *City of God*, *The Motorcycle Diaries* or the Argentine Carlos Sorín's *El perro* (*Bombón: El perro*, 2004) – to name three very different films – I hear nothing but unbridled enthusiasm. If I had one ambition for this project, it would be to encourage these same people, and other *simpatico* individuals, to take a closer look at the continent: to discover and be touched by the deepening well of films of which they are not aware.

The immediate obstacle is obvious: the lack of consistent distribution. But that is improving, both theatrically and on DVD. And one has only to look at the number of Latin American film festivals in the UK over the past few years – led by expatriates eager to promote their cultures – to believe that the appetite is there. There is no reason, given a little application, why people cannot discover not only the earlier work of those familiar directors – Salles' *Terra estrangeira* (*Foreign Land*, 1996), Meirelles' *Domésticas* (*Maids*, 2001), Martel's *La ciénaga* – but also the work of Karim Ainouz, Albertina Carri, Celina Murga, Lisandro Alonso, Martín Rejtman, Matías Bize and Josué Méndez, among many.

Finally, a word on the book's form. At the outset of this project, and throughout my research, I imagined a structure that would involve numerous formal 'dialogues' on the page, a cacophony of voices edited together, to construct the sense of community I was discovering; to portray, in a way, the 'Babel' that both Salles and his fine actor Rodrigo de la Serna described as the pan-Latin American crew wound its way through the continent to shoot *The Motorcycle Diaries*.

When it came to it, I backed off. Perhaps my poor European brain, struggling for order, couldn't take the din. Though actually, I think it was an instinct. I hope that by allowing these individuals to speak, for the most part, in their own space, of their own experiences, the same result will be reached: to convey the sense of a myriad of wonderfully different voices, bonded by blood, politics, strife, courage, ingenuity, and by a shared desire and splendid resolve to make movies.

# Letter from Rio

*Rio de Janeiro, October 2006*

In 1991 Hector Babenco declared that 'Brazilian cinema is dead'. Argentine-born, but a naturalised Brazilian citizen, Babenco was lamenting a calamitous turn of events for his adopted country's film industry. Somewhat ironically, Brazil's first democratically elected president after more than twenty years of military dictatorship had withdrawn all state funding and support for culture, including films – thus decimating Brazilian cinema. An industry that had been producing a hundred films a year under the dictators did not make a single film that year.

But Fernando Collor de Mello's reign was as short as it was corrupt and, by 1992, he had been impeached. Within two years the Audiovisual Law was introduced to help revive Brazilian film-making, and Babenco's obituary for cinema suddenly seemed premature. Fifteen years later, the patient seems in rather rude health.

I'm walking through Rio de Janeiro's downtown district, alongside a small, white-haired man, positively sprightly considering his age and gravitas. José Carlos Avellar, *éminence grise* of Brazilian film critics, has written about and participated in every phase of the cinema scene here for fifty years: he's talked movies with Glauber Rocha and the Cinema Novo revolutionaries of the sixties; during the eighties he worked for Embrafilme – the state distributor and producer of Brazilian films, which Collor subsequently shut down; he was involved, too, with RioFilme, the city film agency that helped to resurrect the industry during the *retomada da produção*, the revival of the early nineties.

'Cinema didn't die,' Avellar reflects with a smile, over a *cafe-zinho*, 'because there was a film culture in Brazil that had nothing to do with the government or the media, but existed in cine clubs and in individuals' passion for cinema. And, with a very little amount of money, films were made again, by an entirely new generation that during the years without feature-film production had produced short films, video documentaries, video fictions. The Audiovisual Law helped a lot, but only because the cinematographic culture in Brazil was alive and well. And many of these young directors knew each other, tried to help each other, there was a real solidarity between them.'

The government response had been swift. Between 1993 and 1994 the Brazilian Cinema Rescue Act (the name says it all, really) created grants for ninety projects. Under the Audiovisual Law, passed in 1994, any company based in the country could invest part of its income tax in local production, while foreign film distributors with local arms, such as Columbia, Fox and Buena Vista, could redirect seventy per cent of the taxes on their box-office profits to local projects. The incentives provided by the Audiovisual Law, and the associated Rouanet Law, have continued to encourage considerable involvement in production, the biggest investors being the state-owned oil company Petrobras and BNDES, the Bank of Economic and Social Development.

Between 1994 and 2000 nearly two hundred feature-length films, fiction and documentary, were made. And with the success in 1995 of the historical satire *Carlota Joaquina – Princesa do Brasil*, audiences started to join the party. Phase two of the recovery was accomplished in 1998 by Walter Salles' *Central Station*, whose international success – a British Academy Award for best foreign film, awards for best film and actress (Fernanda Montenegro) in Berlin, nominated for best foreign film and actress at the Oscars – drew the attention of international audiences and potential co-producers towards Brazil.

While the fiscal incentives have played a significant role in renewed film production, the solidarity among the local directors, mentioned by Avellar, explains why the resurgence of Brazilian cinema has continued beyond the *retomada* (regarded as having ended with *Central Station*) and why it has such character.

The palpable sense of a film community here derives largely from the influence as director/producers of Salles and Fernando Meirelles, and the spirit of collaboration they engender. With his Rio-based company VideoFilmes, which he runs with his brother João, an accomplished documentary-maker, Salles has nurtured some of the country's most promising directors, including Karim Ainouz, whose second film *O céu de Suely* (*Suely in the Sky*, 2006) – a tale about a single mother finding her way in the country's symbolic north-east – scoops the Rio Film Festival's best film prize while I'm in town.

From São Paulo, Meirelles' O2 Filmes supports such diverse talents as Tata Amaral and Cao Hamburger, both of whom have films at the festival: Amaral, whose *Um céu de estrelas* (*A Starry Sky*, 1996) was one of the stunning wake-up calls of the *retomada*, has *Antônia*, which combines grit and ebullience in its tale of a São Paulo girl band (played by real-life singers and rappers Leilah Moreno, Cindy, Negra Li and Quelynah) attempting to sing their way out of the slums; Hamburger wins the audience award with *O ano em que meus pais saíram de férias* (*The Year My Parents Went on Vacation*, 2006), a skilled and enormously enjoyable reflection on the moment in 1970 when World Cup success offered a distraction from the pain of political repression.

The films by Ainouz and Amaral touch on common themes of contemporary Brazilian cinema – the search for personal identity and fulfilment, the concerns of young people in a country with deeply embedded social problems; Hamburger's offers a tentative look back – something atypical of the Brazilian psyche – to the country's dark political past. Among other commendable festival offerings with similar concerns are *Os 12 trabalhos* (*The 12 Labours*, 2006), a gritty urban fable about a young, black motorcycle courier tackling the daily injustices of the São Paulo underclass, and *Proibido proibir* (*Forbidden to*

*Forbid*, 2007), concerning three middle-class students out of their depth discovering the reality of life in a Rio *favela*.

Avellar believes that one can trace a line between much of today's cinematic endeavour and that of the politically engaged Cinema Novo of the sixties and early seventies. 'When you look at film production now, there is not a single agenda that runs through it, like that running through Cinema Novo,' he observes. 'It's difficult to put all the films together in one group, in one movement. But, even if they make different kinds of films, these directors are often working in a tradition that started with Cinema Novo.'

Brazil's most famous film movement, forged amid the revolutionary optimism of the sixties and driven by Glauber Rocha's motto, 'A camera in your hand and an idea in your head,' involved a number of approaches: from Rocha's allegorical provocations *Deus e o Diabo na Terra do Sol* (*Black God, White Devil*, 1964) and *Terre em transe* (*Land in Anguish*, 1967), to Nelson Pereira dos Santos's startling, neo-realist account of life in the *sertão*, *Vidas secas* (*Barren Lives*, 1963). What these directors had in common was a belief in cinema as a vehicle for consciousness-raising and social transformation. Indeed, in his essay 'The Aesthetics of Hunger', Rocha, the polemicist of the movement, spoke of their 'ugly, sad films, those screaming, desperate films' designed 'to make the public aware of its own misery'.

That's a bitter pill, which may explain why Cinema Novo, as tremendous as much of it was, never did engage with the public. It's also an inappropriate way of describing the intentions of today's film-makers, since engaging with the public is precisely what they most want to do, by making entertaining, accessible films that will succeed in a much more difficult market. Yet it would be fair to say that many seek to raise or acknowledge important social issues, as well as revealing the different faces – social, ethnic, geographical – of their immense country.

And if anything, the problems of poverty and social exclusion in Brazil have intensified over the past twenty years, to be joined by a virulent crime scene – notably the heavily armed drug wars

Urban Brazil on screen in 1955:
Nelson Pereira dos Santos's *Rio, 40 Degrees* . . .

© Marcelo Vigneron

... and fifty years later: Tata Amaral's *Antônia*

that have become synonymous with *favela* life and have given Rio de Janeiro one of the highest murder rates in the world. Film-makers as diverse as Walter Salles (in *Central Station*), Meirelles (*City of God*), Babenco (*Carandiru*, 2003), José Padilha (*Bus 174*, 2002), Karim Ainouz (*Suely in the Sky*) and Tata Amaral (*Antônia*) have all dealt with such issues head-on.

One major meeting point between today's cinema and that of the past takes place in what the American scholar Randall Johnson has neatly termed 'the territories of crisis': the *favelas* and the drought-plagued north-eastern hinterland, or *sertão*. '*Central Station* could have taken place in any part of the country: you have poor people in the north-east, but you also have poor people in the south,' says Avellar.

Yet Walter's choice of the north-east was because it is an emblematic space, a well-known dramatic space, which belongs to the time of Cinema Novo and where there is, already, a relationship between cinema and the audience.

At the same time, the *favela* is a real problem of daily life in Rio and São Paulo. The first time we started making films that investigated this relationship between the rich part of the city and the *favela* was in the fifties with Nelson Pereira dos Santos. I remember a discussion with a Brazilian exhibitor, who did not understand why Brazilian films were so eager to speak about the poor. And that's because the bourgeoisie think that the poor don't belong to society. They keep asking, 'Why do you have to deal with the *favela*? Why do you have to deal with the poor?'

In fact, Rio is one of the few cities in the world where the margin is in the middle. The *favelas* are not outside the city, they are in the middle. It's impossible not to see a *favela*, wherever you are. So you cannot ignore them. And you should not ignore them. For a Brazilian audience today, the big successes are often the films that present themselves as connected with the real situation. *City of God* was a big success: it was partly due to the fact that it's a marvellous film, but also because it's a true story. *Carandiru* [about the eponymous, and infamous, São Paulo prison] was the same.

It's interesting that such a hard-hitting, in many ways depressing tale as *Carandiru* can do well at the local box office. But in Brazil directors and audiences seem to share a powerful belief in the resonance, as material, of their own lives. Moreover, Brazil is a country for which the maxim that truth is stranger than fiction could have been invented: where else in the world can police and drug gangs be attacking each other with machine guns and rocket launchers, while down the hill, in chic Ipanema, say, the middle classes obliviously shop?

However, there is another, parallel trend in Brazilian cinema: alongside *City of God* and *Carandiru*, the recent domestic box-office successes have included lowest-common-denominator films, many influenced by *telenovela*-obsessed Brazilian television and granted valuable marketing by the TV behemoth Globo, in return for a credit. The all-inclusive Rio festival opened with a vacuous teen music comedy and ends with *Muito gelo e dois dedos d'agua* (*Lots of Ice and a Little Bit of Water*, 2006), the latest big-budget, instantly dispensable number by former Globo television producer Daniel Filho, whose body-swap comedy *Se eu fosse você* (*If I Were You*, 2006), starring well-known TV stars, has been one of the biggest hits of the past year.

Walter Salles' impassioned speech against this perceived dumbing down, at his friend Ainouz's festival premiere, garnered cheers and the next day's headlines. It suggests a battleground of sorts, with film-makers on one side, television the other – the soul of the country's cinema as the prize.

That said, as ever on this continent there is a greater enemy in their midst: Hollywood. The perennial problem is the US stranglehold on exhibition, a problem compounded by a reduction of Brazilian cinemas from 3,000 in the seventies, to around 1,700 today – many of which are multiplexes allied to US studios. Here, the stream of celluloid offered from America makes it all too easy for exhibitors to give local films short shrift. 'There is at least one thing that we never succeeded in recovering from the time of Embrafilme,' laments Avellar. 'We do not have a national distribution house. And that's a pity.'

Thus, despite as many as seventy Brazilian films now being produced annually, the market share for local fare will barely exceed ten per cent. Whatever the balance of factors – between a film's exposure, audience preference and their ability actually to afford to go to the cinema – a comparison of two hits across three decades speaks volumes: in 1976, twelve million Brazilians (from a population of ninety-five million) saw *Dona Flor and Her Two Husbands*, still the most successful film in Brazilian history; in 2005, with the population doubled to 186 million people, Breno Silveira's 2 *filhos de Francisco* (*The Two Sons of Francisco*) – the biggest hit since *Dona Flor* – attracted, at five million, less than half the audience.

There may never be a way of competing with America. The more important task is to prevent Hollywood hegemony from bankrupting Brazilian production – or, put another way, to make Brazilian cinema sustainable.

Andrucha Waddington, not only one of Brazilian film's brightest lights, but also one of its most pragmatic film-makers, has an interesting perspective on the American presence in his country:

he believes that if you can't beat them, you should join them – or at least get them to pay for your films.

As a young man, and before the industry was shut down by President Collor, Waddington gained work experience on the film sets of Salles, Babenco and Carlos Diegues; during the crisis he worked in commercials; after the *retomada*, he became a partner in Conspiração Filmes, which now vies with Meirelles' O2 as the biggest multimedia company (films, television, commercials, music videos) in Brazil. It's an environment in which Waddington himself can direct his own, extremely good art-house films – notably the smart love-triangle comedy *Eu tu eles* (*Me You Them*, 2000), which derives much comic mileage from the dour life of the dusty *sertão*, and the sumptuous, epic family drama *Casa de areia* (*House of Sand*, 2005) – and at the same time is home to as shamelessly commercial (though admittedly well-crafted) a film as the aforementioned *The Two Sons of Francisco*, about Brazil's famous country-music duo, Zezé di Camargo and Luciano.

'The bottom line is that we want to make good films,' says the adrenalin-rushing Waddington when we meet in his office.

We don't have an agenda. We can have producers' projects, directors' projects, director-producer projects. What we do is develop the script to the point where the director and producer feel that it's ready to go. Then we make a budget, have a reading with the partners, everyone talks about it, then it goes to the market, where we find if it is possible to raise the money for the film, or not. And so the market decides for itself. We don't judge the quality of the genre in choosing which projects to do. So the steps are really clear.

And in Conspiração's marketplace, the US studios, using the tax breaks offered by the Audiovisual Law, have a major stall. Columbia Filmes do Brasil has co-produced all of Waddington's three films to date, along with Silveira's (actually bringing the idea for *The Two Sons of Francisco*, in a neat reversal, to Conspiração). The company is now talking with Fox, Buena Vista and Warner. 'They are very easy to work with,' reports

Singer-turned-actor Seu Jorge with Fernanda Torres in Andrucha
Waddington's *House of Sand* (2005)

Waddington. 'For me, relations with Columbia have been fantastic. They invested in *House of Sand* from the beginning: I asked for $18,000 for development and they said, "Consider it done." Then three months later we had a meeting with a two-page storyline, and they were in.

'There is never an attempt to impose themselves on the project,' he adds, noting my scepticism. 'Actually, this is an important point: it's not money they are risking, because it is a tax they would pay anyway. So it gives us much more freedom.'

Although some have voiced the criticism that Hollywood's Latin satellites impose their own values on films, while also limiting their interests – and thus a film's potential – to the local markets, Waddington's experience again suggests otherwise. Both *Me You Them* and *House of Sand* were released in the US, to good business. Moreover, *House of Sand*, whose stunning desert locations and accompanying visual ambition were reminiscent of *The English Patient*, did much better there than it had at home, showing that US involvement can enable a Brazilian film to reach its strongest audience, wherever that may be.

The director is not immune to the irony of such a positive experience. 'And now you get the devil to work at your side,' he laughs.

You know, I think we can't beat the Americans, because they are very smart. What they did is create an industry with the idea that 'Where our films are shown, our products will be sold and our way of life will be sold.' This is something that they work very hard at, very aggressively. Film is a strategic industry for the American system.

They are not wrong: we are wrong to accept it, and to not do the same. I think the only way to establish a film industry against or at least competitive with American films is to directly subsidise it. And that will take thirty, forty years.

In the meantime, an alternative approach to financing films, one taken by another of Brazil's major players, involves bypassing (rather than relying upon) the tax-incentive cash, and seeking traditional co-productions, particularly in Europe. Salles has championed this approach since *Central Station*. *Suely in the Sky*, produced by VideoFilmes, is a case in point: the $1.3-million film was co-produced with Celluloid Dreams in France, Shotgun Pictures (Germany) and Fado Filmes (Portugal), the inbuilt value of such co-production being that it virtually guarantees distribution in those territories.

Prior to that experience, *Suely* director Karim Ainouz had found it much more difficult to obtain financial support:

The only reason that my first film, *Madame Satã*, exists is because of Walter and the French [Wild Bunch]. I got nothing from Brazilian funding. Because the state money for film is pipelined through private companies, you have to go to a marketing director of a private company and convince them. And the subject of *Madame Satã* was not something that marketing directors wanted to be associated with.

I'm speaking with Ainouz the morning after the colourful Ipanema premiere party for his film. And the young director reveals himself to be a sharp, thoughtful personality, with an outsider's perspective, having spent some formative years in New York.

I think that Walter has made our generation viable. I'm not saying this because of his direct advocacy of certain films – he has concretely produced mine – but because of the kind of figure that he is. He will write about something that's being released and his word will attract audiences. He is somebody, also, who's made it possible for international investors to believe that Brazilian film is possible, because of *Central Station*.

His influence has been fundamental. He's not only a film-maker, he's an ambassador. The way that he presents Brazilian cinema, and articulates it, is really important. He's also a key figure in challenging certain structures. You were there when he presented my film. Oh man. That was big. The headlines the next day weren't about *Suely*, they were about his speech. He has had that role throughout. It's not a bitter role, but one of advancing the discourse. If you think of the role that [André] Bazin played for the French new wave: Walter's not a critic, he's a film-maker, but I would say that he has had a similar role in Brazilian cinema.

Another figure who acknowledges the importance of Brazilian films travelling internationally is one of the Rio festival's two directors, Ilda Santiago. Santiago is much more than a festival programmer: she is also a founder of the exhibition and distribution company Grupo Estação, which has been promoting world cinema in Brazil since the mid-eighties and now operates a number of screens in Rio, São Paulo and Belo Horizonte. She and her colleagues would be the sort of 'keepers of the flame' of film culture lauded by José Carlos Avellar. She recalls:

In the late eighties we ran a festival, Mostra Rio, the aim of which was to show world cinema and to open the door to some kind of distribution in Brazil for international films. The idea now is different. Now, the main purpose of Festival do Rio is to attract people to Brazil to see Brazilian films, and to help those films to travel.

And not just Brazilian films, but Latin American films. We have to start looking at this industry as a regional thing. Yes, we have a different language in Brazil, and a different history of colonisation, so there is a different soul to our culture. But we South Americans have a whole continent in common, and more of a cultural bond than we sometimes think. It's about time we tried to bring our continent together, in relation to film. If we don't do that, we're doomed.

Doomed might be a bit strong. But Santiago's belief in the urgent need for South American films to have better distribution around the continent (she cites a co-distribution agreement between Brazil and Argentina, providing financial aid to the distribution of six films in each direction a year, as a beginning) and in the synergising potential of the positive image overseas of 'Latin American' cinema is perfectly justified.

Arguably, Brazil is making too many films at the moment – certainly more than there are screens available to show them. Avellar believes that while the Audiovisual Law was crucial in shocking Brazilian film-making back to life, it's now outmoded, failing to make provision for script development (guaranteeing the quality of films) and distribution (so that once made, audiences can actually see them). There's also the tiny problem that, with some honourable exceptions such as Petrobras, too many of these tax-avoiding companies have as their driving forces (and, therefore, as arbiters of Brazil's renewed film culture) marketing officers concerned not with cinematic excellence, but with product-placement opportunities and consumer targets.

The debate is ongoing. Yet one thing is beyond dispute: these Brazilian producer/directors find themselves in a far stronger position than they were a decade ago. At least now they can worry about the quality and success of their cinema, rather than whether there will be any cinema at all.

# Conversations with Walter Salles

*London – Rio de Janeiro – London, 2006–8*

During my conversations with the Brazilian director Walter Salles, which spanned the summers of 2006 and 2008, and London and Rio de Janeiro, he was involved in two projects that epitomise his work. One, *Linha de passe*, which he was co-directing with fellow Rio native Daniela Thomas, marked a return to the territory of his breakthrough films *Foreign Land* (also with Thomas) and *Central Station*: like those films, it reflected on what it is to be Brazilian, on questions of identity and personal fulfilment, particularly for the country's under-class. The other was *On the Road*, a film based on Jack Kerouac's classic account of fifties America. While Robert Redford had entrusted Salles with bringing the early life of Che Guevara to international audiences in *The Motorcycle Diaries*, Francis Ford Coppola had gone a step further, handing to the Brazilian the story of this intrinsically North American icon – a testament to the international regard in which Salles is held. True to his *modus operandi*, before embarking on his principal commission he spent several months making a documentary on the influence of Kerouac and the Beat movement not merely to research the era, but to investigate and tease out the possibilities for a feature rendering.

As this book was being completed, *Linha de passe* had appeared in competition at the Cannes Film Festival and was beginning to be released around the world, and Salles was location-scouting for *On the Road*. However, we were to shape our conversations around three films: *Terra estrangeira* (*Foreign Land*, 1996), *Central do Brasil* (*Central Station*, 1998) and

*Diarios de motocicleta* (*The Motorcycle Diaries*, 2004), films that I feel reflect not only the director's development, but the themes of this book, of emerging national film industries and a growing continental mentality. These are films that breathe with the spirit of South America, its exuberance and volatility. I have a feeling that because of the accessibility of Salles' style, and a certain narrative digestibility, the director is under-valued by those who equate quality with discomfort – who can only conceive of Latin American film with a blade and a gun. It's a narrow view, of course, suspicious of warmth. I would argue that while Salles' work rarely holds back from the harshness that society can bestow – whether it be the illiteracy, murder and child-trafficking on view in *Central Station*, or the zero-option world of *Linha de passe* – what makes it so accessible is the director's humanity, which informs everything he does.

Moreover, Salles is a director who is endlessly working on the correlation of style and content, often to dazzling effect. There are moments in *Foreign Land* and *Abril despedaçado* (*Behind the Sun*, 2001)* of sublime, sometimes savage beauty; in *Central Station*, meanwhile, the formal language enables every frame to delineate emotional experience. These are intricately realised films.

A quick word about *Foreign Land*. Salles' first feature, *A grande arte* (*Exposure*, 1991), is atypical of the director's oeuvre – made for hire, a conventional thriller, shot in Brazil but with an American hero and driven by plot, rather than character. And so, in all meaningful respects, *Foreign Land* is his debut feature, certainly as an auteur. It also has all the enticing characteristics of a first film, of someone discovering himself behind the camera: it is raw, personal, at once angry and romantic, stylistically ambitious and enjoyably imperfect.

---

*With co-writers Sergio Machado and Karim Ainouz, Salles adapted the novel *Broken April*, by Albanian novelist Ismail Kadare, transferring the story from the Balkans to Brazil's north-eastern Ceara state. Set in 1910, it concerns a young man's desire to break the cycle of death and revenge imposed by a family blood feud, a travelling circus offering a possibility of escape. The high point of *Abril despedaçado*, a breathtaking chase through a sugar-cane field, is one of the very best sequences in Salles' work.

Walter Salles directs Gael García Bernal on the set of *The Motorcycle Diaries*

Co-directed with Daniela Thomas, the film opens with a brief, dramatic caption:

Brazil. March 1990. Fernando Collor, the first elected president since the military coup of 1964, announces the freezing of all savings accounts. The country stalls, chaos ensues. In the next few years thousands of young Brazilians will leave the country.

Hereafter it follows a young man, Paco, the first of many father-less characters in Salles' work, who, when his mother dies and with no clear future in his own country, decides to leave. Without money, he accepts an offer to deliver a suitcase to Portugal. When he arrives, he waits endlessly in a Lisbon hotel for the mysterious case to be collected.

What ensues is a plangent neo-noir, whose protagonists are exiles, adrift in a fatherland whose inhabitants despise them; Paco and the woman with whom he falls in love go on the run, having already run halfway around the world. Evocatively shot

33

in black and white, it is steeped in Godard's doomed romanticism yet deepened by an empathy for its exiles, one of whom mourns, 'As time goes by, I feel more and more foreign.'

## Beginnings: Parisian picture-houses, country in crisis, *Terra estrangeira*

*Could we start at the beginning: your family background?*

Of course. My family comes from the interior of Brazil. More specifically, from a state known as Minas Gerais, eight hundred miles away from urban centres like Rio de Janeiro or São Paulo. Both my mother and my father come from small towns in that state, towns which, when they were born, had fewer than five hundred inhabitants. And they both migrated to Rio de Janeiro, where they met.

Pouso Alegre, my father's town, didn't have a school or hospital. As a result, he had to be schooled five hours away from there. His parents had a small dry-goods store, selling hats, toothbrushes and barbed wire to farms. It was a fragile commerce that nearly died during the 1929 Depression. He ended up being the first person in my family to reach university, in São Paulo: he was the oldest of his brothers, so the one to whom my grandfather was able to give a better education. He was very lucky to have that possibility. Also, he was lucky to reach São Paulo at the right moment, the early thirties, when the university was being redefined by the structuralists. Claude Lévi-Strauss and a few other French intellectuals were vitally involved with the university at that time and ended up having a strong influence on my father's generation.

My mother, on the other hand, never reached university. Her father worked on the State Railroad System for several years. He came to Rio to find work and ended up bringing his family with him. Here's an interesting story. Once an old woman I didn't know approached me in the street. *Central Station* had just won the Golden Bear at the Berlin Film Festival and was reaching the theatres in Brazil. And she said, 'I worked with your mother at the Central Station [the principal train station in Rio] when we were twenty, we were both secretaries.' It came as a complete surprise. I didn't know that, at all. My mother died in 1988. But I went to talk to my older aunt, who was the intellectual of my mother's family – she directs the library at the Catholic University in Rio – and she confirmed it. It's an incredible irony. I had filmed in the same building where my mother had worked, without knowing it.

*That epitomises the organic relationship between reality and fiction throughout your work. But back to your father: he prospered after university.*

Yes. He was the first to break through that lower-middle-class barrier. He was a financier, he founded a bank with my grandfather and two friends, Unibanco. Then in the late fifties he changed lanes and became a diplomat, a profession he loved and ended up embracing for many years.

He was also a man of culture. He created cultural institutes that bear his name, the Moreira Salles Institute. These centres, in Rio, São Paulo and his home town, host exhibitions and publish studies on Brazilian literature. So he was a businessman who really cared about Brazilian culture. And that balance is reflected, in a way, in what my brothers and I do today: my younger brother [João Moreira Salles] is a documentary film-maker, our middle brother is a businessman, and my older brother works in a company, but also publishes poetry and has written plays.

*It's interesting that your family is extremely well known in Brazil, and perhaps thought of as quite rarefied; yet the roots are humble.*

My brothers and myself have always had an awareness of the privilege that we had, while at the same time a strong sense of where the family came from at the very beginning, which is not a privileged background at all. That awareness has nurtured the desire to talk about those who have not had the same possibilities. The fact that the families both of my father and mother came from very small towns is, somehow, very alive in me today. I tend to feel much more at ease outside the urban environment. When I first lived in Rio it was outside the city. And travelling is also a way to create a distance from cities.

*And this taste for travelling, and inadvertently I suppose for being displaced, was instilled at a young age.*

Yes. And the idea of leaving as a *leitmotif* returns again and again in my work. My father's career as a diplomat coincided with my youth. I was born in Rio de Janeiro in 1956, but three years later left Brazil when my father was sent to Washington DC. We lived there from 1959 to 1963. Actually, I lived in different latitudes until I was thirteen or fourteen. One of these places was Paris, where we lived for six years.

*So he became a diplomat before the military coup – and during an amazingly rich cultural chapter in Brazilian history.*

He was sometimes sent on special economic missions, but was also an ambassador for the government of Juscelino Kubitschek, the president who built Brasilia. This was the most creative time in Brazilian culture, the moment when Bossa Nova erupted, when Cinema Novo erupted, of Oscar Niemeyer's new architecture; but also, I would say, the most democratic moment in Brazil, when the country was redefining its goals and reinventing itself. And then came the coup in 1964, and then in 1968 the coup within the coup, and it all became unbearable.

*And away from that, in Paris, you were discovering cinema.*

Very near to the apartment where we lived in Paris was a revival house that only played double features. Studio Grande Armée, I think it was. And its programme was very diverse. This is where I ended up discovering Italian neo-realism, the French *nouvelle vague*, the early German films from the Filmverlag der Autoren, even the Cinema Novo films that were at that time forbidden by the military regime in Brazil. I was eleven or twelve years old at that time, and that discovery had a very strong impact on me.

Also, it was at that early age that I became captivated by the work of photographers like Cartier-Bresson, André Kertész and Robert Doisneau. The humanism in their work was unique. That aesthetic current had as much an impact on my life as works by Rossellini and Antonioni: neo-realism was not only an aesthetic revolution, but an ethical one, and the same could be said about the work of those photographers. So, at that same age I started to do a lot of photography, influenced by those guys, looking for what we could call a 'human map', faces that were from a specific place and time.

At my school in Paris, there was a photographic lab, where I learned how to develop and print in black and white. The miracle of the image being formed by grain still has a deeply resonating effect on me today. This is why I'm not taken by digital cinema, for instance.

*How were you allowed in alone to a cinema at that age? These were not exactly children's films.*

It took some time! But eventually the owner let me walk in directly. I was probably the person who went there most often. And also he could see me entering my home just adjacent to the cinema, so little by little he accepted me.

One funny memory. There was this one-week vacation, at Easter, and I spent the whole time watching double features. I studied at that time in a very strict and incredibly boring school in Paris, a Jesuit school, where they used to put the sons of diplomats. The day we came back after Easter the teacher asked us to put on paper what we had done over the holiday. I wrote out a list of maybe twenty films. And he grabbed my list – this was the first time I was told off – and he said, 'You've made this up.' And I said, 'I'm so sorry, I can tell you the story of each and every one of those films.' In the middle of that list were films like *Jules et Jim* [François Truffaut, 1962] and *Weekend* [Jean-Luc Godard, 1967], which for that school were considered liberal, dangerous films that shouldn't be seen! I still remember that confrontation as being the best moment of school, when I stood up against authority and actually won.

*When did you go back to Brazil?*

In 1969. While we were away I had been back to Rio for two months every year, and always missed it tremendously. I missed that kind of street vibration that you have here, but not in Paris. When we returned for good I completely fell in love with the country. But I continued to study in the French schooling system: I did a baccalaureate of philosophy in the Lycée Franco-Brésilien, as a way of not losing a year.

*What effect did being away from Brazil for much of your child-hood have on you? It could go either way: did you feel less or more Brazilian?*

Living at different latitudes made me, paradoxically, aware of how Brazilian I was. But that discovery, too, I owe to cinema. When I saw the films by Nelson Pereira dos Santos, Glauber Rocha and Luiz Sérgio Person, I realised that they talked about a human and physical geography that was essential to me. From that moment on, I also realised that you cannot dissociate cinema from national identity. 'A culture without cinema is like a house without a mirror.' The sentence is not mine, it's by Luiz Carlos Barreto, who is one of the fathers of the Cinema Novo movement, and Bruno Barreto's father. And he's absolutely right in saying so. What we didn't have in the beginning of the nineties was that reflection.

Nelson Pereira dos Santos's Cinema Novo classic, *Barren Lives* (1963)

Allow me a small bifurcation of this theme: the understanding that I had, for example, of Iran before discovering the films of Abbas Kiarostami, Mohsen Makhmalbaf or Jafar Panahi, was extremely limited. Watching Kiarostami's *Where Is the Friend's Home?* [1987], among other films, allowed me to understand that in Iran people smile or cry most of the time for the same reasons as in Brazil. Cinema is, or should be, about what brings us together, and not what dissociates us. In many ways, it is one of the most powerful instruments with which to understand the complexities of the world surrounding you.

But getting back to your question. The discovery of the Cinema Novo films created the desire in me to understand my country better than I did, or could from a distance. This desire is what led me to do documentaries first. Twenty years later, I continue to believe that there is no better way to dive into a specific reality than by directing documentaries.

NEW SOUTH AMERICAN CINEMA

NEW SOUTH AMERICAN CINEMA

*Can you say something about those Brazilian directors who had this influence on you?*

Nelson Pereira is at the heart of the Cinema Novo movement. His *Barren Lives* had – and still has – a long-term impact on me. It tells the story of a family that has to leave its farm in the northeast of Brazil due to a drought. Every shot is essential, every camera move justified. The film has an extraordinarily poetic, but also political, strength, and yet it's never dogmatic. I still see Nelson Pereira constantly. My brother João and I have had the privilege at our production house to be part of the documentaries and one feature film that he has directed in the last five years.

Glauber Rocha's *Black God, White Devil*, shot in 1964, was about the ownership of land in Brazil, and the relationship between the classes that exploit that land. It talks about the racial and cultural roots of Brazil. I was very impressed by his *Land in Anguish*. It's a film that at the same time foresees and explains the future of our social and political system, a beautiful work of anticipation that only a convulsive poet like Rocha could offer. Luiz Sérgio Person is the director of a film that I worship, called *São Paulo S.A.* [1965]. The film follows a character who drifts in a city where industrial expansion has no barriers. It is about the industrialisation of Brazil on one side, and the disintegration of personal relationships on the other. And it's about the beginning of the endemic corruption in the country. It's formally brilliant; nothing as bold is made in Brazilian cinema today.

Finally, I would like to mention a Brazilian film that had a very strong impact on me: *Limite*, by Mario Peixoto. I didn't see it until I was in my early twenties, because this is a film from 1931 that disappeared from circulation for many years. It is the only film directed by Peixoto, who was twenty-two years old at the time. This is a non-narrative, essentially poetic film, and an extremely sophisticated philosophical rumination by a precocious director, one who had an astonishing intuition for cinema. I believe that the film has a distant cousin in Eisenstein's *The*

*General Line* [1929] or *¡Que viva Mexico!* [1932]. *Limite* reminds us that Brazilian cinema is much more polyphonic than we believe it is, from a distance.

*Did any of the world cinema you experienced as a teenager have such a personal impact?*

When I started to watch films the term 'world cinema' didn't exist. So, I guess I would prefer to talk about the films that influenced me to the point where I opted to be a film director. For me, the most important of them all was Antonioni's *The Passenger* [1975]. I discovered it when I was seventeen and I still remember the kind of aesthetic shock the film generated in me – to the point that, when the credits rolled, I couldn't move from my seat. The cinema emptied and I just stayed there by myself, crying. Antonioni's trilogy on identity – *Blow-up* [1966], *Zabriskie Point* [1970] and *The Passenger* – as well as *L'avventura* [1960] and *La notte* [1961] were films that had a long-lasting resonance for me.

As I said, up to that point I did a lot of photography. But cinema seemed a very distant possibility. It was too sacred a medium for me to even think about doing. I knew the films of the *nouvelle vague*, Cinema Novo, the Cuban cinema, neo-realism, I worshipped those films to the point where they became like sacred objects on an altar, to which I could relate only as a fan or a spectator. But when I saw *The Passenger*, when I saw Wenders' *Alice in the Cities* [1974], here were film makers talking about themes that somehow had a direct relation with the times we were living in; and in a direct or indirect manner were talking about themes that were very important to me, to my personal life. It was always linked to the question of finding one's identity. I could understand Philip Winter, the main character of *Alice in the Cities*, really well, as much as I could understand David Locke's character in *The Passenger*. They were very close to me.

*In what way close to you? In terms of being on the move, root-less?*

Partially to do with my personal history, but way beyond that. It had to do with the fact that these were characters who were trying to re-baptise themselves. And I come from a country that tries to do that, that tries to redefine itself all the time. Why are our films the way they are? Because our identity is not fully crystallised.

*And you perceived that as a seventeen-year-old?*

I felt an emotion I had never felt before, and this was when I decided to do cinema, to pursue that emotion. I became much more of a cinephile from that moment, seeking to study cinema and find friends who also wanted to do that.

*So what, if any, training did you undertake?*

I felt that documentaries were the vehicle through which to enter into this milieu. But when I went to university in Brazil, cinema was not an academic option. Today most universities carry cinema courses, but this was not the case back then. I ended up studying History and Economics at Rio University, and later followed with a master's degree programme in Communication at the University of Southern California – which I never completed, by the way. I left the course as soon as I had the opportunity to make my first documentaries for Brazilian television, in the mid-eighties, at the moment when the military regime was starting to break up and give way to a more democratic society. This is when Brazilian cinema started to blossom again and when television became open to independent productions.

So this is what I did at first – independently produced documentaries for television. And cutting back to your question: I feel self-taught, more than anything else. I started to do super-8 films, to shoot and edit them myself, and little by little I started to do documentaries.

*What were the subjects?*

I started making portraits, really. About Kurosawa, Fellini, John Huston, in which we accompanied a film-maker or an actor for several days. Those were sixty-minute documentaries. The next project I did was a five-hour documentary on the clash between modernity and tradition in Japan. That was a really interesting moment for me, because I was thrown into a culture that was completely different to mine and tried to understand its quality. We were helped by Kurosawa, who was part of the documentary, and by Mitsuo Yanagimachi, who made *About Love, Tokyo* [1992].

But during those ten years I made documentaries that investigated many genres – from portraits of Brazilian painters and sculptors, to documentaries on such singer/composers as Caetano Veloso and Chico Buarque. A Brazilian psychoanalyst and writer once said that there are two Brazils: the one that you see every day on the streets, an unjust country plagued by social problems; and, conversely, the utopian Brazil described in verse by our composers, the country that we all like to dream of. Brazilian music is therefore the best mirror of Brazilian society – it not only exposes our inner chaos, but also talks about our desire to live in a society that would be just and creative at the same time.

*You also made a series called* The Brazilians.

Yes, the initial series – I produced it, but did not direct – was a ten-hour series on Brazilian society. And that was followed by an eleven-hour series on the Xingu Indians, an indigenous nation in the Amazon region.

*So you really did use documentaries as a way of discovering your own country.*

I felt that documentaries were a way to understand the complexities of the Brazilian identity. You see, Brazilian reality changes at such a pace that our efforts to fictionalise that reality often can't

43

keep up. When they are good, documentaries can capture that transformation as it happens. That's the case with José Padilha's *Bus 174* [2002] for instance.

Also, in Brazil, events that you never thought could happen, do happen. One example: on 15 May 2000, more than forty policemen were called into São Paulo on a vendetta sponsored by the prison gang PCC, the First Commando of the Capital. The city stopped, for two days, while this battle went on. And more than 180 people were killed. One of the reasons for art and cinema to exist is to anticipate, yet it becomes more and more difficult to anticipate what's going to happen in a society in which reality continues to surprise us in such a manner that the extraordinary becomes ordinary.

*I wonder if this is why documentary has such significance in Brazilian cinema, and this very active, almost symbiotic relationship with fiction.*

The proximity of documentary and fiction in Brazil has been ever-present, since the birth of Brazilian cinema. The first projections were in circuses, in tents. In 1909, ninety films were made in Brazil. Few were fiction. The first Brazilian film-makers were trying to register a geography, physical and human, that had never been seen before, in moving pictures. There were an incredible number of explorers, adventurers who went through different regions of Brazil to register the country in that first wave.

Godard – always Godard – used to say that the best fiction films drift towards documentary, and the best documentaries drift towards fiction. Robert Flaherty was the living proof of that. Both in *Nanook of the North* [1922] and in *Man of Aran* [1934] he was inspired by reality, but he also constructed his own perception of what that reality was. He used non-actors, real people from those environments, but he cast them as families that did not exist in real life. What he was proposing was

44

somehow an enhanced perception of reality, yet one that allowed you to understand how those societies functioned.

This dialogue between fiction and documentary is one that interests me a lot, and it is a main concern of people working in Latin America. It's directly perceivable in Tomás Gutiérrez Alea's *Memories of Underdevelopment* [1968].* I should say that this film, when I discovered it, was almost as important to me as *The Passenger*. I still find the film striking, both in content and form. Gutiérrez Alea created a unique narrative about a young bourgeois drifting in post-revolutionary Havana, where fiction and non-fiction blend – or collide – constantly. And the result of that is a synthesis that transcends all the limits of neo-realism and moves cinema language forward, incredibly. The film is endlessly creative.

*Iracema,*† Jorge Bodanzky's film from 1976, starts from a different point. He takes a professional actor and propels him into a completely realistic environment – and films that relationship. The man becomes the igniter of a film that is constructed in front of your very eyes. There is no screenplay to start with, just a hypothesis.

This is one of the most important Brazilian films of the last few decades, and one that has had a long-lasting influence on many directors. I saw it a long time after it was made, because the film was censored by the military dictatorship and then, once the censorship was lifted in the eighties, had a very confidential

---

* Tomás Gutiérrez Alea (1928–96) is Cuba's greatest director, and *Memorias del subdesarrollo* his masterpiece. Gutiérrez Alea began as a documentary film-maker much influenced by Italian neo-realism, which he absorbed first-hand when he studied film in Italy in the early fifties. Returning to Cuba in 1953, he aligned himself to Castro's fight against Batista. After the revolution he made features and documentaries that cast an objective and critical eye on the socio-economic realities of the Castro regime.
† *Iracema: Uma transa Amazônica*, directed by Jorge Bodanzky and Orlando Senna. A trucker, Tião, nicknamed 'Brasil Grande', travels the Trans-Amazonian Highway into the country's interior, trading timber; when he meets the prostitute Iracema he takes her on the road with him. Tião and Iracema were played by actors (she a non-professional enlisted especially for the project), but this was concealed from those they met on their travels, who were also led to believe that the cameras were there for reportage. The film was banned by Brazil's military dictatorship.

release. But Fernando Meirelles saw it, for instance, when he was at university. And if you see his work today you can see the influence that *Iracema* had on him – again, we're talking about the correlation between fiction and reality.

In Pablo Trapero's *Mundo grúa* you can see that same tension defining what the film is about. Several of the Latin American film-makers working today follow this quest, of blending fiction and non-fiction, and they do it in different manners, following different principles. And it transcends generation. If you look at Carlos Sorín's *Historias mínimas* and *El perro*, he's using non-actors and developing the story around them.

*There's also a more literal relationship between the two forms, namely in shared subject matter. For example, before she co-directed* City of God *with Meirelles, Katia Lund made* News from a Private War, *the documentary about the* favela *drug wars, with your brother João.*

And the same thing is happening now, with *Bus 174*. First José Padilha made his documentary, and since then a feature has been made about the same hijack story. You're right, there's this constant synergy at play.

Actually my new project, *Linha de passe*, originated in the work that João developed in his documentaries – more specifically, in two of them. One of his projects, *Futebol* [1998], was about the *via crucis* through which millions of young soccer players, ranging from fourteen to eighteen years old, go in attempting to play for a second- or third-division junior team in Brazil. The other was a very resonant story about the evangelist phenomenon, where churches are mushrooming in every single part of the country. These two documentaries added drama, density and conflict to two subjects that are never treated as I believe they should be in Brazil. Some of the characters in them were very inspiring to me for the fiction work.

*Did you ever do commercials?*

Yes, during the eighties. We needed sponsors for the documentaries, so one of the agencies suggested that I direct the commercials that went with the programmes. That's how I ended up doing the two at the same time, for about six years. But if I hadn't worked primarily in documentaries, I would have lost my sanity.

*You've suggested that the Brazilian film industry was starting to blossom again in the mid-eighties, after the end of the dictatorship. But as I understand it, that promise was short-lived. When Fernando Collor de Mello became president in 1989 he all but destroyed the industry.*

In the mid- to late eighties, there was a transitional phase in which the country was moving from a military dictatorship to a democratic regime. At that time, a number of small independent production houses appeared in Rio de Janeiro and São Paulo. Interestingly, this is when my brother João and I founded our production house, VideoFilmes, and also Fernando Meirelles' production company in São Paulo appeared. This 'Brazilian spring' lasted for three or four years. Then Collor was elected, in 1989, in our first so-called democratic election in twenty-five years. 'So-called' refers to the fact that the private Brazilian television stations had a strong impact on that election, supporting Collor.

What was supposed to take democracy even further ended up being a disaster on all levels. His discourse was all about integrating Brazil into the 'First World', as if you could do that by decree. What he did was create complete chaos in the economy – unemployment, inflation were completely out of control. All savings accounts were blocked, as you see at the start of *Foreign Land*. The whole country came to a halt.

It wasn't a period only of economic and social chaos, but of cultural chaos as well: all his decisions in that regard were catastrophic. Because almost everyone from the cultural milieu had supported his opponent, Lula, head of the workers' party – who more recently became our president – Collor started a personal vendetta against theatre, cinema, all the arts. He sought revenge in a very direct manner: by eliminating all forms of subsidy that existed for cinema at that time in Brazil.

They didn't forbid films, they just cut all the financing mechanisms that would make films possible. And the country was in such an economic mess that it was impossible to get money from anywhere else. It was a dark age: cinematic production fell from between seventy and eighty films per year – which corresponded to a third of the tickets that were sold every year – to literally zero in 1990, 1991 and 1992. Maybe one film in 1991. Brazilian cinema ceased to exist for four years. At the same time, the gates were opened for international companies to sink their teeth even further into the Brazilian film market.

Another interesting aspect is that when Collor came to power Brazil had five thousand screens. When he left, there were only 750 – they became evangelical churches. This tells you the extent of the tragedy: when *Central Station* was launched in Brazil, in 1998, after having won the Berlin Film Festival, we couldn't get more than thirty-six screens in the whole country. At that time *Titanic* was occupying around 350 screens and *The Man with the Iron Mask* 250; these two studio movies were actually using more than eighty per cent of the screens that were available in Brazil at the time.

*Are there more cinemas today?*

Yes, now we're at about two thousand screens. But still not even half of what we had before. And these screens are much smaller than they used to be in the seventies and eighties.

*Thankfully, Collor wasn't around for too long.*

And when he was impeached in 1992, and certain film laws were re-established, film-makers suddenly felt a sensation that was quite exhilarating: it was possible again to express yourself in your own language, which was the one of cinema. But what we felt while Collor was in power is the origin of *Foreign Land*.

*Let's talk about* Foreign Land. *To begin, could you say something about the nature of your collaboration with Daniela Thomas?*

Daniela has been my closest collaborator for more than ten years. She is at once a brilliant theatre director and playwright, and an extraordinary art director. A Renaissance mind lost in the tropics. We share the desire to look at Brazilian society together every few years. *Foreign Land* was the first film that we directed together.

Our collaboration works in the following manner: at the start, I bring an idea and, if Daniela responds to it, we start developing it together. I attempt to write what looks like a first draft. Then, she writes her own take. From draft to draft, we ultimately reach a point at which we are at peace with the way the story is structured, the contours of the characters and dialogue. At this point, I usually begin to define the film's grammar, the way in which the story will be told with the camera, while Daniela roots the characters in their own specific environment through her talent in production design and art direction. Then we rehearse the actors together, and she tends to have more input in that period due to her experience in theatre. Every single doubt is sorted out during this rehearsal phase. This is when we can disagree, experiment with new routes. And then, when the shoot begins, we tend to be in full synchronicity; so much so, in fact, that we can heavily improvise together without getting lost – this is what happened during *Foreign Land*. The final film was very different from the actual screenplay.

*You also had other writers on the film.*

A young law student called Marcos Bernstein, who was an intern in our production house at the time, added a number of good ideas. He later became one of the writers on *Central Station*. And Millôr Fernandes collaborated on the film's dialogue, improving it a lot. Millôr is a brilliant Renaissance man – playwright, writer, cartoonist, screenwriter. At eighty, he is also one of the youngest and freshest minds in Brazil.

I should say that the process has evolved with *Linha de passe*, in the sense that there all areas of directing were truly shared, from the beginning till the end. In regard to the screenplay, we started as we did in *Foreign Land*: I developed an initial architecture that Daniela and her co-writer George Moura polished and improved in more than twenty drafts. At one point, the script had to be rewritten in an in-depth manner, when part of the story was unfortunately appropriated in a TV drama. This is when Bráulio Mantovani [the scriptwriter of *City of God*] came to the rescue, in a moment where we were truly lacking oxygen. He was involved with other projects but helped us in a very generous manner, and the end result was a screenplay that departed greatly from the story I had structured five years ago.

*How did you finance* Foreign Land?

When the film was made the state financing mechanisms had just been put into motion again. We were therefore helped by RioFilme, a municipal financing and distribution company created by the city of Rio de Janeiro. It was headed at that time by the film critic José Carlos Avellar, one of the people to whom I owe the most. And the film was shot very rapidly. Due to the pace that we imposed, from the start, it cost less than $400,000.

*You made the film in 1996, but it's set in the middle of the Collor crisis a few years earlier.*

What ignited the film was the mutual desire to talk about what a generation of young Brazilians felt when they were deprived of a future. In the Collor years Brazil ceased to be a country of immigration and, for the first time in five hundred years, became

© Walter Salles

Exiles: *Foreign Land* (1996)

a country of emigration: eight hundred thousand men and women with no perspective on their own country chose to live somewhere else; as do Paco and Alex, the main characters of the film.

*Foreign Land* is about homelessness, rootlessness and exile. Both Daniela and I wanted, therefore, to do an *urgent* film, one directly tied to an experience that we all had in the country, collectively, whether in front of or behind the cameras. It's a film shot very quickly, on three continents, in fewer than twenty days. And yet we never had the impression that we were racing to achieve what we needed. Quite the opposite: shooting *Foreign Land* was one of the most agreeable experiences I've ever had in cinema.

*I believe you were actually one of those Brazilians who temporarily left the country?*

I left, and started working in France, making documentaries for French television. For example, I made a documentary called

*Chico Buarque, ou le pays de la delicatesse perdu* – 'the country that has lost its delicate quality'.

*There is an overpowering sense in* Foreign Land, *in both the Brazilian and Lisbon scenes, of people not belonging.*

During the shoot, we started to incorporate what we were seeing in the streets. When we arrived in Lisbon, for instance, we realised that the city was partly inhabited by a number of immigrants from different countries like Angola, Mozambique, Cape Verde and Timor, former Portuguese colonies. These were people who were in the same position as Brazilians were then: adrift. And the fact that we bumped into them immediately changed what we were doing. These immigrants were absent from the Portuguese films that we saw at that time, and yet there they were, in front of us, in the streets. So we rewrote the screenplay to incorporate these guys who were as lost in Europe as we Brazilians were. We would not have been able to react in that way, probably, without the training in documentaries.

*The film has a very vital style, which evokes a number of film-makers for me, notably Godard. The eerie feeling of alienation in the opening scenes made me think, specifically, of* Alphaville. *Is it fair to say that the film represented a young director's* nouvelle vague-*like aspirations?*

Because young Brazilian film-makers hadn't been able to express themselves for four or five years, the films that appeared in the post-Collor era, beginning in the mid-nineties, were nurtured by this extraordinary gusto for cinema, in its most diverse forms. *Foreign Land* is our homage to a number of films that we loved: the influence of the black-and-white Cinema Novo films, the early Wenders films like *Alice in the Cities* and *Kings of the Road* and, yes, the early *nouvelle vague* films like *Breathless* (I hadn't seen *Alphaville* at the time) and Alain Tanner's *The White City*.

*Did you draw some inspiration from the political nature of the Cinema Novo films?*

Yes, certainly, and more specifically in the first part of the narrative – the one in which Paco has to deal with his mother's death.

*Glauber Rocha spoke of Cinema Novo's aim as seeking 'to make the public aware of its own misery'. Is this a long way from your and your contemporaries' ambitions?*

Yes and no. Yes, because, as I was saying earlier, cinema should function both as a way to offer a country's reflection on the screen and as an instrument to better understand the world. But the difference between our generation and that of the Cinema Novo years has to do with the fact that the Brazilian society of the nineties or at the beginning of this millennium is very different, structurally, from the society that was making its transition to industrialism in the late fifties and early sixties. It's a much more complex world out there, which requires different instruments to comprehend it. Also, cinema viewers today can access a much wider array of films than in the sixties. I believe that today you can, and should, ask questions, but not impose answers on them.

*Paco is the first of a number of young men and boys in your films.*

That's true. The idea of someone who keeps a sense of innocence in the midst of a cynical environment is an element of almost all of the films and documentaries I have done. You will find that in *Central Station*, in *Behind the Sun*. I'm interested in somebody who has moral and ethical values that somehow confront those of their established community.

*And identity, a theme that is so strong in* Foreign Land, *will also come up time and again in your work.*

It's important to remember, I think, that in Western Europe you live in societies whose identities are, for the most part, crystallised. In Latin America we are societies in the making. Our identity is redefined as we speak.

In a country like Brazil, the collision between social classes and the violence that results show that the population wants to redefine the country. The question of identity, as a result of that, is at the core of Brazilian cinema. These very simple questions – where do we come from? who are we? where are we heading? – are at the heart of most of our recent film efforts, from *Foreign Land* to *City of God*, from *Madame Satã* to *Bus 174*.

And what interests me as a film-maker are the actual parallels that can exist between an individual's journey and the way a society or a country itself evolves. This is why most of the characters in my films are characters who re-baptise themselves. This is the case in *Foreign Land*, *Central Station* and *The Motorcycle Diaries*, which form a sort of trilogy of the Brazilian and Latin American identity.

## *Retomada*, rediscovering Brazil, *Central Station*

We hear the sounds of Central do Brasil, the central train station in Rio de Janeiro, before we see it: the announcer, the sound of trains, the bustle of commuters. Then a melancholy theme tune plays as people disembark, and a crying woman speaks in close-up, declaring her feelings to her lover, who is in jail. She is replaced by a smiling old man, who thanks the person who cheated him (we never learn the reason for his gratitude, but it's a fine attitude to take), and a mother, her young boy beside her, who declares, 'Jesus, you're the worst thing to happen to me.'

A parade of people speak to the camera, giving the destinations throughout Brazil to which their declarations, being written down by Dora (Fernanda Montenegro), are to be posted. It is a touching, intriguing, immediately embracing opening to a film which also happens to represent the declaration to the world of the return of Brazilian cinema.

Dora, it transpires, is a cynical, middle-aged woman whose inventive service at the station – writing letters for the city's many illiterates, so they may connect with their loved ones – is actually a ruse: instead of posting the letters, she reads them to her friend for amusement, before throwing them away and pocketing the postage charge. But events conspire to leave the aforementioned boy, Josué, in her care, along with the task of finding for him his father, Jesus. The pair leave Rio for Bom Jesus do Norte, in the northern province of Pernambuco.

Thus *Central Station* concerns a boy's search for the father he has never known, and a woman's rediscovery of a sense of decency she had long forgotten, buried beneath the pain of her own familial losses. It is also a director's discovery of a country that, in some senses, he had known only from other people's films.

There are road movies in which the locations are irrelevant, merely a backdrop to adventure, and those infinitely more interesting ones in which the road and what is found on it are integral to the character's interior journey. *Central Station* belongs firmly in the latter category. Indeed, the road movie is Salles' preferred form, with which he is able to exercise his curiosity about his country and the world, and this is the clue to his films' international appeal: whatever its specific continental or national characteristics, the 'well-travelled' road movie will connect with anyone who has wondered about his or her place in the world.

In *Central Station* we see two aspects of Salles' approach to film-making: the formal and the organic. On the one hand, meticulous care is taken over composition, particularly in the Rio scenes where the framing and shallow focus evoke the alienating effect of city life, and the fear that it can hold for those desperate inhabitants; on the other, real life is constantly permitted to seep into the film, not least when non-actors make their way before the camera, often casually. When Dora and Josué encounter a pilgrimage in the *sertão*, the whirl of preachers, fortune-tellers, musicians and hawkers is patently real. Of course, there are moments – for example, when the boy runs through a candle-lit night – when the two tendencies memorably merge.

This story is told with the heart, head and a great sense of cinematic style. Salles doesn't attempt to ignore the country's problems: the Rio scenes are genuinely disturbing – proving that you need only show one brutal murder in order to establish the danger of a milieu – and the scenes of the *sertão* suggest little promise of a comfortable life. Most of those we encounter are caught in the pincer of illiteracy and blind faith. Nevertheless, while the father is – as always – elusive, brothers provide the key to the film's essential optimism.

With *Central Station*, Salles proved himself to be both a humanist and a pragmatist: caring for his characters and the world he depicts, optimistic on their behalf, and also caring as a film-maker about the accessibility that will help a film connect with a wider audience. This pragmatism – call it commercial savvy if you will – informs all the major Brazilian films, particularly *City of God*, to have touched both local and international audiences since the country's cinema revival.

The late Anthony Minghella said of *Central Station*, 'That small Brazilian movie touched more hearts than almost any other movie I know of. It announced a real voice in international cinema.' The film premiered in 1998 in Sundance, before going on to win the Golden Bear in Berlin. Its achievements, including box-office success around the world and two Oscar nominations (best foreign language film, and actress), cannot be underestimated. Not least, it enabled Salles to enter the ranks of viable international directors, allowing him to begin to influence and support his fellow film-makers in Brazil.

*I'd just like to cast back to that period in which* Foreign Land *is set, the early nineties. It seems ironic that it was harder to get films made under Collor's so-called democracy than it was under the previous military dictatorships.*

Yes, but at that stage you could do certain films, and not others. We should never encourage military regimes or say it was not as bad as it sounded. We were living under palpable restrictions at that point, and I think that they had a very negative effect on Brazilian cinema in the eighties. There was an array of themes that you couldn't touch upon; anything that had a social and political quality was eliminated.

The first part of the *coup d'état* – that is, from 1964 to 1968 – was one where you could still express yourself. From 1968 on, which represents the coup within the coup, freedom of speech was curtailed completely. This is when the censors lived inside the newspapers, to the point where one or two newspapers in Brazil started to fill the blanks that the censor had left with poetry: every time you saw poetry in the middle of a page, you knew the article had been censored. This is also when a number of film-makers and musicians opted for exile – Glauber Rocha left for Paris, Caetano Veloso and Gilberto Gil went to London – in order to be able to express themselves freely.

In Latin America today we owe our existence to the generations that have preceded us and resisted, in one way or another, the military regimes that were in power on the continent during the sixties, seventies and part of the eighties. The fact that there were film-makers who tried to continue to do their work in very difficult times, including Nelson Pereira dos Santos, Carlos Diegues and many other film-makers from the Cinema Novo generation, who fought constantly for freedom of expression when that vital quality was constantly being disrespected in Brazil, laid the foundation, in a way, for a new generation who could express themselves without fear of harm.

*And after the rude interruption of the Collor government, this desire for expression was even stronger.*

I think we had a real sense of mission. Suddenly you find yourself in a world where you are allowed to talk again about your

own country. And obviously at that point you have so many stories that you want to tell and haven't been allowed to tell. And in
1994 you had something interesting, something that corresponded to a national filmic movement, which was called in Brazil the
*retomada*, the rebirth of our cinema. And that movement was
multi-generational. On one hand you had film-makers like
Carlos Diegues, a Cinema Novo director who is still very active
today; you had film-makers from my generation, starting to do
their first and second films; then you had film-makers from an
even younger group, such as Tata Amaral, who made *Um céu de
estrelas* in that period.

Those films had one shared characteristic: either directly or
indirectly, they were all trying to talk about what had happened
in a country that had undergone tremendous transformations
over the previous twenty-five years.

You have to understand that this is something that television
doesn't do in Brazil. Our TV has a very alienating quality, making it almost the opposite of what you have on British television,
which is a very democratic instrument. Firstly, our television is
mainly privately owned, and therefore responding to a specific
ideological agenda; secondly, the schedules of the numerous
channels really mimic each other, therefore leaving very little
ground for reality to find its way through the cracks of that pro-
gramming. The culture of the *telenovela* left an enormous, open
field for us to fill.

*What was the first film of the* retomada?

It was a historical comedy, *Carlota Joaquina – Princesa do
Brasil*, made in 1995 by Carla Camurati, an actress who became
a director. Interestingly, although it appeared to be set in the
past, when Brazil was part of the Portuguese empire, you could
make the correlation with what had just happened to us under
the dictatorship. So in an indirect manner it was talking about
who we were and especially where we were coming from. It was

a very interesting political satire, very caustic, and very revealing of why we were in the situation we were in.

That film had great importance because it brought the public back to the theatres. And then a number of films profited from this regaining of interest, *Foreign Land* among them. When the *retomada* films surfaced, they gathered an immediate public response. And there you have another element, which is the public seeking to see themselves on the screen. For five years they were not able to do so.

*Do you think it was Brazilian stories, plain and simple, that they wanted? Or perhaps some answers about this appalling political period?*

Inversely, it's about going to the theatre in order to understand what the questions are. Cinema should not automatically hold all the answers; on the contrary, it should raise the questions. This is what *Memories of Underdevelopment* does so brilliantly. It puts you face-to-face with a reality that is extremely complex, leaving you with more questions than you had when you entered the movie theatre.

Abbas Kiarostami gave a very interesting interview in Brazil, a few years ago, when he was asked to compare a commercial film and an independent film. He said it's very simple: a commercial film is a film where we understand everything, and an independent film, or a film that comes from a country like Brazil or Argentina, or his part of the world, should help us understand what the questions truly are.

*We've spoken about the correlation between documentary and fiction in terms of subject matter. There's a direct example in relation to your next feature,* Central Station, *which was prompted by your documentary* Socorro nobre (Life Somewhere Else, *1995). Can you tell me about the documentary?*

It tells the story of the written relationship between a woman,

© Walter Carvalho

The eponymous *Socorro Nobre*, in Salles' 1995 documentary

Socorro Nobre, who was an inmate in a prison in Brazil, and an elderly sculptor, Franz Krajcberg. She discovered the work of this man, who goes into the Amazon and takes up burnt wood and sculpts it. She read something in a newspaper about him and made a connection, somehow, between his granting a second life to something that had been burned, and her own experience, her desire to start again. So she wrote to him. And he wrote back, and they started a correspondence. Franz happens to be one of my best friends, and told me about their exchange, which is how I came to make the film.

We were in the prison for three days, but didn't film on the first. I learned that from Sebastião Salgado: 'Look first.' It took us a month to get the authorisation. In the end I think the woman who ran the prison hoped the film could help Socorro. For my part, I was shocked by the importance that a letter can have. On the verge of the twenty-first century, in the age of the Internet and so forth, here you had lives that were changed by a letter. And I started to think about what could happen if letters were written but did not reach their destination. And what if this happened on purpose? This is how the story of *Central Station* was born.

*In fact, Socorro is the first person we see in* Central Station, *in the station itself, dictating a letter. And she's crying.*

Yes, she is. That was the first week she was out of prison. And it was a real letter that she was dictating, to someone she left behind.

*I loved the close-ups of the different people, effectively dictating their letters to the camera.*

That's one way in which the film is modified by the contact with life. The letters in the film are real letters. People saw Dora's little table and came there and asked whether they could dictate letters, and we accepted that.

This was a major challenge in the movie, intermingling an actor – the magnificent Brazilian actress Fernanda Montenegro – with non-actors, in order to achieve, if you like, Godard's 'truth, twenty-four frames a second'. The 'real Brazil' passes through Dora, and the letters dictated to her shape the tone of the film. I wanted *Central Station* to open in such a way that for several minutes the viewers wonder whether they are watching fiction or documentary. The whole texture of the film was constantly transformed by the contact with reality.

*Just out of interest, what was Socorro's crime? You don't raise it in the documentary.*

There was a conflict in her family that ended in a fight, and the death of one brother. She wasn't there when it happened, but was considered a collaborator and given the harshest possible sentence. I didn't want to go into that, because it was not a film about guilt and punishment, but about the possibility of healing, about someone giving themselves a second chance. I wanted to show how Krajcberg's sculptures gave her the desire to survive in prison.

*What does* Central Station *as a fiction lend to our understanding of what had been a real-life situation you had already documented?*

The documentary was about two people whose lives were changed by the fact that they wrote letters to each other. That led me to try to imagine what would happen to people who could have gone through the same process: if their letters were also delivered, destinies would be altered, but they are not, because Dora takes their money and does nothing. Then that question was linked to the much broader question that was at stake in Brazil at that time, which was really a question of ethics. We were coming out of the military regime, we were coming out of the Collor years, always the end justifying the means. Dora is the

Shoe-shine boy Vinícius de Oliveira finds his voice in *Central Station*

expression of that very cynical period. And what the documentary showed me was that there was something burgeoning in the country which is the opposite of that. This is what helped me create the character of the little boy, Josué, who would challenge Dora's cynical perception of the world.

By the way, if the film had resonance in Brazil, and also outside Brazil, I think it's because the characters were representative of that ethical question, a question that transcended the personal journeys of Dora and Josué.

*This raises an interesting point. Many British film-makers, among others, make the mistake of trying to follow American formulas, with the result that the films usually die somewhere over the Atlantic. In contrast, a number of Latin American directors are making non-genre, highly personal films, rooted in their environments, which are striking a chord internationally. In other words: having faith in your own culture pays.*

I completely agree, and I think that's the reverse angle of globalisation. You look around you, you sit in front of the television, and what you see is a multitude of the same thing. You're witnessing the McDonaldisation of the world. So whatever offers you the possibility of understanding that the world is much larger, more complex, more polyphonic than it seems when you're watching CNN is, I think, necessary.

I think we have a very clear understanding of this in South America. If our narratives start to mimic a Hollywood narrative, or a classical commercial narrative, we will fail for a very simple reason: that form of narration has to do with a specific culture that has nothing to do with ours. Our films would immediately feel artificial. On the other hand, the way we structure our stories is never oriented towards three acts, the conflicts tend to be internal as opposed to clearly external, the sense of time and the way the shot breathes are radically different. And just as Hollywood narrative tends to be about characters responding to an input brought by another character, our narratives are most of the time about characters changing when they are confronted with specific political or social environments. Their plots are rarely integrated into a social context; for us the context is as important as the characters. *Central Station* is a clear example of that: it's to do with the harmful cynicism of the Collor years, which tried to turn Brazil into a First World country, whatever the cost.

*It's also, literally and metaphorically, a journey through the country.*

We were living in a time where the interior of Brazil was seen as archaic. *Central Station* answers a need to show a contradictory argument. I wanted to go to the interior of the country and again show that there was something to be learned from looking in that direction. It's no accident that the beginning of the film, which is in the station, in Rio, talks about Dora's individualism, her solitude, and the cynicism of this woman who is unable to shelter the boy, and even tries to sell him – which relates to the ethics of the time. The return to the heart of the country allows for a certain understanding to develop. The further she goes, the more she sees what she had completely forgotten, which is the humanity of our culture. The intention in the film was really to frame what hadn't been framed, literally, for a long time. And to say, 'This is us,' or 'This is also us.' Only by the understanding of who we are can we actually move forward collectively.

*My memory of the Rio section is almost monochrome.*

That's the idea. It is very monochromatic; we eliminated all vivid colours from the Rio de Janeiro section. Also, at the beginning of the film there is very little depth of field, people are kind of lost in the frame, you have no skies, very limited perception of the geography in the city. The impression is of individuals isolated in those large urban spaces, with a desire to communicate yet unable to do so.

Then, little by little, the further they go into the hinterland, the more vivid the palette becomes. For the first time the characters in the frame gain focus. The film language we used was really about recuperating your vision, the vision of the country that you belong to, perceiving it in a different manner.

*I'm interested in the dynamic between such evident, formal planning, and the sense of spontaneity in your films.*

I think that cinema has a little to do with jazz, in the sense that the screenplay is the melody from which you have to start, but also depart, if you want to have something that is truly original and fresh. In Portuguese, screenplay is *roteiro*, which comes from *rota*, a specific road. It's the thing that shows you what the road is, but once you're on it I think you should have the autonomy to decide how far you should go on that road, or whether to explore the side roads as well. This is when the possibility of doing something transcendent in cinema occurs, when you blend a work that is truly solid and consistent with an experience that works in a sensorial and responsive manner.

So *Central Station* was thought out item by item, before I shot it. But thanks to the fact that so much thought had preceded the film, we were able to improvise quite a lot. For example, when we bumped into the religious gatherings in the countryside, we thought it would be interesting to use them: more from an anthropological standpoint than any other – the film's themes are not religious. Those religious scenes were not in the screenplay, but we started to incorporate them as we went along, because they certainly enrich the story, they were completely pertinent.

The same thing happened in *Behind the Sun*. The girl from the travelling circus actually came from a circus. One day she was exercising outside the hotel and was doing this fire-eating trick. The crew were all spellbound. So we immediately included it. And again with her rope trick: she showed us this amazing skill, and we immediately created the possibility for it to be included.

*And those scenes resonate with the themes at play.*

Absolutely. If it was just a gimmick, the film would disintegrate.

*As with* Foreign Land, *there is an absent father. This time, though, there is an active effort to find him.*

In Portuguese the word 'country' and the word 'father' are almost the same: father is *pai* and country is *pais*. Thus, the search for the father that is at the core of the film is in fact a search for the country. Again, I think the film touched a chord in Brazil because we were not talking only about two characters trying to find their own roots; at the same time, it was a film trying to find a country's roots, its identity.

*How would you say the two films complement each other?*

*Foreign Land* is a film about two characters who try to re-baptise themselves, or to redefine themselves by fleeing Brazil during the Collor years. And *Central Station* is a film about two people trying to re-baptise themselves by going to the heart of the country. Interestingly, *Foreign Land* goes towards Portugal, which is our stepfather. *Central Station* does the opposite: it tries in many ways to understand what makes us intrinsically Brazilian.

*I think this desire is one direct connection between your work and that of Cinema Novo.*

I agree. It was not by accident that Cinema Novo happened, in the late fifties and sixties, at a moment of extraordinary political freedom in the country. For the first time Brazilians had the certainty that they could define their own future and create a society that was truly unique and original. And all the different art forms – music, poetry, architecture, film – tried to respond to that need. That was the moment when you can really say that a national cinema was born.

Here you had a group of directors, who came from different

parts of the country, yet had the same aesthetic and ethical principles. It is true that they were influenced by the Italian neo-realists, but they blended this with the heritage of Soviet cinema – most specifically Eisenstein's technique of montage – and in certain cases with a *nouvelle vague* influence. But while drawing from these different movements, they somehow went beyond them, in responding to a very local culture. That's the most important thing, to capture a specific human geography, a specific physical geography, capturing stories that are local and transferring them to the screen; while also, of course, because it was the fifties and sixties, combining that with a political and social discussion that had to do with what kind of society we wanted to live in. It was a fascinating time, because the destiny of the country was totally open. And cinema was reflecting that.

*You've used the phrase before: can you elaborate on 'aesthetic and ethical principles'?*

Let's start with the neo-realists and understand what they did. Before Rossellini did *Rome, Open City* [1945], what you had was film production that was basically straitjacketed, shot in the studios and obliged to mirror the 'realities' of the Mussolini era. What Rossellini, Pasolini, De Sica, Visconti, Fellini and later Antonioni do is take the camera out of the studio and bring it close not only to the faces, but to the stories of the people in the street. For the first time in the history of cinema, what they do is almost to eliminate the distance between the observer and the one who is being observed, thus creating an aesthetic, but also ethical, revolution in the cinema – those things go hand in hand.

And it was a very liberating movement. You didn't need to film in studios any more, you didn't need to work with big cameras or well-known actors. *Rome, Open City*, or Visconti's *La terra trema* [1947] open an array of possibilities. The next-door neighbour's story can literally become the material of a feature-length film for the first time. This had a tremendous impact on world cinema, particularly in emerging cultures and emerging economies, where you need to work with whatever means you have. And when your stories are happening in front of your very eyes in the street, when you can use non-actors as the main characters, it's tremendously liberating. I think that our cinema movement owes a lot to these doors that were opened by the neo-realists.

*It's worth noting the similarities of process with documentary.*

Absolutely. There are similarities in the decision to work with as small a crew as possible; to incorporate as many newcomers behind and in front of the camera as possible; to use as little artificial light as you can during the process. And there is the incorporation of anything you find on the road that is pertinent to the story.

*Is there any way in which, when you use the word 'ethical', you also mean political?*

I think the terms are intrinsically linked, in the sense that every ethical and moral decision that you take is a political decision. Gael [García Bernal] says that in Latin America even the choice of what you're going to wear is political. Of course it's a figure of speech, but it is also true.

*This conversation makes me think of Ken Loach.*

Well, if you talk to film-makers as different as Fernando Meirelles or Pablo Trapero or Andrés Wood, I think they will all tell you how important *Kes* [1969] or *Raining Stones* [1993] or *Riff Raff* [1991] were for them: in the way those characters are portrayed and evolve you can see reflected a lot of the struggles in our own films. Also you get a sense that the cinematic struggle – that is, the economic struggle that Ken Loach goes through to make his films – has a lot to do with the cinematic struggle that a number of film-makers in Latin America go through to do their own. The correlation relates not only to what is seen on the screen, but to how the film itself is made.

*Picking up the earlier question: do you feel that with Dora and Josué's journey to the north-east you are reaching back to Cinema Novo, which of course became synonymous with the* sertão?

We're getting back to a geography that was 'named', made known visually for the first time by Cinema Novo. But I'm conscious that I'm doing it in a different manner and especially at a different time. The political, historical conditions of the fifties were very different to those of the nineties. In the earlier period you had the impression that the possibilities were endless – you could even recreate a capital in a no-man's-land. *Central Station* responded to a different country. And so the film could not be one of the Cinema Novo tradition. There are correlations, but also differences.

*Since we've mentioned* The Passenger, *I can't help making this observation. When I first saw* Central Station, *the key scene when Dora and Josué arrive at the house where he hopes to find his father reminded me of Antonioni's famous sequence in his film, when the camera leaves Nicholson's room, passes through the square and back again. It's just a moment, an echo.*

That's interesting. I never thought of that. That scene from *The Passenger* is, I think, the most extraordinary final scene in cinema. Every single element in that square becomes part of the story.

*And camera movement around space, when it's done that well, adopts a psychological dimension.*

I completely agree with you. And I think that Antonioni is the film-maker who best translated the correlation between physical geography and human geography. It's interesting that you're associating it with a scene that was very complex to do. Maybe it is not evident now, but the actor who plays the mistaken father, who appears in the middle of the sequence, and Vinícius, who plays the young kid, never get to act with each other. Vinícius became ill for three days and couldn't shoot, and the father was doing theatre in Salvador, so I had to shoot that sequence in a manner I had not anticipated. And I thought it was extremely interesting and appropriate that, since this was the false father, the father not-to-be, in reality the kid would never actually see him. The shot/reverse shot: they are never in the same frame. It's the magic of cinema.

*How did you find the boy who played Josué?*

Vinícius [de Oliveira] was a shoe-shine boy. I tried to find a boy for a whole year, I did fifteen hundred tests. And in the end he found me. He just came up and asked me to lend him some money for a sandwich. I remember I was wearing sneakers, so he couldn't offer to clean my shoes. I said, 'Of course I will buy you a sandwich, but do a film test with me.' And he said, 'I can't, because I've never been to the movies before.' But ultimately he came, he did a test, and was brilliant in it.

*Was he at school at the time?*

No, he had abandoned school for a year and a half, but went back after the film. He was a very honest kid, poor but very honest, with a very sound family.

*And he appears in the new film,* Linha de passe. *You've kept in touch all this time.*

After *Central Station*, Vinícius and I stayed in close contact. We became friends and he has visited me and my family constantly during the last ten years. This was also due to the fact that, in order to do *Central Station*, he had to promise that he would go back to school and go all the way to college. Vinicius is a serious, smart guy and he kept that promise. As a matter of fact, he's just entered university and is now enrolled in the best cinema department here in Rio. His aim is to become a film director. As for acting, he kept the flame alive and did several plays between *Central Station* and *Linha de passe*, as well as cinema and television.

He's magnetic on stage, and seeing him maturing as an actor was an unforgettable experience. *Linha de passe* will exist in great part due to the desire to work with him again. I've always been fond of directors who revisit characters in their films or who worked continuously with an actor, as Truffaut did with Jean-Pierre Léaud.

*I think it's fair to say that* Central Station *pretty much announced the* retomada *to the world. That's almost a decade ago now.*

And I think you can follow that movement, that renaissance all the way to *City of God* and *Madame Satã*, or even Babenco's *Carandiru*.

*If Babenco was premature in 1991 to talk about the death of Brazilian cinema, what is the state of the patient today?*

I think what you have now is, on the one hand, films that still try to answer those questions of identity, about characters transformed by the social and political reality around them, with on the other hand films that are products or sub-products of television, with no relation to reality. You can see now in Brazilian cinema these two paths that diverge greatly. If you're asking me about the state of the patient today: I think that we're on the analyst's couch trying to make sense of this dichotomy.

*But on the road to recovery?*

I think that the *retomada* was all about the recovery. And actually it acquired strength much earlier than I thought it would. The dialogue that Brazilian films created in the nineties and the beginning of this decade with the public was more than we could expect. Think of the number of spectators that a film like *City of God* had in Brazil – more than three million people came to see that film, at a time when everybody said that the public would not pay for a ticket to see a story about the *favelas*. Well, not only did they, but they really discovered a reality that was not shown on television.

The film had such an effect on the social fabric of this country that it ultimately went to television, as *City of Men*, and did extremely well. That was the first time that you had a series on television with young black kids as the protagonists and, I think, the first time you could see the world of the *favelas* on TV. Up to that point, when you saw black characters in soap operas they were limited to stereotypes, characters who were always at the service of white families and white stories. And the periphery was very rarely represented.

*So film is fighting back against television?*

Absolutely. I think that Fernando Meirelles is mainly responsible for that. We have to applaud him for having really altered, or shaken, this barrier that had existed in TV. And he's continuing to do that. His company has produced Tata Amaral's film *Antônia*, which is also a mini-series, with four black actresses representing the outskirts in São Paulo.

*How is television achieving this negative impact on cinema?*

The state system of financing films in Brazil relies on a tax-shelter device that allows enterprise companies to invest part of what they would otherwise pay in tax, in culture. In 1994–5, when Brazil started to see the rebirth of its cinema, that was a very important device, which allowed us to re-emerge from the ashes. The problem is that, little by little, the private Brazilian television companies have started to use this same device to finance their own films. And these films for the most part are derivative of what they already have on air, sub-products of what you see on television.

So there is an inversion of what has happened in Europe, where Film Verlag in Germany, Arte in France, Channel 4 and the BBC in Britain have allowed film-makers to have a voice. When television comes into the world of cinema in a non-imposing manner, when it respects the necessary difference between the two media, respects diversity, we should be all for it. On the other hand, if television comes into the territory of cinema to impose its own aesthetic perception of the world, or to launch what become sub-products of its programmes, then I think we should be against it and voice our discontent.

*I understand there is a product-placement award here.*

Yeah, I heard about that. Why would you allow public money to finance films that actually believe in cinema as 'product' and are full of merchandising events that permeate a narrative?

*The problem is, presumably, that these films have a ready-made audience in the cinemas, squeezing out the bona fide films?*

And, also, the perception that the public has of cinema becomes very blurred. For that special relationship between spectator and national cinema to exist, the cinema has to have a very strong identity.

You know, the problem between cinema and television is that you always make cinema – at least the independent cinema that interests us – *against* something, either from an aesthetic or a political standpoint. And television is exactly the opposite of that: television, especially commercial television, is *for* something. So it's very dangerous to create a system where cinema and television are in competition. And that's the situation in

Brazil. At the end of the day what we're talking about is the difference between those who see films as a possibility of mirroring one's society and those who see cinema as new commercial territory that needs to be controlled.

*Is there a danger, in any case, in being dependent on state money? Look what happened when the Collor government pulled the funds – the industry collapsed. Is there a future in private, independently secured financing, and co-productions with overseas companies?*

This is basically what we do at VideoFilmes. Since *Central Station* we've been trying to find the co-productions, mainly with Europe, that will allow our film-makers to express their personal voices. *Suely in the Sky*, for instance, was done in this manner.

On the other hand, think about a young film-maker who is coming out of film school: he's in his early twenties, he's got talent and ideas and a screenplay that is ready to go. With Brazil's world of tax-shelter private financing, that guy, unless he has extraordinary luck, is going to have to fight for years to have his first film made. I believe that outside the Hollywood and Bollywood worlds, a national cinema can't exist without a form of state protection.

I compare what is happening in Brazil with Argentina. I prefer their system of a state-controlled fund, in which a commission, INCAA, finances a number of films based on the quality of the screenplays and the history of the film-maker, as opposed to the marketing potential or the audience potential of a project. This is what has allowed Argentine cinema to become as good as it has in the last five or six years. It's direct funding, as opposed to trusting the marketing directors of privately owned companies to select a project. What you do is create a fund and determine in a democratic manner who are the film-makers who are going to be considered.

Argentine films are not a hundred per cent state-funded, because they're also looking for possible co-productions, with European countries, or to access grants. But the fundamental state system allows for much more independence than we have in Brazil.

*Does VideoFilmes in any way use this indirect state money?*

We do, mostly from the main financier today of Brazilian cinema – Petrobras, the state-owned oil company. But Petrobras really functions like the INCAA. José Carlos Avellar was one of the people responsible for that fund. Here is the most knowledge-able person about Brazilian cinema, an ex-film critic, helping to put the system to good use. The Petrobras programme is a very democratic and well-run programme that really allows film-makers to access tax-shelter money without any kind of imposi-tion. So there are a few companies, mostly state-owned, who are allowing true cinema to exist in Brazil. They are not worried about product placement. I think they are responsible not only for the best projects in Brazilian cinema, but also for the best dance and theatre and other forms of expression.

For most of our projects we try to look for co-productions. At the same time we bring them to the Petrobras fund. Sometimes our projects are accepted, sometimes they are not, but at least you get a level of independence when funded by Petrobras that you don't get when funded by a burger chain.

*There is also the chief obstacle to a national cinema, which is dis-tribution. How can you compete when Hollywood dominates the market?*

Since 1918 we have had to compete face-to-face with an indus-try that has privileges that we don't have. For example, a car that is made in Brazil has all the fiscal advantages of being home-made, while cars that are imported have to pay considerable tax. There is no such law protecting Brazilian cinema from the competition. And there never has been. But in many territories you have rules that protect the local film industry from unfair competition, France being the best example. Every time you buy a ticket for an American film there, you are contributing to a French fund that will finance French films. There is no such thing in Brazil. After all, you are in Adam Smith's land.

I personally believe that the fairest manner to allow a local film industry to exist is to tax the import of films and films on television. We don't have such a thing. And that is in part due to the power of the American lobby. It shows how conscious the American government is not only of the fact that Hollywood films are one of their main export items, but also that those films contribute to the marketing of a lifestyle. They are a form of cultural as well as economic colonialism.

*Did the contacts established while you were making documentaries in France, such as Canal Plus, help when you started to direct features? And perhaps set a European co-production template for VideoFilmes?*

Not before *Central Station* won the Berlin Film Festival. This is when things truly started to change – and allowed the creation of an international production network that helped not only the films that I would direct from that moment on, but also the ones that I was able to produce here in Brazil.

*You've nurtured a number of film-makers, at different stages of their careers and in different ways. But I'm interested in how you came across Sérgio Machado and Karim Ainouz, who were not based in Rio or São Paulo.*

I met Sérgio before Karim, and the circumstances in which we met for the first time were quite unique. Twelve years ago, I received a call from Jorge Amado, who was one of our most extraordinary writers here in Brazil. I admired his work, but didn't know him very well and thought at first that a friend was calling and pretending to be Jorge Amado. But no, it was really him.

Amado was known to be an extremely generous person, and this call proved it: he had seen the work of a very young director from Bahia, the part of Brazil he gave life to in most of his novels, and wanted to suggest Sérgio to me as a possible future collaborator. He had seen *Foreign Land* and liked it, and he thought that the match would be a good one. He sent me a forty-minute television drama that Sérgio had directed for the state TV in Bahia, and I was thoroughly impressed by the density of the work, which seemed quite mature for a director of such a young age. We then met and I was again impressed, this time by how much of a cinephile Sérgio was. We had common references, and that led me to invite him to be an assistant director on *Central Station*, together with Katia Lund. Sérgio also coordinated the casting process for me. This was a film that was done with as small a crew as we could, and guys like Sérgio would fill several roles on the film.

I first heard about Karim through the Sundance screenwriters' programme. *Central Station* won a Sundance/NHK screenwriting prize in 1996, which was a defining moment for the film – it literally made happen a project that was very unstable up to that moment. I was then part of the jury for the same prize the following year and Karim's *Madame Satã* was one of the screenplays that made it into the final round. I didn't know him, but was truly impressed by how he managed to convey the journey of a real-life character, who had been marginalised in so many different ways, in such a vivid, layered manner.

The screenplay stayed with me and, many months later, Karim and I met in Paris, where I was mixing *Central Station*. We talked a lot, and it soon became clear that we had similar views about different aspects of film-making. Then, when *Central Station* won the Berlin Film Festival and other prizes, I found myself in a position from which I could help young directors make their first films. Karim was the first one we chose to support. It took him seven years to get *Madame Satã* made. And he made it with such integrity and talent that I would start from scratch to help him again and again if I could.

After *Central Station*, we also produced Sérgio's first documentary, on the director Mario Peixoto, whose extraordinary *Limite* I have mentioned. So to help him in his fictional directorial debut, *Cidade baixa* [*Lower City*, 2005], was a logical step. Sérgio is also a writer-director, and one of those few directors able to understand all the different aspects of film-making, which is something that is becoming rarer and rarer these days. As it happens, his next film is based on a Jorge Amado novel, *Quincas Berro D'Agua*. I've just read the adaptation – you could shoot his first draft. When I write, it takes me at least five or six drafts to reach the level of development that Sérgio is able to get on his first try. This is quite upsetting, actually!

*Their own collaboration with each other started through working with you.*

When the time came to adapt Kadare's *Broken April*, which in English was translated into *Behind the Sun*, I wrote several drafts but was never truly pleased with them. This is why I asked the two directors who were close to me, Karim and Sérgio, to come in and help me through the process. Without them, I would probably still be trying to solve the many pitfalls I was facing at that time.

By the way, a collective process defines what happens in our small production house today. Every single film that is made at VideoFilmes is discussed by all the film-makers who work around us, and I can tell you that that discussion can be heated and painful sometimes. Just to give you an idea, our most important documentarian in Brazil, Eduardo Coutinho, asks questions such as 'Does this film truly need to exist?' And that is an important, defining question that all directors at VideoFilmes have to deal with. One recent example is that Sérgio Machado had two projects he was considering. The first one did not pass

Coutinho's test; he was actually relieved to be able to concentrate on the second idea.

Also, when we finish the first cut of a film, we invite these directors to come to the editing room and give us feedback. In the case of *Linha de passe*, this has helped us immensely.

*Regarding your help to first-time directors in Brazil, or indeed across Latin America, to what extent is this the result of a conscious feeling of responsibility, a sense of mission?*

In Brazil, there is more talent for cinema than ways to express this talent. This doesn't give us an option: we either work collectively and strengthen national cinema, or we will slowly disappear in the long run. So here, we have an *obligation* to do what we do, but what comes out of it also gives us immense pleasure. At the end of the day, the exchange that we have with young directors keeps us alive: they feed us with different ways to see the world, they shake our beliefs and our understanding of the society in which we live. Pablo Trapero just told me that he has been working with screenwriters who are twenty-three, twenty-four years old, and he does so in order to connect with the younger generations of Argentines. I completely identify with what he is doing.

*We were talking of the periphery. Ainouz, Machado, Katia Lund all deal with this in their work – the* favelas *and the* sertão, *the people they choose to portray. Arguably what you and your colleagues are doing in your films is moving the fringe to the centre ground of cultural discussion.*

Certainly it's all about trying to hear voices that have been unheard up to this point. But you know the Cinema Novo directors also did that. Nelson Pereira dos Santos, who is our most important film-maker alive, did a film, *Rio, 40 Degrees*, about life in the *favelas* in the fifties. That film, which is really the groundstone for the Cinema Novo movement, was the first to capture and express the desires of those people who live on the fringes of Brazilian society. It comes as no surprise that it was banned by the authorities at that time. The allegation was that in Rio the temperature never went as high as forty degrees!

But it's true that the generation of film-makers that has appeared since the nineties has sought to incorporate the voices that were completely unheard on television and were not represented enough on the big screen. Having said that, I think we now have to go one step beyond. In an ideal world what I would like to see is young directors coming from within the *favelas*, representing their own world, or looking at the world of those who do not live in the *favelas*. We should now invert the point of view, or enrich it by integrating film-makers who up to this moment have not had the possibility to express themselves.

## *The Motorcycle Diaries* and a renewed spirit of Latin American film-making

> This is not a tale of heroic feats. It is about two lives running parallel for a while.

This self-effacing opening to *The Motorcycle Diaries* typifies a film of deceptive simplicity. It might be easy to read the film as a smooth account of the early life of revolutionary Che Guevara, before he became interesting: a cheery tale that does not sully itself with politics. What it is, in fact, is a subtle and persuasive account of political awakening; of a man in the very midst of transition, not from boy to man (coming of age would be a cheap phrase here), but from a man dimly aware of the reality of his world to one whose blood races with that reality. As we watch Gael García Bernal, who is vitally relieved of explicatory or polemical dialogue, it is like watching a man whose DNA is being subtly recalibrated before us.

The idea to adapt Guevara's diary of his first, formative journey around South America came from Robert Redford, whose

Gael García Bernal and Rodrigo de la Serna stride into the unknown
in *The Motorcycle Diaries*

Sundance Institute had been instrumental in bringing *Central Station* to life. He now gave Salles the opportunity to tell a story that has always had a worldwide resonance: of a driving force of the Cuban revolution, an eternal icon, and a man who was motivated at first by curiosity, allied to a deep compassion. From a practical, as well as spiritual, point of view, the project was ideally suited to a man whose natural first instinct was to replicate the trip made by Guevara and his friend Alberto Granado – twice – before embarking on a third journey that would create the film.

The result is another of Salles' road movies, following as it does Guevara and Granado from Buenos Aires, through Patagonia into Chile, then north to the Peruvian Andes and into the Amazon, before leaving the pair in Venezuela, where they were to part company until after the revolution. At first their trip aboard an unreliable Norton motorcycle, *La Poderosa* (The Mighty One), is concerned with the adventure of the road and the pursuit of girls, its biggest consequence a broken heart. Eventually, once they ditch the bike and travel on foot, they make a greater connection with the people they meet, discovering countries riddled with inequality and peopled by indigenous Indians who are homeless in their own land.

In *Central Station* the experienced Fernanda Montenegro controlled the centre of a film populated by non-actors; the further the film moved from Rio, the greater the number of ordinary people before the camera. Salles repeats that approach here. While the story takes place in Argentina, Bernal and his co-star, the Argentine actor Rodrigo de la Serna, share the screen with fellow professionals. As they venture into Patagonia and beyond, the pair liaise with real people they meet on the road, the exchanges become more spontaneous, and the life of the film is led by those in front of the camera, not those behind it.

Bernal and de la Serna must take enormous credit for what ensues. Not only do they develop the most palpable friendship, which has the character of a grouchy old couple who know each other a little too well (much of the dialogue is comedic – at times Bernal and de la Serna could be Hope and Crosby, on the *Road to . . . Havana*), they also present an enlightenment that is shared but not developed at the same speed or in the same depth. Moreover, very little is said of what these men think, or feel, for each other or of themselves; the sea changes in their personalities all take place behind the eyes.

Salles engaged the Puerto Rican–American playwright José Rivera, who had studied at the Sundance Institute, to write the film, drawing from both *The Motorcycle Diaries* and Granado's book *Con el Che por Sudamerica*. Rivera was nominated for an Oscar for his work, with Jorge Drexler winning for best song. The film won a British Bafta for best film not in the English language, and the equivalent award from the London Film Critics' Circle, while the Argentine film critics honoured Rivera, de la Serna and composer Gustavo Santaolalla.

The film was also selected for competition in Cannes, where it was awarded three prizes, two for Salles and one for his accomplished French cameraman Eric Gautier. *The Motorcycle Diaries* enjoyed a healthy worldwide distribution, including a box-office return of more than $16 million in the US, a significant amount for a non-genre film in Spanish.

*There is a clear thematic progression from* Foreign Land *to* Central Station *to* The Motorcycle Diaries.

I agree. But at the same time, they're all linked. I think there is a definite thematic correlation. *Foreign Land* has to do with the moment when Brazil suffered an identity crisis, and talks about trying to find one's identity outside Brazil's frontiers. It studies the relationship between the colonial power and the colonised country, between the father who refused us – Portugal – and Brazil. *Central Station* is again a film about missing fathers and the relationship between the centre and the margin. It is again a film about the search for a national identity. *The Motorcycle Diaries* expands on that search and the main theme becomes Latin American identity – what does that mean, to be part of a continent that has very specific qualities?

*Brazil seems to sit almost uneasily within the continent, in some way apart from the other countries.*

Brazil is the only country in Latin America that speaks Portuguese as opposed to Spanish. Therefore we have always had the impression that we were a continent within a continent. The generation that my parents belonged to knew more about Europe than they did Argentina or Chile or the countries surrounding us. Spanish was never the second language in the schools, it was French and now it's English – to the point that in order to direct *The Motorcycle Diaries* I had to learn Spanish.

When Collor came to power he took this sense of isolation even further. He tried to link the country economically to the United States, more than anyone had ever done before: not only refuting what he considered backward (culturally and economically) in Brazil itself, but also generating an even greater distance between us and the rest of Latin America. So when he was impeached, we all started to be attracted by the 'reverse angle' of what he represented, and that was the possibility of being integrated into a continent that is our home but which we didn't fully understand. The desire to understand where we come from on that larger scale is at the heart of *The Motorcycle Diaries*.

If you take a look at the position in which Ernesto and Alberto, our two main characters in *The Motorcycle Diaries*, found themselves in the fifties, they were in a state not very dissimilar from ours in Brazil today: that is, they had very little information about the rest of the continent. Alberto Granado told me that in school he was taught about the Egyptians and the Greeks and the Venetians, he knew all about the unification of Germany, but on the other hand he had very little information about the Incas and the Mayans and the indigenous cultures, and very little information about the social and political structure of Latin America as a whole.

*And today?*

I think that today we're much closer to Latin America as a whole than we were ten years ago. And we want to be. Absolutely.

*To what extent is your desire to understand your cultural identity in this way shared by your fellow Brazilians?*

You know, these themes respond to an impulse that transcends my own desires. It may be one of the characteristics of this cinema from the mid-nineties, that we were confronted with situations so drastic that the stories we created reflected not only our own desires to tell those stories, but also had built in them a collective quest, related to where this society was going or wanted to go. And whenever you lose that sense of the collective you're bound, I think, to follow a very solitary route; one that in my case would interest me much less. I would probably prefer to dive into video art or into writing.

Somehow I associate the need to express myself in cinema with the need to discuss what kind of culture I belong in and want to live in. And maybe this is why when I develop a film it takes me so long to arrive at a point where I think it is right. It's not only about the characters, it is also about how I sense that the country we're living in is represented within that story. And of course that is something in constant transformation.

> *The Motorcycle Diaries* seemed like the perfect way to collaborate with Walter, especially since Che Guevara can be such a tricky subject. I knew Walter would handle the story with lyricism and humanity, rather than focusing on the politics of who Ernesto would later become.
> ROBERT REDFORD

*Were you familiar with the book when Robert Redford approached you?*

Yes, and it really had had an impact on me because of the things we've been discussing: it is about a journey to discover not only one's place in the world, but also what I think we could call a Latin American identity. I was very moved by the intertwining of this personal search with one that had a larger meaning for all of us who come from these latitudes.

Also, the beauty of the journey lies in the fact that their perception of the world changed, that they did not refuse to see. In turn, they would go on to try to change the world, according to what they had come to understand on their travels. And when you finish reading the book, you too have the impression that you can actually change the world.

*I gather you had some initial reservations about adapting it.*

I felt that it had to be done in Spanish, and that we had to work with actors from Latin America. And for those reasons I told

Redford it would be difficult to fund the film. And it was. It was refused by almost all the American studios. If it hadn't been for Film Four in the UK, we might not have been able to move forward.

*What was Redford's personal response to your desire to make it in Spanish?*

He thought about it for ten seconds and said, 'Let's try it like that.' Robert Redford is the most extraordinary producer I've ever worked with. He gave complete freedom, but was also present in the important moments: never interfering, giving us slack when he had to, but inspiring us to move forward.

*Considering the finished film, I can imagine a studio executive being quite indifferent. The transformation of these two guys would just be too subtle for them. There are no great, heart-wrenching scenes every ten minutes.*

This is probably why no American company wanted to fund the film to start with. They couldn't see the conflict. Many times we heard that the film had no interest and blatantly lacked conflict. Actually, I feel these people blatantly lacked sensibility, because what was at play here was an internal conflict, and not one that you could easily pinpoint through action. It was about delicate layers of transformation that would operate in such a manner that at the end of the journey the man who reached Venezuela was very different from the young man who had left Argentina.

You know, this is not surprising. There are so many books that are published telling you how to respect the three-act structure and how characters should be defined throughout, and so forth, that it creates not only a fixed mode in which a screenplay is written, but also in the way it is read – thus making it much more difficult for a non-traditional story to be financed and accepted. On the other hand, this is what makes the whole idea of transcending this mode more interesting.

*So how do you pitch the film?*

*The Motorcycle Diaries* can be seen as a rite of passage, a journey through a continent that would utterly define, both emotionally and politically, who these two young men would become. It's a film about the choices we have to make in life. It's also about friendship, about solidarity, and about finding one's place in the world.

Alberto told us many times how decisive this trip was for both of them and how much it helped to shape their future. You have to remember that this was the first time they had ventured throughout Latin America. These two young men lived in a relatively protected environment in Buenos Aires, in a country that was connected to Europe much more than to Latin America at the time. When they went on the road, on this old motorcycle, they were confronted with the remains of the Incan culture and were exposed to theoretical works of such Latin American thinkers as Mariátegui.* Such extraordinary, diverse experiences helped them rethink their understanding of the world around them.

So it's about eight crucial months in the lives of these men, during which they were confronted with a reality that departed completely from the one they were used to in urban Argentina, and after which they would elect the bank of the river on which they wanted to spend the rest of their lives – which is not a small decision, it's a defining one. We had to fully seek and understand what it was they fell in love with. And for that to be truthful we had to go through the same journey.

The challenges were many. How do you even begin to approach an iconic figure like Ernesto Guevara? How do you humanise the myth? How do you honour the

*José Carlos Mariátegui (1894–1930) was a Peruvian journalist and Marxist, and one of the most influential political theorists in Latin America in the past century. His most famous work, *Seven Interpretive Essays on Peruvian Reality* (1928), influenced later indigenous revolutionary movements.

memory and serve history? How do you give the companion Alberto equal weight? How do you capture
the inner geography of a boy turning into a man?
How do you capture that flickering pre-sixties Latin
America, poised, it seems, between centuries? How do
you capture the mind-boggling variety of faces, tem-
peraments, cultures, races and voices?

JOSÉ RIVERA

*This is conspicuously not a film about Guevara the revolution-
ary, about 'Che'. Did you even dally with the notion of in some
way referencing the myth?*

I think it was the opposite of that: it was about taking Ernesto
Guevara off the pedestal and bringing him closer to the average
man. It seemed much more interesting, to us, to understand his
fallibilities and his desires, to film the untold part of his life that
people do not know. And not so many people have read *The
Motorcycle Diaries*; the content of the book was found in a
backpack, way after his death, so it was only published for the
first time at the beginning of the nineties.

We certainly did not wish to increase the mythologising that
was already at play. The film is about Ernesto Guevara before he
became 'The Che'. It aims almost to demythologise the historical
character. This is what will allow people to eventually say, 'Well,
I can be extraordinary too, you know.' Very early on, when we
were researching in Cuba, I was taken to the Guevara memorial
in Santa Clara, three hours from Havana by car. This is where
Guevara is buried now – his ashes, with the other men who died
in Bolivia. I was quite impressed by that place, especially because
of the photographs: the young man in Argentina, then the photographer in Central America, then the first images of Guevara
meeting Castro in Mexico, then the Sierra Maestra campaign. If
you walk backwards from the end of the exhibition to the young
boy, towards a stage of innocence, it is very interesting, and very

moving. And I think the film is about that innocence being lost. When you take a stand you say goodbye to part of your innocence, because you have a responsibility now. There's something at once very tragic and very beautiful in that.

By the way, a woman I like a lot, who works at the Cuban Institute for Cinema, said she brought her ten-year-old son to this same museum. And suddenly something caught the boy's attention. She asked him what it was and he said, 'Is this Che Guevara's school report?' And she said yes, and he looked at the marks, which were really average and some were frankly not very good. And he said, 'But I can be like Guevara.' Somehow you can relate this story to the film, when you see this young man with his fallibilities.

*Actually, when I first read the book, one thing that struck me was how amusing an account it was of the change in someone who was a bit of a lad, a carefree rogue, into this nascent revolutionary.*

That's an honest description of what the book is. José Rivera retained the humour that is so vitally present in Guevara's book, as well as in Granado's account of the journey. I would say that Ernesto's book is more impressionistic and sometimes philosophical, while Alberto presents the point of view of the people they meet during the journey, and has an indefinable sense of humour. The two books are really complementary.

*And José Rivera's script is a blend of the two?*

Yes. And then we had hours of interviews with Granado, which I'd done in Cuba before the screenplay was finished, and which informed it.

*Why did you choose Rivera to write the screenplay?*

Of all the writers I met, José was the one who had the most discerning vision of what the screenplay should be. He never allowed the young Guevara to be confused with his future, mythological image, and was more interested in revealing the human side of these two young men, as who they could have been, in that moment. He retained their humour. And most importantly, he added layers of gravity as the two travellers went deeper and deeper into their journey – not unlike Ettore Scola's screenplay for *Il sorpasso* [1962].

*Can you describe both men's personalities in the period of the film? What were their reasons for wanting to make the journey?*

Alberto is twenty-nine, lives in Córdoba, Argentina, and works at a local hospital where he is somewhat uncomfortable at the way the patients are treated. He's been dreaming about this journey through Latin America for years and is determined to do it before he is thirty.

Ernesto is the best friend of Alberto's younger brother. He comes from an upper-middle-class family, but his curiosity and interests go way beyond the limits of his class. He's well read, and has travelled throughout Argentina on a bicycle, on which he installed a small engine. His asthma has been a constant concern from a very young age, but he has learned to fight it. He's a medical student, and he's not far from graduation when he opts to take the trip with Alberto. When they leave Buenos Aires, in January 1952, he is twenty-three.

*Granado is not going to espouse the revolution, as you put it, in the same way as Che.*

He doesn't make the same decision immediately, but he gets there. I'm very fond of Alberto and have the highest respect for him, because I think he is a man who is faithful to his friends and his principles at the same time. That's a rare feat. He didn't fight the revolution, that's not his role, he's a scientist. But he espoused that ideology because he believed in it, and went to work in Cuba in the early sixties, to complete the personal journey that had started with that motorcycle trip.

Actually, at the beginning of that trip he was a much more politicised animal than Ernesto. There was a moment when they traded places and Ernesto became the more articulate voice of the two, politically. But Alberto is a man who kept his integrity and was faithful to himself until the end. It's quite admirable.

*Why did you cast these actors?*

Gael I met in 2001 when I saw *Amores perros*. I was really struck by the visceral quality of his acting, everything coming from within. And he is able to hit you with very light strokes, like gentle rain. I invited him before *Y tu mamá también* came out, but seeing him in that film just reinforced my desire to work with him.

Rodrigo's physical resemblance to the young Alberto is staggering, but this is not why I ended up choosing him. I think that he's in the tradition of the great Italian actors like Vittorio Gassman and Alberto Sordi – always ready to surprise us, blending humour and drama in a unique manner. Then there was an incredible coincidence, which I realised only after casting him, which is his relation to Ernesto Guevara de la Serna.*

You know, they are both excellent actors, but their quality transcends being a good actor or not. It has to do with the level of embracing a project, the willingness to be completely in synchronicity with the character you are portraying. And that requires a state of total giving, which both Gael and Rodrigo brought to this film. Only the film mattered. Really. I've rarely been in a situation where I felt I was totally on the same boat as the actors.

*Each of those guys has become synonymous with this new wave of Latin American cinema.*

* Rodrigo de la Serna: 'Second cousin isn't exactly correct; there's not one word that describes the relation. We are connected way back on the family tree, on my father's maternal side. My father has the same face. So it's there. And I'm very proud of it.'

I think the great cinematic movements can't be dissociated from extraordinary actors. Can you think of Italian neo-realism without Giulietta Masina, or Mastroianni, or Gassman? Not easily. Or *nouvelle vague* without Jean-Pierre Léaud or Belmondo? I think not. Can you think of this new wave of Latin American cinema without Gael, without Lázaro Ramos or without Rodrigo de la Serna? It would be difficult.

*You've mentioned research.*

The research took more than two years. José and I read all the biographies that had been written about Ernesto Guevara, including the one that was the most interesting to me, by the Mexican writer Paco Ignazio Taibo. I went to Cuba several times to meet with Alberto Granado – then a young man of eighty-two! – and with Ernesto Guevara's family. The support of his widow, Aleida, and his children was very important for us to move forward. Finally, we retraced the motorcycle journey and scouted extensively throughout Argentina, Chile and Peru: journeying in Patagonia, crossing the Andes and the Atacama Desert, entering the Amazon Basin, ultimately reaching the San Pablo leper colony, in Peru. I did the journey three times: twice for location scouting, and the third time to actually shoot the film.

*That's what I call dedication to the cause. How did the first journey affect you?*

The first impression I had in retracing their steps was that the structural problems that caught Ernesto and Alberto's attention in 1952 – relating to the distribution of land and wealth – are mostly still present today. What was transmitted onto the page was pretty much what I felt in taking the journey. What came as a revelation was how modern and contemporary both books felt. And that may be because the political and social realities of Latin American culture have not changed all that much since the fifties.

It was particularly difficult for Walter, because he was in charge of everything, every detail. Coordinating that kind of production, in three different countries, and using in each country a local crew – an Argentine crew, a Chilean crew, a Peruvian crew, with Brazilian people alongside them. It was like a South American Babel. And Walter learned Spanish for the film. He spoke more correct Spanish than any of us.

RODRIGO DE LA SERNA

*I've heard you describe the pre-production as a sort of boot camp.*

The preparation for this film was different to anything I'd done before. We asked the two main actors, Gael and Rodrigo, to be in Buenos Aires two months prior to the shoot, so that they could learn how to drive a motorcycle and study tango, rugby, everything that was needed for the characters to perform what they needed to in the film. But it was also so that everyone on the crew could understand the cultures that we were going to depict. We put together a series of seminars, which most people attended, ranging from a study of the Inca civilisation to a study of Peronism and the popular music of the fifties. We also talked to experts on asthma – because of Ernesto's condition – and leprosy. And we saw many films, not only fiction but documentaries and newsreels, to learn about the way that society was represented on screen in the period.

That was an extremely informative phase of the production and one that also allowed that group to become a family. And that sense of family developed little by little, as we progressed on this very arduous physical journey.

*Was it an immediate decision to have a pan-South American crew?*

Yes. The crew in Argentina was not the same as in Chile and not the same as in Peru. The idea was to integrate technicians from these different countries, so that the film would really reflect a Latin American experience. I did not want to impose, for instance, a Brazilian crew that would just go and do the film from beginning to end: I wanted the Argentine part to be basically done by Argentines, the Chilean part to be done by Chileans.

The core crew – the production designer, cameraman, art director, costume designers – remained from beginning to end, and was international. But we had assistant directors, for example, from each of the countries we were going through. So that was a very organic way of looking at it. We all needed to share the same sense of a quest. I was helped by the fact that we were being inspired by a book that many in the crew knew, and worshipped. That, of course, is an extraordinary starting point.

But to go beyond that starting point, to transcend it, I wanted to give everyone the possibility of having the same level of information before we started. That was an extremely interesting process, I think, one that I want to, not replicate, but find in different forms in the next films I do: to create a process by which you can search for the heart of a film before actually doing that film.

Conversely, I think that when you reach a point where you know a lot about a subject, you have to try to forget everything before starting to shoot. Because it's important to start the film in a state of innocence and not to have preconceptions of the work you are going to frame. So it was about understanding as much as we could, then forgetting that on the first day of the shoot.

*Your budget and schedule?*

The shooting budget was $6 million. The shooting schedule was a very specific one, because in any one week we rarely had more than four shooting days; mostly we had three and a half, because of the travelling that was involved. So it was sixteen weeks: sixty-four days roughly.

We shot in sequence and, as much as we could, we used the

original locations that Ernesto and Alberto travelled through. There were more than thirty in all, in Argentina, Chile and Peru. In reality, a large number of the more distant locations have not been dramatically transformed by what we know as 'progress'. But when we couldn't use a particular place, we tried to find alternatives that would be very similar to those our friends cruised through on *La Poderosa*. The extensive research conducted by Carlos Conti, our production designer, was very important in this sense.

*It's no coincidence, I think – and it's time we mentioned this – that* Foreign Land, Central Station *and* The Motorcycle Diaries *are all road movies of one kind or another. Considering that you're currently working on adapting Jack Kerouac's* On the Road, *this is a definite genre of choice.*

There is a sentence at the core of *On the Road*: 'I was halfway across America, at the dividing line between the East of my youth and the West of my future.' The first image I actually remember – I must have been two years old at the time – is of a road fading away from the rear window of a car. And if you think of the films that brought me to cinema, films like *The Passenger* and *Alice in the Cities*, they are road movies.

At first I couldn't explain why they touched me so profoundly. Little by little I realised it had to do with characteristics that were particular to this form of storytelling. I believe that the most interesting road movies are the ones in which the identity crisis of its main characters mirrors the identity crisis of the culture these people originate from, or are passing through. Also, because they deal with internal transformation, road movies are not about what can be verbalised, but about what can be felt. That's very appealing to me as a film-maker.

*There's always the sense, of course, that the journey is more important than the destination.*

Exactly. Road movies are about experiencing, above all. They are about what can be learned from the 'other', those who are different from you. In that sense they challenge the culture of conformity and the sort of vicarious experience that is promoted, for example, by reality TV shows, and which is so depressing.

In *The Motorcycle Diaries*, the social and political reality of Latin America takes over these men, little by little. That's what I tried to convey, with the help of Gael and Rodrigo. I always thought that the film should be constructed in layers. A road movie has by definition an episodic quality, but that can be a danger if you don't grant time for the information to sink in, slowly and delicately. There was not a single, defining moment where everything changes.

*What have you learned about road movies by making them?*

After directing three, I believe that a defining aspect of this narrative form lies in the word 'unpredictability'. You simply cannot and should not anticipate what you will find on the road – even if you have scouted a dozen times the territory you will be crossing. You have to work in synchronicity with the elements. If it snows, incorporate snow. If it rains, incorporate rain.

We travelled around twenty thousand kilometres to do the film, twelve thousand miles. And as Latin America is still pretty much a last frontier, there were moments where in order to go to point B we had to go to point D and then come back. The roads didn't exist. But that was actually in perfect synchronicity with the story we were telling: we were living what the characters were supposed to live on screen. And that kind of synchronicity or connection was very positive for the film.

*Was it not regarded as high-risk? Film production, after all, is reliant on keeping to its schedule.*

Of course it was high-risk. Many times we didn't know if we would reach the next stage of the shoot. It was an extremely tough experience, on a physical and emotional level, as you can imagine. We endured temperatures that were way below zero in the Andes, to more than forty-five degrees Celsius in the Amazon. Of course, when you go between those extremes in a few weeks, you are not making it easy on yourself. But that was the rule of the game. Most of the time we were in small hotels, a little bit scattered around. It was a rough journey, but at the same time the most inspiring and fulfilling one I've ever gone through. When we reached the end we didn't want it to finish, really.

> It was not an easy film to make. You had to be one
> tough nut, because they went through some really
> extreme conditions that were next to impossible in
> some cases. There was the weather. You had the threat
> of political violence along the way – they were going
> into some pretty hot areas. And that's all evidenced in
> this film. But what they went through to tell their
> story was exactly what the characters went through.
> You see that and, more importantly, you feel it. And if
> you feel it, you're gonna feel how Ernesto Guevara
> was affected by it.
> ROBERT REDFORD

*When I saw the scene in Machu Picchu, I couldn't help thinking of Werner Herzog, who famously filmed there and in the Amazon. He, of course, has a marvellously volcanic love–hate relationship with nature.*

In *Burden of Dreams* [1982] he says that everybody has the perception that nature is governed by a sense of equilibrium, when it's exactly the opposite – there's an immense chaos, it's really about species trying to destroy each other. Actually, he also brings this up in his quite extraordinary documentary *Grizzly Man*,* saying, 'This is when Timothy Treadwell and I depart – he thought nature was beneficent, and I don't.'

*So how do you feel about it?*

Coming from a documentary background you realise that you are totally insignificant in comparison to the nature surrounding you; nature is much stronger than any human resources. And if you don't bend with it, you will be broken by it. Therefore, if the screenplay says 'Driving through Patagonia on a sunny day and talking about the heat', but as you're about to film the wind starts to blow and the rain is going to fall, you immediately transform that into 'Driving through Patagonia through the rain and talking about the cold'. You would never bend nature to serve your own purposes; on the contrary, you have to accept what nature is bringing you as a gift, and try to transform that into a filmic expression.

We did that all the time in *Motorcycle Diaries*. When we arrived in Patagonia in the beginning of the summer and were met by a snowstorm, we immediately filmed the storm. I still remember it well. It was on a Sunday and we were not supposed to film, yet Rodrigo and Gael agreed to do it. We were totally unprepared for it. It was freezing cold – we thought we were going to have temperatures of twenty degrees Celsius, and it was minus ten. We had no gloves. We couldn't see anything. There was so much snow that we could barely film.

We were maybe seven or eight, very few. I was driving the car, Eric [Gautier] was freezing out there with the camera, the sound guy was by himself also, there were the two boys on the motorcycle – and off we went. There were no snow tyres. Nothing. Imagine, if this was a Hollywood film that scene would never

---

*\* Grizzly Man* (2005) was Herzog's documentary on the life and death of Timothy Treadwell, whose life was dedicated to studying grizzly bears in the Alaskan wilderness, until he and his girlfriend were attacked and killed by a rogue bear.

© Walter Salles

Acting up a storm: the cast of *The Motorcycle Diaries* adapting
to the weather

have been shot in the first place, due to insurance limitations. We
did it, despite it not being scripted, because it was completely
organic with the story. Interestingly, after having shot it, I told
Granado, 'Listen, we did something in the spirit of the book, but
which doesn't exist in the book, because you don't have snow.'
And he said, 'Oh, we went through some snow, we just didn't
write about it.' So there you go. The most important thing when
you adapt a book is that you have to understand what the spirit
of that book is, and try to be faithful to that spirit.

*Did they always fall off their bike on cue?*

No. The snow was pouring down and the difficulty you see was
real and unpremeditated. They fell when they fell.

*And how difficult was the filming in Machu Picchu?*

Actually, it was one of the easiest parts of the shoot. The only
difficulty was that we had to ask the tourists not to come into the
frame. They understood what we were doing, and that we were

doing it passionately. And we were so few – only eight or ten people at that stage – that they totally respected us. Also, we started very early in the morning and tried not to repeat the same scene more than once, so we weren't disturbing anyone. We were moving really fast – you know, the smaller the group the faster you can actually progress.

Today, a lot of people ask us, 'How did you shoot that? Did you bring cranes? Did you ask permission to close the park?' No, we never actually closed the park, the camera's handheld all the time, and the stones are already there. What else do you need? You are at Machu Picchu, which is one of the most extraordinary places in the world – not only because of the geography, but because of what it means – and that somehow translates to the screen. The actors were feeling the shock of discovering that sanctuary for the first time in their lives. And that also is transmitted onto film.

*So what were the hardest moments of filming, and the personal highlights?*

Filming in the Amazon is extremely hard, due to the heat, the humidity, the impossibility of predicting the weather. On the other hand, the most fascinating part of the journey for me was the one centred in the San Pablo leprosarium, in the middle of the Amazon. This is where Ernesto and Alberto spent more than three weeks of their journey and entered a reality that was drastically different from anything they found elsewhere. Several people who played lepers in the film had been patients at the actual leper colony, and I wanted to be porous to their input, which granted an additional gravity to our work.

*I'm not clear if you shot in a real leper colony or not.*

I am very honoured by that. It wasn't. Again, there was a lot of research done to understand how the leper colony was at the time, and very careful preparation. We worked hard to make that environment appear not to have been constructed at all. In reality, we filmed in a fishermen's village, to which Carlos Conti added a few buildings in order to create a sense of the colony. It was, again, a collective effort, which really made that part of the film credible.

*That was presumably the production at its biggest.*

We were a hundred and twenty, a hundred and thirty at that time. The crew changed drastically during the course of the journey, depending on where we were. So for example: in Buenos Aires, we may have been thirty-five. And then in [the Peruvian city] Cuzco we were almost a large documentary crew, ten or twelve people. Then in the leper colony you had ninety extras, and fifteen make-up artists to prepare the patients.

Interestingly, or symptomatically, the fewer we were, the more we were in absolute synchronicity, and doing much more than we thought we would be able to do. And the fewer we were, the more we were allowed to improvise.

*Just as in* Central Station, *you had professionals surrounded by non-actors.*

More than ninety per cent of the characters were played by non-actors. The Chilean sisters were students, for example. And most of the people in the leper colony came from the little towns near where we filmed. But I didn't just arrive and film straight away. We played football with them, arranged jam sessions, tried to create something like a collective history. You need a bond before you can introduce the camera into their midst.

*You've spoken of the 'side roads' off the script, which are worth exploring. The most rewarding side roads on* The Motorcycle Diaries, *I imagine, were gained in the interaction between the actors and the people that you met on the road.*

That would be a fair assumption. Alberto and Ernesto's trip was shaped by the encounters they had on the road, and I tried to keep this quality alive in the film. In places like Cuzco or Machu Picchu, for example, we encouraged the actors to mingle with the people they met, as Alberto and Ernesto would have done fifty years ago. This purely improvisational material was then blended with the more structured screenplay by José.

*And this seems to occur more often when they are on foot.*

That's right. This direct contact with people happened, more specifically, from the moment when the bike breaks down and they were obliged to hitch-hike and walk: this is what both Alberto and Ernesto relate in their respective diaries, and the same thing happened to us, as we were entering deeper and deeper into the heart of Latin America; most especially, when we arrived in Peru and were confronted with the Inca heritage. There we were approached by Indians who spoke Quechua, who were asking us to initiate a dialogue. In some ways the scenes that result from those encounters are closer to the spirit of the original journey than scenes that would simply revisit specific events told in the book.

*And the actors were essentially improvising, reacting directly to these people?*

When we were in Cuzco, for instance, and bumped into that boy and those Indian women, who spoke Quechua, Gael and Rodrigo were so intelligent and had such a sense of where their characters were, emotionally, that they could easily improvise in the logic of the screenplay and in the logic of the characters.

*How did that come about with the boy, the cheeky little guide?*

He came to us outside the hotel, the day we arrived. 'Do you want to know Cuzco?' Yes, we said, if we could take our super-

16 along and film him. 'Bring whatever you want.' We told him what it was about, and he never actually asked more than two or three questions. He totally got it. There's no take two in what he does, and nothing that is scripted.

*It's a wonderful exchange.*

Gael and Rodrigo were in Cuzco for the first time and had a genuine interest in what he was saying. That exchange really took place before us, as we were filming it. And the same thing could be said about the scene with the four Indian women. By the way, that conversation that you see in the film – which concerns the political and economic situation of the indigenous people living around Cuzco – may have taken place in 2003, as we were filming, yet was very similar to what you find in Ernesto Guevara's book. This shows how little progress has been made in Latin America, in social terms, in the past fifty years.

*The problems of distribution of wealth, for example.*

Problems you would find from Mexico to Patagonia: bad distribution of wealth, an education system that is nowhere near as fair and democratic as it should be, a health system that works for a part of society, but not the major part. These have been chronic problems in that part of the world probably for a hundred or two hundred years.

*I'd like to draw a line between your documentaries and that aspect in your fiction film-making of confronting real people when you see them. A favourite word of yours is 'porousness'.*

I think that's an important part of this profession, really, the way I see it. Again, when Rossellini and Pasolini and that generation started to tell stories of the Second World War in Italy, they were telling stories about things that they had seen, or heard of. And they were totally open to integrating non-actors and any element

© Paula Prandini

'You don't need to be from one specific milieu to understand another one.'
The Peruvian leg of *The Motorcycle Diaries*.

that could actually transmit a better understanding of what living under those circumstances might be like.

In documentaries, when defining the theme that I want to develop, I try to study as much as I can about it, but I never try to start with a structured screenplay. I have some lines, some possible vectors of development, I follow them, then there's something in there that leads me to an unexpected ending. And in doing so, porousness becomes an essential factor, because you have to allow yourself to be permeated by what reality brings to you. Otherwise you are going to repeat the same film endlessly; otherwise, you are going to be judging and not proposing.

Also, in documentaries, I try to put myself into a situation where I can be constantly surprised, and then try to transmit what I felt, being surprised, to the screen. That's what I aim for. And that has somehow instructed me, when proceeding in fiction. There are certain themes that are conducive to this approach in fiction, and others that are not, or much less so. But if you are working with a very small crew, and you have a good screenplay that frames a contemporary story, it's going to be much easier to integrate whatever accidents you may find into the narrative.

*From a practical point of view, I don't imagine everyone is able to operate on the streets amongst real people, in such a way. You have to have an empathy, a* simpatico *nature, otherwise they simply won't respond. It's interesting how often people, not least children, seem to come up to you, rather than the other way around. Do you think your roots have anything to do with this?*

You don't need to be from one specific milieu to understand another one. Visconti may be the best example of that, because he somehow found an equilibrium in that improbable blend of aristocratic background and communist tendencies; it allowed him to make at the same time *Rocco and his Brothers* [1960] and *The Leopard* [1963], which looked at very different facets of Italian society. It says a lot about his sensibility to be able to really dive into worlds that are so different. I don't know if I would be able to do so.

  I simply think that a film-maker should not judge, should try not to have a fixed perception of where his narrative is going before he starts to shoot it. Something should be transformed by the act of filming itself. The shooting should be an act of revelation and discovery.

*Did you have anything like the same formal approach to the cinematic grammar, here, as you did in Central Station?*

Yes. *The Motorcycle Diaries* is really about revealing a continent and being transformed by what you see. So how do you translate that into cinematic grammar? Well, first of all the camera. When the two characters are in Buenos Aires, it is much steadier, often on a tripod, reflecting that kind of anchored, upper-middle-class, bourgeois life that the characters lived. I did very specific breakdowns of the scenes in Buenos Aires, with camera placements and lenses.

Then, as they go further and further into the heart of the continent, and are destabilised by what they witness, the camera becomes more and more handheld, and the filming becomes much less reasoned. We basically tried to film the story as if it were unfolding before our very eyes, so the breakdown of the scenes becomes more intuitive and less Cartesian.

I had the opportunity to collaborate with one of the most brilliant directors of photography that I've ever worked with, Eric Gautier, who not only has an extraordinary eye but also an intuition and intelligence that are unique. He immediately understood what was at stake and we collaborated in trying to reach that goal together. We opted for a direct cinematic grammar to tell this story, with the simplicity of the super-16 format, blended with a few night shots on 35 mm.

*Would you say there is a consistency in your style?*

I think that there are correlations between all of the films: the blending of actors and non-actors, which I think really defines the quality of the acting you're going to have; the refusal to use certain technologies, and basically film on location; opting for a handheld camera that is very close to the bodies; filming with as small a crew as you can get, with urgency. So I think that you can eventually find not only thematic correlations, but grammatical ones.

*By technologies you mean special effects?*

Special effects, or even Steadicams or cranes. In *The Motorcycle Diaries* there's not one crane shot, there's not one Steadicam shot. In *Central Station* there's no Steadicam and three crane shots that I knew I wanted to do, but only three. Again, what you exclude from the narrative becomes as important as what you are including, and ends up creating a unity between films.

One thing that Eric suggested on *The Motorcycle Diaries* was to push the film, as the journey progressed, so that the texture becomes grainier, edgier, rawer, as you go further into the continent – because it's what these guys were feeling. There is a senso-rial quality in cinema, those elements that you cannot explain verbally, but should be felt. I think they are extremely important for a film to have a resonance. And that's the beauty, actually, of film as opposed to digital. I was talking once with a French photographer and he said the beauty of film lies in the impression-ability of the grain. You cannot predict how an image will be composed. Digital technology eliminates the grain, therefore it is way more difficult to add texture to it.

*There is a very poignant conclusion to the film, when the two men part. Was your impression that just as Guevara and Granado were deeply affected by what they found, there was a similar, revelatory experience for your cast and crew?*

Definitely. And up to this day we still talk about it. And that in turn makes it much more difficult to jump into other films, because the level of expectation will never be the same after such an unforgettable journey.

One of the most resonating aspects of *The Motorcycle Diaries* was that, little by little, silently, we all understood that we would either survive collectively or the film would collapse. This specif-ic film required that everyone would help each other. If you lim-ited your work to what you were actually supposed to do, we wouldn't reach the end. The small resistance that may have exist-ed in the beginning gave way to a collaborative instinct that real-ly allowed the film to exist. And it has never dissolved. It's really interesting: there's rarely a day when I don't receive two or three emails from people from the crew.

I must tell you this. Jean-Pierre Melville was once asked by a film student, 'What makes a film a good film? Which elements are more important than the others?' His answer was, 'Well, young man, it's very easy to respond: fifty per cent is the quality of the story that you want to tell, fifty per cent is the screenplay, fifty per cent is the choice of the actors who are going to give life to the characters, fifty per cent is the lighting, fifty per cent the editing, the music . . .' and so forth and so forth. And then he said, 'If one of these elements goes in the wrong direction, you will have fucked fifty per cent of your film.'*

At the end of the day he's totally right. In a film, all the elements have to go in the same direction, you have to have that unity, that collaborative aspect. The great films are the ones where everybody is collaborating, understanding what is to be done, working in the same direction.

*Talking of collaborations, can you say a little more about the connections that you made with film-makers across the continent: the support system and ethos that you established for the film, which seems to have forged lasting links with other directors? For example, in Chile Andrés Wood gave you assistance; in Argentina Daniel Burman.*

The structure that Michael Nozik, who directed Robert Redford's production company, Wildwood, and the French–Argentine producer Edgard Tenembaum set up was that in each country we would film in – Argentina, Chile and Peru – Wildwood would be associated with local producers. So the film was basically line-produced by different entities in each. In Argentina, Daniel was a film-maker who was barely thirty but had made four films – he's a wise young guy, very experienced and talented – and he gave us the production support, and was constantly on set, with his partner Diego Dukovsky. In Chile, Andrés was not the producer that Redford's company retained, but he was extremely helpful in many different ways, such as introducing me to people who would later work in the film.

In Chile and Peru, Edgard and Michael opted for Sahara Films and Inca Cine. In each country, these companies brought a local

---

*Jean-Pierre Melville (1917–73). Renowned French director whose films include *Bob le flambeur* (Bob the Gambler, 1956), *Le Samouraï* (1967) and *L'Armée des ombres* (Army in the Shadows, 1969).

understanding of the culture and also a number of collaborators who were essential to the film. I had never lived a similar experience before: in every country, it was as if we were starting again and had to learn how to operate as a team, respecting the specific cultural aspects of each. It was a challenging process, but beneficial to the film. At the beginning it was very Babel-like: we were trying to find a common way to make a film, which was sometimes very hard to find, because we were coming from different latitudes in the continent, with different ideas of how to organise a film crew that changes from country to country. But little by little we found a *modus operandi* that allowed the film to exist.

The interesting thing is that at the end we ceased to be a film crew and became a filmic family. I have since participated, as an associate producer, in the first film by my first Assistant Director in Argentina, Julia Solomonoff, called *Hermanas* [2005]. And we're taking part in a film by Samuel León, who was my second AD in Chile, and has just acted again as second AD for my new one, *Linha de passe*. And so the ties have remained very solid.

*A key line in* Memories of Underdevelopment *is the character's definition of 'underdevelopment' as the inability to establish links, share experience and grow. Your enthusiasm for collaboration suggests that you absorbed the lesson.*

If there is one art form that needs to be collective, it is cinema. Not just in the way you make films, but in the way you watch films. If you take a look at the important movements of cinema, the ones that have at least had an effect on my generation – the Cinema Novo or the new Cuban cinema that Gutiérrez Alea is so representative of, the *nouvelle vague* or the Italian neo-realism, or even the independent cinema in North America in the seventies – one thing that defines those movements is their collective quality. Take a look at neo-realism and you immediately understand that Fellini was writing for Visconti, who was being assisted by Pasolini, who himself had a link to Antonioni, so all of these extraordinary directors, who would blossom and make Italian cinema what it became, were helping each other.

Now transfer that reasoning to what we're witnessing now. I don't think we in Brazil have the possibility of making a difference in world cinema, or even of survival, if we don't have that desire for collectiveness. And this is why my brother and I, or Fernando Meirelles, are not interested in just doing our own films, we're basically interested in being part of a larger whole. And this, I think, goes beyond the frontiers of Brazilian cinema. For instance I'm a huge admirer of Argentine cinema and I believe that the closer we get to the Argentine film-makers such as Pablo Trapero or Lucrecia Martel, the stronger we will be in Brazilian cinema.

*Could you elaborate? By 'get closer' what do you mean exactly? Co-produce, share ideas, open dialogues?*

All of that. Pablo and I have just spent some time here in Brazil talking about all the possible future projects we are contemplating as directors. We do share ideas and screenplays on a constant basis, and I hope that this exchange will continue in the years to come.

We Brazilians are much closer to Argentine cinema than we are to cinema from other parts of the world. This is one of the reasons why we have been fighting for several years for the establishment of a co-production agreement between our two countries. This agreement is finally coming together. It will probably be similar to the one Brazil has with Portugal, in which committees from the Brazilian film commission and the Portuguese film commission elect a number of films each year for co-production purposes. It is still too soon to know the parameters that will guide this co-production agreement, but it should probably be effective in 2009 and will have an impact on Brazilian and Argentine film production from 2010.

Up to this moment, there are no mechanisms that allow us to extend the financing that comes from the Brazilian tax-shelter system to Argentine films, but that will probably change in the near future as well. Until now, we have been limited in terms of how we can co-produce. So with VideoFilmes, we have basically sent cameras, lenses and similar technical equipment to help the production of Pablo [Trapero]'s films. We did this for his three last projects, *Familia rodante*, *Nacido y criado* and *Leonera*. So you see that relationship transcends the physical boundaries of our countries, and is very much alive. That kind of connection will, I believe, nourish and fortify Brazilian and Argentine cinema as a whole.

*Ironically, when I speak to directors around the continent, while voicing admiration for each other's work some also admit to only being able to see that work at European film festivals.*

It's true that eight or ten years ago you would rarely see an Argentine film in Brazil. When I myself saw work by Pablo and Lucrecia for the first time, it was elsewhere. Their films just weren't distributed here because of the control the major studios have over distribution. But we have had laws now, for two years or so, which create incentives for the distribution of Argentine and other Latin American films in Brazil, and vice versa. Today it is mostly impossible to pick up a newspaper and not see an Argentine film playing here. And I hope that this will continue to improve.

*So can we speak of a continental cinema?*

You can really say that there is a point of union that transcends the boundaries of national cinema at play in Latin America. Was it Tolstoy who said that the more you talk about your village, the more universal you get? Maybe what will unite us is the fact that we're all talking about our 'villages', and sometimes the same problems that affect Brazilian society also affect Argentine and Chilean societies. What we're talking about is not that different from country to country. Sometimes when I see a film from Argentina it reminds me so much of things that are happening just outside my door. Also, the manner in which some of us want to do cinema creates a link: the desire to work with smaller crews, to film fast, allowing improvisation, incorporating non-actors.

*It's hard to imagine speaking this way about Europe.*

There's a reason for that. With the exception of Eastern Europe, you're talking about cultures, firm identities that have become fixed over hundreds of years. Whereas on this continent Brazilian, Argentine, Chilean film-makers are dealing with societies that are still being defined as we speak. And this is why I think that *urgency* is really the common denominator of this new Latin American cinema, the necessity to grab what is going on in our streets and transfer that in a raw manner to the screen. I think that we're all, actually, trying to do the same thing, which is to understand what characterises our cultures now. We share this collective desire. Of course, there are differences that have to do with diverse cultural imprints, or diverse cinematic traditions. But what unites us is much stronger than what separates us.

Sometimes there is a generation that appears with an extraordinary talent. You had that in Taiwanese cinema, you had the Fifth Generation of Chinese film-makers, then you had three generations of brilliant Iranian film-makers. There are cultural, political conditions that can create a climate for such talented generations to rise up.

*Do you connect the 'flowering' of this generation of directors across the continent with the emergence of comparatively stable democracies? Put another way, has political freedom inspired creative expression?*

Absolutely. As Daniela Thomas often puts it, we were the first generation of film-makers who were able to think about cinema in a completely free manner. But if we were able to do so, it was only because previous generations resisted the military regimes during the dark ages and created the conditions for a local cinema to continue to exist.

# War zones: the making of *City of God* and other *favela* films

Cannes 2002 was one of those years when La Croisette was crackling with buzz about a film that wasn't in the official competition and wasn't familiar to one and all, yet was building up a frenzied word of mouth as the festival progressed. It would be mentioned in almost hushed excitement, as if the Brazilians on everyone's lips were going to burst into the room, guns blazing, or else whisk you off to a party that, unlike most festival revels, would actually be cool.

*Cidade de Deus* (*City of God*, 2002) was undoubtedly the hot ticket that year. It would go on to be distributed around the world and win four main-category Oscar nominations, including best director for Fernando Meirelles – something quite unprecedented for a Brazilian film.

The title – not a film-maker's conceit but, presumably, a town planner's – is at once a beautiful and bitter illusion. 'Cidade de Deus' is the name of a housing project in Rio de Janeiro which had disintegrated into an infamous slum, more akin to hell than heaven. The film itself would also confound expectation. Here was an entertainment that was visceral, inventive, funny, dangerous, which could stand for cinematic and narrative flair alongside anything that the young Quentin Tarantino was making at the time, or for that matter even Scorsese. Yet there was another, surprising dimension: social content. *City of God* was about something. As much as people laughed at the runaway chicken or wished they had some of the style of Knockout Ned or Bené, they could also feel the authenticity, and hence the genuine pathos of small boys being herded into a life of crime. As with *Central Station* three years before, it wasn't just Brazilian cinema that was being rediscovered: it was Brazil itself, a Brazil light years away from soccer, sand and samba.

Brazilian film-makers have always dealt with the country's social issues, although the fundamental concerns of, say, Nelson Pereira dos Santos and Glauber Rocha – poverty, political powerlessness, the inequitable distribution of wealth – have been ever more compounded in the past forty years by another affliction: crime. As Walter Salles has already suggested, film-makers can never keep up with Brazilian reality: Pereira dos Santos's *Rio 40 Graus* (*Rio, 40 Degrees*, 1955), which offered a kaleidoscopic view of Rio, from the hillside *favelas* to the beaches, seems positively cheery when regarded alongside Hector Babenco's *Pixote* (1981), with its grim, melancholy depiction of a child losing his soul somewhere between institutions and the street; and while that film's conclusion was extremely pessimistic, it hardly prefigured a world in which kids like Pixote would be armed with military hardware, turning their communities into veritable war zones in which a person is shot dead every few minutes.

This is the Rio of today, an early version of which *City of God* (which spans a period between the sixties and the end of the seventies) first revealed to international audiences. By the very nature of the beast, this film is already out of date. Nevertheless, it sits at the heart of a very particular phenomenon in contemporary Brazilian cinema: films that not only tackle Brazil's highly charged social and civil issues in the *favelas*, on the streets and in the prisons, but do so in a manner that has attracted considerable domestic audiences; films which, in other words, are at once socially conscious and 'blockbuster' popular.

*City of God* had a Brazilian audience of 3.3 million (not huge in relation to the country's population, but nevertheless a significant number), while winning forty-nine awards worldwide. In 2003 Hector Babenco's *Carandiru*, about one of the country's most notorious penitentiaries, had 4.5 million admissions at home, and was selected for Cannes competition. In 2007 José Padilha's *Tropa de Elite* (*Elite Squad*), concerned like *City of*

*God* with the drug war in the *favelas*, but from the perspective of the police rather than the gangs, attracted 2.4 million people (alongside the incredible eleven million who saw a stolen, pirated copy before the film was even released). The next year it won the Golden Bear in Berlin. All three were the most popular Brazilian films of their respective years.

As well as winning popularity and festival acclaim, these films are also notable for their highly synergistic relationship with documentaries made about the same subjects. The following interviews chart the patterns of correspondence – in subject matter, personnel and in some cases film-making practice – between the features *Domésticas* (*Maids*, 2001), *City of God, Elite Squad* and *Cidade dos homens* (*City of Men*, 2007), and the documentaries *Notícias de uma guerra particular* (*News from a Private War*, 1999) and *Ônibus 174* (*Bus 174*, 2002). It will be seen how documentary-makers first took the plunge, exploring slums that were effectively self-governing cities within the city, ruled by drug-dealers; then how feature film-makers entered the fray, taking the same considerable risks to their safety, in order to give those real-life stories flight. The result is a cycle of films by like-minded, committed film-makers, contributing to a contemporaneous chronicle of their city's underclass.

It will also be noted how the film-makers have emerged from the *favelas*, effectively bringing a number of boys and young men with them. *City of God* may be a 'fiction', yet Meirelles and Lund's decision to cast non-actors from the *favelas*, to select and train boys to bring to life experiences they lived every single day, not only lends the film authenticity, but instilled in these kids a realisation that there was an alternative life to that of the gang. The school that the film-makers created to train the boys was, on completion of the film, turned into a permanent film school and NGO, Nós do Cinema.

I know of a number of Brazilian expatriates who despair that the chief stories distributed abroad are of a violent Brazil, in their view giving an unduly negative picture of their country. I would suggest that the objection is moot: in that the films actually sell on their cinematic merits, as well as distributor confidence in their explosive stories; and that in the year in which the controversial *Elite Squad* was released in the UK, British audiences also had a chance to see Walter Salles and Daniela Thomas's mellow, reflective *Linha de passe*, as well as the touching Uruguayan comedy-drama *The Pope's Toilet* (produced by Meirelles and co-directed by his regular cameraman, César Charlone) and the mature, gender-questioning Argentine drama *XXY*.

Moreover, one has to ask how often films with similarly violent content or similar levels of excitement from other parts of the world (particularly Hollywood) also contain a social message, sparking widespread debate. It is that amalgam that makes this aspect of Brazilian cinema almost unique in the early twenty-first century.

## News from a Private War

In 1997 the documentary film-maker João Moreira Salles teamed up with Katia Lund, who had just worked as assistant director on *Central Station*, directed by Salles' older brother Walter. The project, initiated by Walter Salles and produced by VideoFilmes, was to direct together a documentary on the drug-dealing in Rio's *favelas*, which had been escalating since the mid-eighties, bringing with it a sharp rise in homicides.

When *News from a Private War* was filmed in 1997–8, it was estimated that 100,000 people worked in the drug trade, the same number as was employed by the city authorities. One person was being murdered every thirty minutes, usually by a high-calibre bullet. By speaking with dealers, police and the *favela* residents 'caught in the crossfire', Salles and Lund were among the first to expose a war – both among dealers and between dealers and police – costing thousands of lives, conducted within the city limits, yet somehow and conveniently ignored by the general population.

Documenting a gentler world. João Moreira Salles' *Santiago* (2007)
featured the family's childhood butler

Having come to documentary, João Moreira Salles jokes, 'out of sheer luck, or lack of luck' – his brother engaged him to edit hours of footage he had shot for a documentary on Japan, at which point the younger man was hooked – he has since become one of the pre-eminent documentary-makers in a country that thrives on the form. Among his best-known works are *Entreatos* (*Intermissions*, 2004), about the election campaign of President Luiz Inácio Lula da Silva, and the award-winning *Santiago* (2007). The latter, ostensibly a series of recollections by the Salles family's long-serving (and multi-talented) former butler which subtly evolves into a reflection on memory, language, class, history, storytelling, family identity and film-making itself, is an extraordinarily beautiful and resonant film.

It is also, one suspects, the film of which Salles is most proud, because, according to his philosophy of documentary, it is as concerned with form as it is its subject. In that regard, *News from a Private War*, a fairly straightforward reportage, falls short for him. Yet, even coming to it after the shock and rush of *City of God*, or returning to it after experiencing the soul-destroying pessimism of *Elite Squad*, the directness and vividly orchestrated interviews of *News from a Private War* maintain their own, revelatory power.

Watching the film, one glimpses some of the personnel who will carry the baton of *favela* storytelling over the subsequent decade. Among the interviewees are Paulo Lins, who at the time was awaiting the publication of his novel *Cidade de Deus*; and Rodrigo Pimentel, a fresh-faced and blatantly media-savvy police officer who conducts the film-makers through the work of BOPE, the army-like police battalion charged with tackling the drug-dealers – Pimentel will later lend his insights and experiences to the script of *Elite Squad*. 'Would you like to have been in a war?' he is asked here, having related how happy he is to experience armed combat, to which he answers, 'I am in a war. I'm in the middle of a war. The difference is that I go home every day.'

## Rio de Janeiro, 2006

JOÃO MOREIRA SALLES: In retrospect, when the film industry in Brazil basically stopped for four to five years, maybe that was not such a bad thing. Because when it started again, in 1994–5, people were hungry to film. And Brazil had changed a lot. After the end of the dictatorship, and with democratisation, suddenly you had a new reality: you had democracy, you had years and years of hyper-inflation, which had a very strong impact on Brazilian social life, you had violence, an urban chaos that became very significant by the late eighties and early nineties.

I think that that's when documentaries really became important. It was like a crowd trying to enter a rock concert and the gates are closed, then suddenly they're opened and people flood in. There was a whole new society to be explored and we were eager to explore it.

It's easier to do a documentary than a fiction film, as far as logistics and money are concerned, so Brazilian documentary film-makers were able to get to the topics first. Take religion: Eduardo Coutinho, the most important non-fiction film-maker in Brazil, made *Santo Forte* in 1995–6. Politics: Eduardo Escorel made a film about four or five guys entering political life, *Vocação do poder* [*The Vocation for Power*], in 2005. And I made a film about Lula, which is called *Intermissions* in English, in 2004. Violence: I could name two or three, including the one I directed with Katia Lund, *News from a Private War*.

So in a sense all the major topics of Brazilian life that had been untouched by cinema, for quite some time, were explored by non-fiction film before being explored by fiction. And I think the influence of non-fiction film on those fictional films that came afterwards is not something you should dismiss.

KATIA LUND: I was working in advertising – that was my film school, technically, from 1990 to 1995. In 1995 films were being made again, Walter [Salles] had made *Foreign Land*, and Cacá Diegues was doing a film in Bahia called *Tieta*. And I worked as an assistant director on that film. Then when the production moved to Rio, in 1996, I moved here. And soon afterwards I was invited to prepare the production for a Michael Jackson music video in one of the *favelas*, 'They Don't Care About Us', which Spike Lee was directing.

I knew nothing about the *favelas* in Rio, really, at the time. I used to go to *favelas* in São Paulo, but I just saw them as poor neighbourhoods; they didn't have a culture of their own, to me. I was working as the location person as well as an assistant director: I had to work for three weeks in the *favela*, Santa Marta, to prepare the ground, with eighty kids, doing construction on three different sites. And that was the first time that I saw the drug-dealing situation and started to realise that there was a completely separate organisation and hierarchy, a way of thinking, a whole different logic to the *favelas*. I realised that we don't know shit about our own country.

I was really thrown back, because I was twenty-nine years old, I had travelled the world, I was well read, I read the newspaper every day. But the newspapers here are completely misleading: in Rio they would talk about 'public enemy number one' and 'terrorists'. Then I'm in the *favelas* and I'm looking at a twelve-year-old kid and thinking, 'Is this a terrorist?'

These kids are great when they have something to do. They were so excited about being part of the video production. I remember being floored by one situation. I asked one of my best kids to take a hammer from one construction site to another. So he ran down the stairs – this is a vertical *favela*, it's all stairs – and when he went round the corner he ran into five policemen with machine guns. I was following, and saw him transform from being this vibrant, incredible kid to . . . he completely cancelled himself out. And the policemen were trying to provoke him, slapping him around. I went to them and said, 'He's working with me.' And the policeman looked at me and said, 'What are you doing here?' That's when I realised that as a 'privileged' Brazilian woman I was co-responsible. I'm not separate from this reality, I pay taxes so the police will go there and do that job.

At that time Walter, who I didn't really know, called me up and wanted me to be his first AD on *Central Station*. So I went to talk to him at VideoFilmes, and he started out by teasing me about these newspaper articles. 'So, I hear you've been making deals with the dealers.' I explained that I was talking to them, yeah, because you have to, but the whole way it was portrayed in the newspapers was not the way it happened. They didn't charge us money, because they thought it was an honour to have Michael Jackson in their *favela*.

So Salles is teasing me about this, and I start telling him all these stories, all this stuff that I'd seen. And our conversation goes on for about six hours. And at the end of the conversation – this is the first time I've met Walter – he said, 'How do you feel about making a documentary about this?'

In the beginning I was doing it with Walter: while we were shooting *Central Station* – the end of 1996 into 1997 – he and I shot a few things. But then when Walter was editing, he didn't have the time any more. So Walter left the project and João came in. In early 1997 João and I started shooting together.

*In his three-part television documentary* Futebol *(1988), João Moreira Salles had filmed in the dangerous Morro do Alemão favela, where at that time twenty-five people per month were killed in the drug war – one reason why parents hoped their sons could start a football career that would help them escape the favela. The father of one soccer hopeful is seen clearing bullet shells from his corrugated roof.*

JOÃO MOREIRA SALLES: Making my documentary *Futebol* put me in contact with the *favela*, so when the idea popped up about doing a film on violence, I already knew the stage. And because the idea appealed to me, I asked to join in.

I would say that *News from a Private War* is an urgent film, which stems from the desire of two citizens of Rio to tell what was going on in the city we lived in and liked so much. It was not a thought-through documentary, a film that took a lot of pre-production time. As I remember it, between the first conversations we had about the film and the first day of shooting no more than three weeks elapsed.

It's not a militant film, and certainly not a film that preaches or has the ambition to propose solutions. A friend of mine says that one of the reasons people make documentaries is simply to bear witness. I think this applies to *News*. We just wanted to say: 'This is what we saw.' I've learned something very simple, almost trivial. When you are willing to hear, people are willing to speak. That was true of the drug-dealers. No film crew had ever gone to a *favela* to hear what they wanted to say. That caused great confusion at the time, because people – and the powers that be – decided that to hear was to condone. Well, it was not. We just wanted to know why so many young people decided to become bandits. Economic reasons were not enough. The choice was a much more complex one, and it was useful to understand it. Today, most of what we heard back then is taken as a given.

KATIA LUND: During the Michael Jackson production I met the head dealer of that *favela*, Marcinho VP, who was later arrested.

So I started going to see him in prison, for research, and to create trust. On my first visit I told him that I didn't know what the shit was going on in the *favelas*. And he said that the only film that had anything to do with his life was the French film, *La haine* [1995]. It's funny, he had seen that on video but didn't know of any Brazilian films that referred to his reality in the same way. When we started shooting in 1997, he had broken out of prison. And he gave us access to the whole network.

JOÃO MOREIRA SALLES: I went to Minas Gerais to meet Marcio in his hiding place, with the mission of explaining what we wanted. Shooting started a few weeks after that in Santa Marta. Because we had the go-ahead of the drug leader who ran the *favela* where most of the documentary was shot, there was no sense of danger at all.

KATIA LUND: Of course we *were* in danger, in some ways. I just don't think we really, fully realised. The crazy thing is I felt this sense of immunity, which was partly stupidity and partly this belief that if you had a camera you would not be harmed.

I think the community had a similar idea about cameras. One time I had a call, around 6 a.m.: 'Katia, you have got to come here because the police have surrounded the house where the dealer is. Do you have a camera?' So I got there, with my little camera. The fact that an outsider was there with a camera was so important to them. Also, the people in the *favela* are disposable people, but if I get shot – upper-class, white – it's going to be front-page news.

JOÃO MOREIRA SALLES: In the end Marcio does not appear in *News*. He said he wanted to speak without a balaclava – to show his face – and the agreement we had with the television channel was that it could only be shown if, at the time of the screening, he had left the *favela*. Well, when *News* went on air, he was still there, so I kept the agreement. The dealer you see a lot of, Adriano, was his lieutenant, who died a little bit after the interview.

© Walter Carvalho

Rio police chief Hélio Luz, *News from a Private War* (1999)

*As well as speaking to a number of disguised drug-dealers, of numerous ages, Salles and Lund interview two notable members of the Rio police. One is Pimentel, the other police chief Hélio Luz, in many ways the most surprising interviewee of the film. 'I'll say it myself: the police force is corrupt,' he declares. 'The institution was designed to be violent and corrupt . . . because it was created to protect the state and the elite.' He also admits that the only way to control 'two million underprivileged people' is through repression.*

KATIA LUND: Hélio Luz was an extraordinary person to be the chief of police. He had been a leftie, a militant, he used to go into the *favelas* to try to mobilise people to revolution. When we interviewed him we asked, 'Why are you the chief of police, when this is what you think?' And he said, 'So that I can speak from this position, basically.' They say that there's a direct relation not between poverty and crime, but police and crime. And we asked him, is there such a thing as organised crime? And he said, 'I'm tempted to say that the only organised crime exists in the police force.' And he was the chief of police.

Rodrigo Pimentel also did an interview for José Padilha's *Bus 174*. He was getting into a lot of trouble for being so honest. He finally quit and went into sociology, and now he's a scriptwriter. In fact, the time that was really terrifying for us was when the film came out, because of the reaction of the police and others.

The first time it was seen was in São Paulo, in a museum, a little private screening which was being televised. And João was up on stage with a policeman and Paulo Lins – *City of God* came out at the same time, so we were doing these debates together. And the audience was packed with the pro-gun lobby and the police force. And we were just being attacked. The fact is, as the opening line of our film says, we thought we were doing a documentary about drugs, and realised we were doing a documentary about guns. It happened, you know, but it wasn't the initial intention. And it was such a volatile environment: people were standing up in the audience and screaming. There's always been a fear that the people of the *favela* are going to come down and take over the middle class of Brazil. João was saying they will not come down, because now they're just fighting each other. And this person stood up and said, 'What do you mean they haven't come down, they're here, we have to have our own guns.'

JOÃO MOREIRA SALLES: I don't think the film is important as a documentary, in terms of its form. But I do think in Brazil it was an important film because it was the first that brought the theme of that kind of violence into the country. It has an historical value, let's say.

*Whereas Katia Lund has since directed fiction, as has José Padilha, João Moreira Salles has no intention of doing the same.*

JOÃO MOREIRA SALLES: I'm very militant about that. It's a very common question, not a bad question, but it is a funny question, because you never hear a feature film-maker being asked, 'When will you finally make your first documentary?' I don't need to move into features.

Something quite significant has happened now in Brazil which really allows us to speak about the Brazilian documentary movement. When I started teaching documentary in university back in the early nineties, most of the people I taught were there because they thought documentary was a necessary step before reaching 'nirvana', which was fiction. It's like a long-haul flight when you have to stop in Arkansas before reaching Los Angeles.

Views have changed now, which is a very good thing. I think that you will find in Brazil more people, proportionately, than anywhere else in the world who studied cinema and who want to become documentary film-makers. Non-fiction is not a step in the direction of fiction, but an end in itself. There are a couple of reasons. The first is that some of our most interesting films have been non-fiction. Secondly, you have someone like Eduardo Coutinho, who has influenced a whole generation of young film-makers. Unfortunately, his films depend on the spoken Brazilian language and therefore don't travel well; but for Brazilian audiences it's an extremely powerful cinema. If you ask the very talented film-makers who are in their late twenties or early thirties to name two or three of their most influential Brazilian film-makers, I'm absolutely sure that in all the lists, all of them, the name of Eduardo Coutinho will show.

Now, in general terms, people want fantasy. The oneiric co-efficient of documentaries is usually very low. As the man said, humankind cannot bear much reality. Therefore, features will always have a wider reach than docs. Depending on the circumstances, there might be good reasons to expand the audience for the discussion of certain subjects. Even if *News from a Private War* could be seen as the documentary precursor of *City of God* (which it is not), there would be a good argument for making *City of God*. Besides the technical skill of Fernando Meirelles's work, which helped bring Brazilian cinema to world attention, the fact that he chose his cast from the same *favelas* where *News* was shot had deep political implications. Suddenly, we realised that there was an immense pool of talent waiting to be discovered, where most people only saw violence and dystopia.

## Fernando Meirelles

Alongside Walter Salles, Fernando Meirelles is the most successful and best known of contemporary Brazilian directors. Like Salles, he made his name with an intrinsically Brazilian story, in his case *City of God*, which struck a chord with audiences all over the world; like Salles, also, he went on to build an international reputation and strong connections in America and Europe, while using his influence at home to develop Brazil's film-making community.

Meirelles' follow-up to *City of God* was *The Constant Gardener* (2005), a film set outside his country, albeit with a physical milieu – the shanty towns of Sub-Saharan Africa – he would have understood after his time in the *favelas*, and which he brought to life just as vividly. Based on the political thriller by John le Carré and produced by the late, highly respected Briton Simon Channing Williams, the film confirmed its director as a consummate storyteller, here interweaving the personal and the political, romance and thriller with great dexterity and feeling. The film, shot by *City of God* cinematographer César Charlone, was also one of the most visually arresting of that year. It received four Oscar nominations, with Rachel Weisz winning for best actress.

I met Meirelles in February 2008, when he was in New York on a double mission: to discuss the soundtrack for his new film as director, *Blindness*, and to promote the release of *City of Men*, which he was producing with his São Paulo company O2 Filmes. The first project served, among other things, to illustrate Meirelles' status and pulling power as a director, with an A-list cast that included Julianne Moore and Danny Glover; the latter completed a cycle of Brazilian films and television series about the *favelas*, by Meirelles and others, the centrepiece of which remains his own *City of God*.

Before speaking in detail about *City of God*, I wanted to gauge Meirelles' views on the ongoing phenomenon of *favela* films, and to chart his unusual path from architecture student to the point when he would make one of the most successful movies in his country's history.

*I've just seen* Elite Squad *in Berlin, where it's caused quite a stir. And your company has just finished* City of Men. *Six years after* City of God, *which seemed so definitive an account of the* favela *problem, what's to be gained from more films on the subject?*

These films are valuable because they show other aspects of the same neighbourhoods, the same environment. *City of God* is the story of the drug-dealers, and behind them you see the lives of ordinary people, like the narrator, who's not a drug-dealer, he's just a guy trying to live his life. In *City of Men* we do the reverse: we talk about normal people in the foreground, and behind them are the drug-dealers. *City of God* and *City of Men* are very complementary. And we could say that *Elite Squad* is another point of view: of the police who come into this place and who affect *everybody*. So there you have three angles on the same kind of community.

*You evidently think it's important for cinema to keep the spotlight on the country's social problems.*

Definitely. But I'm not going to do any more of these films myself. O2 Filmes made *City of God*, then we did twenty episodes of *City of Men* on television, and we also produced a TV series called *Antônia* – Tata Amaral made her feature, and we produced two TV seasons – which is about the suburbs in São Paulo. And we have released the movie *City of Men*. And so after five or six years dealing with this subject, I'm moving on to different pastures.

But there is a phenomenon in Brazil right now, which I think is one of the most interesting things happening in cinema anywhere in the world, which is the work of really, really super-independent film-makers in the slums. All the big *favelas* have cultural centres, and all have groups of boys – eighteen, nineteen, twenty years old – shooting their own films. In São Paulo there are forty, in Rio probably sixty. Every year there are a hundred shorts made by boys from the *favelas*. They are not very good in technique, yet, they don't know how to write, but they're learning how to shoot and how to edit. And every year I see better films.

It's so different to having a guy like me, from the middle class, with my background, going to a *favela* and telling their story. Now they are telling their own story. I think it's sensational.

*Presumably one of these groups is Nós do Cinema.*

Yes. After we finished *City of God* we didn't want to say to this amazing cast, whom we'd worked with for a year, 'OK, thank you very much, see you around.' So Katia and I kept in touch with them. Every weekend we would bring them together, to try to see what other films we could do. And from these meetings Nós do Cinema was created, and later this became an NGO. I gave them cameras and a cutting machine and space – I bought a building, a small house in downtown Rio, so they could attract kids from different *favelas*. Now it's become a kind of school, with three hundred boys who go there every day for different classes, not just cinema, but English classes, other things. They raise their own money for their projects, and now they are running themselves. It's great. And they are doing very interesting cinema.*

*What about the kids in* City of God? *Have many of them contin-ued to appear in films?*

---

*Nós do Cinema, now named Cinema Nosso, is, in its own words, 'a media-based arts organisation, which uses film and video as a means of education, empowerment and cultural expression'. It offers training by professionals in basic communication skills (writing, computers, etc.) and specific training in areas such as directing, screenwriting, journalism, lighting, sound, photography, production and computer science.

There were nine or ten who became professional actors. Some of those you see in *City of Men* were from *City of God*, and are doing television, soap operas, theatre and other things. Douglas Silva and Darlan Cunha – who are in *City of Men* on television, and now this new film – are big stars in Brazil.

*You mention different pastures. Do you see yourself now as a Brazilian director or an international director?*

This is not an issue for me. I make films. But I do want to do Brazilian films, films in Portuguese. O2 is currently working on four film projects, all Brazilian. One of these is called *Xingu*, which is the name of a national park in the centre of Brazil – a huge park the size of Belgium and an Indian reserve. It's the story of the creation of this park by three Brazilian guys, who in my view were among the best Brazilians ever. They've been forgotten; we should tell their story, we should show the Indian tribes, we should compare our civilisation with theirs.

You know, one thing that would be interesting, and which I would consider myself in fifteen or twenty years' time, would be to return to *City of Men*. Because we have those two very strong characters, very successful on television in Brazil, everybody knows them. And by writing a story for these two friends years from now, we would also be talking about the fate of the country in that same period. When kids are raised like this, without the support of the government, what happens to them? And what happens to a country that doesn't take care of its children? Imagine: I'll be seventy-eight!

*How important is it to have your own company? Does it strengthen your position as a director?*

For me personally, it doesn't change much. Because I have had two films that were successful, I can finance my films internationally. But for new film-makers, if O2 is behind their film they know it can happen. We can really push new film-makers.

What I like about O2 is that it has become a cinema and TV centre in São Paulo. We now have a development department, so everybody who has an idea or a script in Brazil sends it to us, because they know O2 is a way to finance films. We're in touch with good writers, good actors. We make our money with commercials and TV – they pay the rent, and we know that. So we only get involved in film projects because of the subject, or the director, or because of a possibility of a partnership. We want to work with Gael [García Bernal]'s company in Mexico, for example. We've never done any project because we thought we'd make a lot of money. Money is a different department.

*This is a good point to go back a bit. Your name is now synonymous with cinema. But you trained as an architect.*

And I am an architect, although I've never worked as such, only for myself. I've just built my own house, and have designed a renovation or two for the company. Paulo Morelli, who has directed *City of Men* and is one of my partners in O2, is also an architect. We're colleagues from the same school, at the University of São Paulo. We started our company when we were still in architecture school.

*So how did you cross disciplines?*

Before doing architecture I always liked films. My father is a doctor, a gastroenterologist, but when he was young he had a 16 mm camera and he made a lot of very funny films, with his friends. After he was married, when we were very small kids, he made more films – parodies of westerns, or thrillers, using the family. So I grew up watching my father's films, with me in them, with my mother and my father's friends. Then when I was twelve, thirteen years old, I did some little shorts of my own, experiments, with my father's camera. And I liked it. Making film for me was something fun to do at weekends, you know, like going to the beach.

Then at architecture school we had a group who liked to draw together, a kind of atelier, and we decided to do an animated film, just to see our drawing move. And that's how we started. We did a first cartoon and it worked, and we did a second one. And I liked to work with films, cutting. So I bought U-matic video equipment. And for my graduation thesis, instead of writing something, I made a forty-minute video, about architecture and city planning.

By my fifth year in architecture school we had created this company – me, Paulo and two other friends. 'Olhar Eletrônico', Electronic Gaze. So when I left architecture school I was already doing experimental videos. At that time I never thought about making films, because in Brazil in the eighties it was nearly impossible to make a living making films. So we started to do video, really experimental: art videos, things for museums, installation and performance. But then some people came and asked us to make some videos for their companies, institutional programmes, and to make some money we started doing that.

*Working in video in the early eighties must have felt like cutting edge.*

The first video festivals in Brazil were in 1982–3. There were only a few people who had video equipment at that time. I think in the second of these festivals there were ten awards – and we got seven of them. The next day there was this article in the press, 'Who is this group of boys?' A guy from Brazilian TV visited us and said he had a slot at eleven o'clock, with no audience at all. 'I have one hour, do you want to do a show? I won't pay you anything, but you can use my time just to do whatever you want.' So we did TV. It all just happened.

*In what way was your video work experimental?*

The experiment was mostly with the editing, which was often very fast-paced. It was about cutting. One of the videos that won, *Time*, for instance, was the story of mankind told in two minutes. The images were two or three frames. Ten images a second. Now we see this very often, this machine gun of images, but it was not so common in the early eighties. Really, everybody was quite shocked. We went from cave to space in two minutes, with everything – religion, war – in between. It's a bit clichéd now, but in the eighties it was, 'Wow!'

*I can't help thinking of the opening of* City of God: *not just the fact of the frantic cutting of the chicken chase, but the way you use editing to organise time and space, convey information quickly.*

I never thought about it, but it's true. Another video that won awards was all about rhythm, all the cuts were used like sound, like a beat. It was the story of a woman who wakes up in the morning and goes to bed at night, her life is so boring. Four minutes, just images and sounds of her. And it worked.

*So you had this carte blanche offer for TV.*

It was crazy. We had five days to prepare a one-hour TV show. And we decided to do it live. We arrived at the TV studio just an hour before the broadcast, with some friends, including a friend who had published a book, a very big hit, so he was our star, our *pièce de résistance*. We did the interviews ourselves. The set was whatever we found in the studio. All improvised. It was terrible.

In this programme we also used some of our recorded tapes, of our famous videos, and those were very good moments. So the following week, the programme was half and half – we spent the week recording things, including interviews on the street, and then we had a live part. To make this long story short, after two and a half months, eight or nine programmes, this same guy moved us to a Saturday slot, where he presented his own show, to produce that. It was a night-time show – everything that happens at night in the city. And after six or seven months producing that, he gave us our own space on Saturday afternoon, and we created a show for teenagers called *Crig-Ra*.

*What does that mean?*

Nothing. It's what Tarzan would shout! Crig-Ra! It was a one-hour show which only ran for three or four months, but became a cult. Even today I meet guys who are six or seven years younger than me, and they talk about watching *Crig-Ra*. It was a bunch of boys having fun on air. And that's how we started on television. I did independent television for ten years.

*You also made an important children's programme.*

*Ra-Tim-Bum*. It was for two- to six-year-olds. Pre-school. Between 1992 and 1993 I did 180 episodes. It was an interesting challenge for me to create a programme for kids who are learning to speak. It took the educational idea of *Sesame Street*, teaching the letters, counting. Then there was the challenge to keep a two-year-old boy watching for half an hour. At that time my young boy was exactly the same age. I had a four-year-old girl and a two-year-old boy. So they were my audience. The show was very successful. They are still repeating it today. It was very funny, creative, with a lot of interesting ideas.

*The thing to say, up to this point: you're self-taught.*

Exactly. We were just doing it. With our first company, for seven years we never hired anybody from outside. Not even a driver. We would do everything. Everybody knew how to operate the camera, how to cut, how to present a programme, how to write scripts. Everyone worked as the grip. It was a very good school.

*How did you segue from television to commercials?*

An advertising agent asked us to use one of our television characters in a campaign and so we produced seven or eight commer-

cials with him. We were all starting to get married and we needed to pay for diapers and all that. And we thought, 'OK, we can
make money with this.' And because this campaign was successful, other agents called us. So at the end of the eighties, beginning
of the nineties, Olhar Eletrônico became this very avant-garde
commercials company in Brazil; we were all very young, creating
very different commercials for the time. One of the things that
our work brought to the commercials market was that we used
ordinary people. At that time commercials looked like commercials – all perfect lighting, pretty faces, blond people. And we
proposed to our clients that they start using black people, something that is very usual today.

But as the commercials work grew we started to fight in the
company. One of the partners didn't want to do commercials,
and another started his own business. So in 1990 Paulo and I
opened O2. And in four or five years it became the biggest commercials company in Brazil.

*So at a time in the nineties when there was no money for cinema,
the world of Brazilian commercials was thriving.*

Nobody wanted to finance films. When we started making commercials we were always thinking that we were stealing money,
that they would realise they were stupid paying all this. And then
we realised that we were charging a fifth of what any other company charged. That's why we grew so fast, it wasn't just because
we were young and different, but because we were so cheap.

*I've seen you quoted as saying that eventually an 'internal alarm'
went off, in relation to your career.*

That's true. I think it was around 1996–7. I was in a big crisis. I
wanted to change my life, I had been doing mostly commercials
for ten years, it had become so boring. I said, 'I've got to stop
this. I want to move on to films.' And I started reading books,
looking for an idea. The first book I tried to buy the rights of, in

1997, was *Blindness*, actually. The book had just come out in Brazil. But the author, José Saramago, didn't want a film to be made at that time. Then the same publisher offered me *City of God*.

## The Making of *City of God*

It starts with a runaway chicken and the swish of a knife and the cut-cut-cut of film to the beat of a whooping whistle; and a stand-off between a gang of youths and the police and an outsider with a camera round his neck, who could be Eastwood with a cheroot in a Sergio Leone show-down, if he didn't look so scared, and is spared his sticky predicament – for now – when the camera makes a jagged 360° pan and retreats into the past.

The film will circle back and end where it began, guns facing guns, boys playing at being men, by which time these youths will have a history and we will have seen enough to know that violence is inevitable, and to accept Walter Salles' interpretation that 'the chicken caught in the crossfire is not only a chicken. It is the reflection of so many Brazilians trapped in an unjust country.'

*City of God*, directed by Fernando Meirelles, with Katia Lund as co-director, is a remarkable film. It has all the accoutrements of a crime drama – psychotic hoods, power struggles, innocents and tarnished angels, corruption, danger, needless tragedy – yet is rooted in reality, a reality that we accept as a given every time one of these urchin boys opens his mouth and speaks in the dancing, expressive patois of the *favela*. Its narrative plays with every cinematic trope at its disposal – voice-over, captions, split-screen, flashing backwards, forwards, sideways – yet every trick serves a more intimate storytelling: that of oral history. When we're told, 'It's now time to tell Knockout Ned's story,' we could be sitting on an outcrop of a *favela*, glancing over the lights of Ipanema below. And it deals with a world saturated in violence, yet never attempting (despite criticism at the time) to glamorise it, conveying instead the terrible sense of a world where a gun really does have the currency of a toy, to be popped as pleasure, where premature death is a given, stoically accepted, and where there is only one peer group to which to aspire. 'A kid?' jeers the sweet-faced Steak and Fries. 'I smoke, snort, I've killed and robbed. I'm a man.'

It was adapted, by Bráulio Mantovani in close collaboration with Meirelles, from the acclaimed novel by Paulo Lins, itself born of the author's personal experience (he grew up in City of God) and painstaking research. It is an adaptation of the very highest calibre, bringing to mind, from recent years, only Anthony Minghella's work on Michael Ondaatje's *The English Patient*, for its alchemical extraction of its story from a complex source.

That story concerns some twelve or fifteen years in the life of the City of God *favela*, in western Rio de Janeiro, a slum designed, as Katia Lund has neatly summarised, 'to draw poor people out of the city centre and keep them out of sight and out of mind of the wealthy'. In the film's three phases, one in the sixties, two in the seventies, we see the community transformed through increasing poverty, ever-congested and congealing living space and, in particular, through the intensification of crime: from amateurish robberies conducted by local Robin Hoods, to drug-dealing – first marijuana, then cocaine. And as the drugs become more and more profitable, so the number of guns increases.

Of Lins' cast of hundreds, Meirelles and his collaborators have chosen to give us an occasional narrator, Rocket: entirely ordinary and unpretentious, and a rarity in his ability not to be sucked into crime (though he comes close). The more interesting characters are those knee-deep in the mess: the psychopathic drug-dealer Li'l Zé, determined to control the *favela*, his right-hand man and jovial party animal Bené, rival dealer Carrot, and Knockout Ned, a peaceful ex-soldier drawn by circumstance into a war with Li'l Zé.

There are three phases, then, but no three-act structure in the manner of Hollywood: there are no contrived plot points, forced confrontations or resolutions. Unlike most crime films, it conveys a sense that it is almost academic who lives or dies: if they don't die on screen, they probably will after this tale is over. That is not callous, merely realistic. When we see a small boy murdered, or a young woman horribly gang-raped, or a family gunned down in its home, the horror is not mitigated by the satisfaction for the viewer of knowing the culprit will be brought to task and the violence ended; there is no end, merely cycles. And even if the film concludes optimistically for its passive hero, Rocket, it is realism that has the last word. 'Who knows how to write?' asks a boy, walking with his friends away from the final carnage. 'Let's make a list and kill them all.'

In keeping with the trend that courses through this book, the film-makers are content to show, to reveal, rather than soapbox. They wish to tell a story; all else will follow. But there is, arguably, one flaw to its inbuilt social critique, and that is the character of Li'l Zé: the film-makers allow the *favela*'s descent into chaos to be presided over by a *bona fide* psychopath rather than – more plausible in this environment – one of the many victims of nurture, not nature. Maybe it is enough that 'the runts', the ragamuffins who *have* been nurtured to disrespect life, walk away with his empire.

Among the film's excellent young cast, Alice Braga went on to star in Sérgio Machado's *Lower City*, excelled in an A-List international cast in Meirelles' *Blindness* and is now established in Hollywood; Seu Jorge is one of the most popular musicians in Brazil, while winning a legion of overseas fans with his soundtrack of Bowie covers for Wes Anderson's *The Life Aquatic with Steve Zissou* (in which he also appeared). And the then eleven-year-olds Douglas Silva (the young Li'l Zé) and Darlan Cunha (Steak and Fries), in real life fatherless children of the *favela*, have become television stars in Meirelles' cheerier depiction of the same milieu, *City of Men*.

While I wrote, I imagined that some day the story
could be made into a film. I have always liked the cinema. I even participated in the Cidade de Deus cinema
club, from 1980 to 1987, which used to show political
films. I imagined that if *Cidade de Deus* became a
film, many more people could participate in the discussion of this reality.

PAULO LINS

FERNANDO MEIRELLES, director: I remember after reading the
book I was really shocked. I was forty-five years old at that time,
had lived in Brazil all my life, and I really didn't know that these
things were happening. Those ghettos are really closed. It's like in
the film – you never see the city, the drug-dealers only live inside
the *favelas*, where they are protected. If they step outside, they're
caught, so they don't leave. And look at [the film] *City of Men*:
the first scene when the gang leader goes to the beach – it's like a
scandal, it's the first time in three years the guy leaves the *favela*.
That's why no one really knows what happens inside these places.

Of course, this phenomenon of drug-dealers has developed a
lot since then. Today the big drug-dealers are like superstars,
everyone knows their names. Ten years ago nobody would know
they existed. I didn't. At that time it was a revelation.

KATIA LUND, co-director: The novel sparked an intense debate in
Brazil about the relationship between violence, drug-dealing,
social injustice, political action and the role of civil society. I participated in many of these public discussions alongside Paulo
Lins. They were often very emotional. For the first time, ordinary
citizens were openly exchanging views on these painful subjects.

FERNANDO MEIRELLES: I gave a copy of the book to Bráulio
Mantovani, and he loved it too. We decided to develop the story,
to see if it was possible. It's six hundred pages, there's no structure, just a lot of episodes happening one after the other – with
no dates, nothing – of people dying, dying, dying. Bráulio had

never written a script before. We had met by chance and I invited him to do a TV project, and then we did a second together and became friends. So when I decided to adapt *City of God*, instead of looking for an experienced writer I decided to trust his talent. We spent two years writing.

BRÁULIO MANTOVANI, scriptwriter: I was very surprised when he asked me. I had no previous experience writing features professionally. There wasn't a market for film writers in those days. Of course, I was also elated. I had been a big fan of Fernando's work since the eighties, when he and his collaborators from Olhar Eletrônico made a small revolution on Brazilian television.

I must say, I got scared when I got to page 100 of Paulo Lins' novel. I actually decided to give up the project, and rehearsed many possibilities of how to tell Fernando that he had gone mad and that it was impossible to adapt that novel to the screen. Then I thought: 'What do I have to lose? Fuck it.'

FERNANDO MEIRELLES: First we made a list of all the 260 characters in the book, on little cards, with little paragraphs relating their stories. Then we selected the interesting ones, and kept about fifty or sixty. And from those we started planning, and combining characters, until we had twenty. Still we had no structure. And so – this is something that Paulo Lins didn't like much – I decided to create a structure for the film. I decided to split the story into three periods: the first moment when the drug-dealers come to City of God, then jumping ahead five years or so to the period when the dealers' business is going well, then to the third period, the war.

To tell the story, we first thought about having several voices, even tried to have different people narrating, like the community telling the story. Then we felt that we needed somebody with whom the audience would identify. And so we decided to create Rocket, who in the book is just one of the many characters, but for us is Paulo Lins. It's his perspective. Like Rocket, Paulo Lins had a lot of friends who were drug-dealers, but he says he was always afraid of being shot, of guns and bullets. That's why there's a line in the film, when Rocket says, 'I didn't become a drug-dealer or a policeman, because I'm afraid of guns.'

Life through a lens: Alexandre Rodrigues as *City of God*'s narrator, Rocket

BRÁULIO MANTOVANI: I wasn't very enthusiastic about using voice-over in the script. Fernando convinced mc that that was the only way to tell a number of stories covering the whole period the novel covers. Once I agreed with that, I realised the real question was: 'Through whose eyes we will see the images of the movie?' Rocket was perfect for that, because he wants to be a photographer. Photographers look at the world in a different manner. They see things that are there that non-photographers simply miss. They can frame fragments of the world around us and create metonyms that open windows to unseen parts of the world. A good photographer knows his subjects from an insider's point of view, yet can register moments from a distance, revealing things that even his human subjects don't know about themselves.

Plus, I thought that still pictures could help the narrative. I could freeze the images, as if they were inside Rocket's camera, and use his voice-over to comment and explain details that would take lots of scenes in a more traditional film narrative.

*At that time the Sundance Institute helped to create a screenwriting lab in Brazil. Mantovani participated in one of those labs, with the first draft of* City of God. *The American writer and director Alexander Payne – later to win an Oscar for his screenplay for* Sideways – *was one of his advisers.*

BRÁULIO MANTOVANI: The Sundance labs meant a great improvement in the screenwriting process in Brazil. The opportunity to have foreign advisers together with Brazilian ones was, and is, very productive in improving the craft.

When I participated in the lab with *City of God*, in 1999, my first session was with Alexander Payne. I had no idea who he was. Back then, he had only one feature released, *Citizen Ruth*, and I hadn't seen it. I was very nervous and insecure about my script. But Alexander started paying so many compliments that I quickly relaxed. I was amazed that he had two copies of the script with him: the English translation and the original in Portuguese. He said that every time he had problems understanding the English version he would go to the original and check it out. I thought to myself: Who is this guy?

As it happens, he has a degree in Latin American history. He speaks perfect Spanish, and when he comes to festivals in Brazil he always presents his films in Portuguese. What I remember most from that session with him, funnily enough, is his saying that I should use more voice-over. He kept asking: 'Where's your narrator?' He even suggested changes for the title cards: the last card that appears in the film, *The Beginning of the End*, is his idea.

*One of Rocket's important functions in* City of God *is to create a glimpse of the world outside the* favela, *as well as an alternative way of living, without recourse to the drug trade.*

FERNANDO MEIRELLES: Rocket is not trying to escape the *favela*. Actually, this was a big discussion for us. At one point we had two endings. In one, after Li'l Zé is killed, the journalist with whom Rocket has spent the night comes in her Volkswagen and they leave together. But we realised that leaving altogether is not a solution. You can't just go away and let the place burn. It would be wrong. All he wants is an opportunity in life: the country needs to give that opportunity. So we changed it. He still lives in the *favela*, but he has a decent job. He effectively says, 'I don't get much money, but I'm included. I'm part of society. I have a life of possibility.' And that's it.

This is one thing that all the scriptwriting manuals are very wrong about. The first rule, especially for American scripts, is that the narrator should be the lead character, telling you his story. But *City of God* is a story about Li'l Zé and Knockout Ned. Rocket is a lead character who's not telling his own story, but somebody else's.

Actually, there's an example of the same idea in a film that was a big reference for us, which is *Goodfellas*. It's a gangster movie, like *City of God*. And who tells the story of *Goodfellas*? Henry Hill. And he's telling the story of his bosses. He wants to be a gangster, but he's not, he's just a boy watching what is happening from the outside, as Rocket does.

BRÁULIO MANTOVANI: I was familiar with *favelas* before I wrote *City of God*. In São Paulo I worked as an actor in a kind of agit-prop theatre group, and performed in many *favelas* in the city. I also come from a working-class family, growing up in a tough neighbourhood, not far from the biggest *favela* in São Paulo. So I didn't need to visit City of God. I went there for the first time after I wrote the first draft.

FERNANDO MEIRELLES: Bráulio is very good with dialogue. And he quickly learned to write in the same way as the boys speak. That's something that is lost in translation – all the slang, the way these boys use Portuguese is so beautiful, and of course when you subtitle it you lose all that.

Take the names, for example. Rocket. It's OK, but it's not the same. His name in Portuguese is Buscapé, which is a kid's toy – it looks like a firework, you light it and put it on the floor and try to catch people's feet with it. You have to jump, because it burns. Rocket is too powerful a name. He's Buscapé, he's not dangerous, just a little fire in the ground. Buscapé, Buscapé. Li'l Zé never remembers his name. He's nobody.

Another joke that is totally lost in translation is at the beginning, with the chicken. The name of the Knockout Ned character is Mané Galinha, which would be Mané Chicken. 'Galinha' means chicken. But chicken in Portuguese doesn't have the same colloquial meaning as in English, it doesn't mean coward, but a guy who gets all the girls. The guy in real life was very good-looking and he really had all the beautiful girls, which is why Li'l Zé hated him, because Li'l Zé was ugly and never had a girlfriend. So when he says, 'Let's kill the chicken,' right before he tries to kill Mané Galinha, that's a double meaning that gets lost in English. He's talking about his enemy.

It was Bráulio's idea to open the film with this. But it was from the book, the beginning of one chapter, with somebody thinking, 'Well, they're going to kill me, I'm tied with this rope, I'm seeing my friends being killed and I'm going to be killed myself.' And you read for one or two pages, thinking he's a person, then in the middle of the chapter you realise that he's actually a cock, thinking. And then this cock runs away and describes how desperate he is with people chasing him.

We wanted to grab the audience in the first ten seconds. First, I thought it would be funny to start chasing a chicken in a gangster movie. Then we realised that there was this coincidence with the names, so we were really talking about what the film is about: Li'l Zé chasing Mané Galinha. And we also thought that the chicken could lead us to our big conflict: the chicken runs and runs and after two minutes you have the police, Rocket, the bad guys, and then Knockout Ned. The chicken takes us to the most dramatic moment in the film, and then we go to flashback and start the whole story again.

'Are you talking to *us*?' *City of God*

*These opening moments of the film, in which a knife is being sharpened not for violence, but for a barbecue in the street, before the group of kids comically gives chase, cleverly relate to the vibrant picture-postcard images we associate with Brazil – drawing the viewer in before the darker story.*

FERNANDO MEIRELLES: If you go to *favelas* at the weekends, they always have these barbecues on the rooftops. And as you're walking down those little streets, there's different music coming out of each window, like tuning a radio, always a rhythm going on. And the huge party in the film – some of the larger *favelas* have events like that two or three times a week. Leandro Firmino, who plays Li'l Zé, he's got some money, he could have moved, but he lives in City of God still today. He says he loves it, he would never leave.

You actually see this reality throughout the film. There are very violent moments, then you cut and there's a party. You see crime and happiness mixed. Only in the third act does it get darker.

*In 2000–1, while developing the script of* City of God, *Fernando Meirelles directed his first feature film, with Nando Olival. Adapted from a stage play,* Domésticas *(Maids, 2001) follows*

*the fortunes of five maids in São Paulo whose dreams or desires
– for a husband, a modelling career, to have an illicit lover – dis-
tract them from their dreary lives. It's a spirited, sympathetic
account of an underclass of women which doesn't shy away
from humour. And while the straight-to-camera reflections
betray its stage roots, Meirelles' use of evocative night shots,
stop-motion and black-and-white photography suggests a man
gearing up for something much more dramatic.*

FERNANDO MEIRELLES: After a period of writing with Bráulio,
I became really enthusiastic about the *City of God* project, but I
had never done a feature before. Meanwhile, I watched this play,
*Domésticas*. And I invited another friend to see it the next day,
and four months later the film was shot. A very simple, low-
budget film, which we financed ourselves at O2. From the first
time I saw the play to the first cut was six months.

I wrote the script with Nando Olival, who directed the film
with me, the playwright Renata Melo and one of the actresses.
There's no plot actually, it's more like a chronicle. The play's a
bit like that: the actresses say their lines to the audience, then
they dance a bit. The idea of doing *Maids*, for me, was really just

Trial run: Fernando Meirelles' *Maids* (2001)

to learn, especially about the post-production process of film. Our work at O2 was all on video: with *Maids* we learned how to produce a feature. And then when that film opened, I was just starting to shoot *City of God*.

It wasn't a casual choice, of course. Actually, I created a specific scene in *Maids* that I wanted to shoot in *City of God*, like a rehearsal, which was the scene where the two boys try to rob the bus. In *Maids* it's very funny: everything goes wrong, they complain that 'there is no one but maids on this bus', they really don't know how to do it, the passenger tells them off and they are ashamed. I put that scene in *Maids*, because I had written the same scene in *City of God*, for Rocket. That was supposed to be the funniest scene in *City of God* – there was supposed to be lots of laughter, that was my dream. But it didn't work.

They come to rob the bus and Knockout Ned is the ticket guy and he says he does karate, and he's pretty cool too, so they just get off without robbing him. They are not prepared to be criminals. But the two actors playing Rocket and his friend, they didn't know how to be funny. So I shot the scene and in the end I just cut it in a different way.

CÉSAR CHARLONE, cinematographer: Fernando called me to work on *Maids* because I came from a film background, whereas he came from video, so it was natural that when he did his first film I should be with him. But I couldn't, because of my Uruguayan background. Brazilians have a sense of humour that Uruguayans don't understand. I just felt that, to my political inclination, this script was very disrespectful to the working classes. But I said, 'The next one, we'll do together.'

I felt very differently about *City of God*. I thought it would be a very useful, socially important film. It did what I had always been trying to do: show people in Brazil a reality that many don't know exists. I remember Walter Salles visiting us when we were filming it. And Walter – I know him, but we're not very close friends or anything – he came up to me and took my arm and said, 'It's important that you guys are doing this film. It has to be done.' And it was that important that I took all my family to visit the set, so they also would know the reality of the *favela*. My three kids were working as apprentices, in different areas. One was in the grip shop, one was in the camera shop, and the other was in the art department.

*When* City of God *opened in Cannes, there developed considerable tension between Katia Lund and Fernando Meirelles over the positioning of Lund's 'co-director' credit, a designation that had already been the subject of difficult discussions and was now, on screen, separate from Meirelles' as director. Lund's displeasure – she felt she was the equal director of the film – was exacerbated when Meirelles alone was nominated for an Oscar. Ultimately, the pair agreed to disagree over the extent of Lund's involvement, and have continued to work together, notably on the* City of Men *television series.* City of God *is Meirelles' film, though Lund's influence was considerable, not least in introducing Meirelles to the* favelas, *and in selecting and training the boys who were to be the film's actors.*

FERNANDO MEIRELLES: I was about to make the film in Rio, where I didn't know many people. And I was looking for an assistant director. And Walter [Salles] suggested Katia Lund, who had been his assistant director on *Central Station*. He said she was really amazing. And I thought that *News from a Private War* was brilliant. So I invited her to be my AD.

KATIA LUND: After *News from a Private War* I was totally involved with the *favelas*. I felt like people were still just starting to get it. Paulo Lins and I had become best friends. We had made this music video together, 'My Soul the Piece that I Don't Want', with O Rappa. And I was writing a script with him, when I got a phone call from Fernando. I knew a feature film was going to reach a lot more people than a documentary ever could. Fernando asked me if I would do research and prepare the cast.

I said, 'I am so involved in the subject, and I've been an assistant director for ten years, so if you want me to be a part of your film, I'll do it if I'm co-director.'

FERNANDO MEIRELLES: Katia brought a lot of ideas to the film. She lived in Rio. She introduced me to people in the *favelas*, which she knew much more than me. It's really through her that I was introduced to this world. Another reason I looked for her was that I knew that middle-class, professional actors would never be able to do the same things, convey the same feeling as boys in the *favelas*. We needed to create actors, to invent actors.

I gave myself six months, during which time I was going to invest my life in the project – I moved to Rio, travelling back and forth at weekends to see my family. My idea was to create this workshop and if after six months I found good actors, then I would go ahead with the film. If not, I would abort.

*The well-known* favela *figure Guti Fraga had established Nós do Morro, 'We of the Hillside', as a theatre workshop in the Vigial* favela. *Many of the actors in* City of God *came from this group. It was to be the first time they had appeared in front of the cameras.*

KATIA LUND: Guti Fraga is really interesting. He's from the interior of Brazil, he's white, he was poor but he's got culture. I'd say he's middle-class now, pretty much. He lived in Vigial and, as the *favela* grew, started giving acting classes in the street. This was fifteen years ago. Now they have two thousand students or something. He's got a Buddha-like energy to him. So I really wanted him involved in this first phase. And because I had wanted to start a permanent school ever since *News from a Private War*, and because we needed more actors than Guti had available, we started Nós do Cinema, 'We in Cinema': to do the casting for the film, but at the same time to prepare for this non-profit organisation that would continue afterwards.

Instead of screen-testing, we were going to have to prepare these people, and to create an ensemble, because we needed the collective energy. We agreed: let's not talk about the film yet, let's talk about a course – we're offering a course for acting in film. For free. And at the end we'll give them a diploma.

We established an office in the centre of the city, an easy place for everybody to get to, and we started researching all the theatre groups, music groups, circus groups that existed in all the *favelas*. Then three actors from Nós do Morro went out to these places with video cameras in their knapsacks and used the loud-speakers – all the *favelas* have these speaker systems – to invite people to sign up for this acting course. And they filmed all those who came forward.

FERNANDO MEIRELLES: We took this material to our little office in downtown Rio: Guti, Katia and I watched 980 faces on a Steenbeck. And just chose the interesting ones. In the end we had around four hundred. We called them. And Guti organised workshops, little improvisations, which we would watch, and reduced those four hundred to two hundred. Then we split those two hundred into eight different groups, and they had to come for two-hour classes, three times a week, from the end of August to November. So we had two hundred boys doing this work-shop. It was really like a circus.

I didn't want the kids to perform to get the part, to create a competition. So at the beginning we didn't tell the boys we were going to do the film. We didn't tell anybody, actually. They knew Guti, so for them it was a workshop with Guti. And he intro-duced myself and Katia as his assistants. The boys were always listening to him, and during the exercises me and Katia were helping. But always Guti was the man.

He had his theatre group for years, so really knew how to deal with these boys. They were coming from very different *favelas*, so the first thing he wanted to do was create an *esprit de corps*, to make the boys feel that they were a group and could trust each other. There were a lot of games, playing with each other, push-ing, making them really close. Then, when they started trusting each other, were not afraid of physicality, they started saying lines.

Every day, in the beginning, we would spend eighty per cent of the time talking about discipline – the importance of showing up on time, of listening to other people, stuff like that. It was very hard to make them understand that discipline means something. Katia really helped to create this school. I'm very disorganised. Katia is the opposite. At the same time as she was very tough with the boys, she was very kind, very friendly. They loved her, because she knew how to support them, she was involved with their private lives.

By the end of this period, the last month, we were doing mostly improvisation. Guti had his routine to warm them up, then we would split them into groups and give them some ideas of theme: you fight here, that's the story you have to play, you are two drug-dealers, you are policemen, you want to get money. We would tell them a little story, then we would give them half an hour to prepare a scene with this idea. And then each little team would present to the group, and everyone would comment. They became very critical of themselves.

The great thing about this process was that at the same time I was writing the story with Bráulio. The script was still being developed: we started the workshop in the fourth version of the script, and finished in the tenth. It eventually went to twelve. If Bráulio and I discussed a scene that was not going very well – I didn't like the dialogue, for example – the next day I would give it to the boys to work on. And every day, they would come up with great lines, or an idea or a moment, I would write it all down, send it to Bráulio, and the next day the script was revised.

The boys would never read the script, but that's how we developed it: I was suggesting lines I had heard from them to Bráulio, Bráulio put them in the script, then I was suggesting them back to the boys. Actually I never gave them the dialogue. And they did not know I was testing the scenes.

I was there from nine in the morning to eight every night. And every two hours was a new group. It was exhausting, but such a good period in my life. And it was a totally different life: one moment I was doing advertising, the next I was with those kids, all day long. Suddenly I'm barefoot and in Bermuda shorts. By the end of the period we knew each one by name, we knew their backgrounds. And I discovered that the drug world is part of all their lives. Almost all the boys had stories – this guy has been shot, this guy's brother was killed, this guy . . . all the boys.

Five were drug-dealers themselves. We didn't find out immediately, but after a while, when they started to trust us. We had this rule: you have to choose. You participate here, or you deal drugs, but you can't do both. So three boys stayed, and two left. One of the boys who left was one of my candidates to play Li'l Zé. I was very disappointed, he was really something: no expression, like Javier Bardem in *No Country for Old Men*. A bit too good-looking, but so powerful. But he left.

CÉSAR CHARLONE: When we shot the film, Fernando would often say to me, 'I want you to be Paulo Lins' eyes.' In that sense, there was one piece from the book that I liked so much that I photocopied it and put it on the door of my hotel, so that I would see it every day as I went down to film. It was the part where Lins describes a killing as casually as I describe this coffee here. *The kid was walking along and a bullet shot his face and his face was spread all over the floor.* He was describing this with no sensationalism, very matter of factly. And that's what we wanted to do, depict violence as a very day-to-day thing.

And, actually, it was a day-to-day thing that I felt when I was shooting the film. Normally during production the van that picks you up is from your department – like the camera van, the make-up van. But because of the geography of Rio de Janeiro they put us in neighbourhood vans. So I was in the van that came from one certain *favela*: it picked the kids up from the *favela*, then picked me up to go to the set. Six o'clock every morning, I would climb into the van and I would immediately start to hear the film that I was doing. Kids would say, 'Oh shit, I was late this morning because there was a shoot-out at my door and I had to escape over the roof,' or, 'There was a body laying there, I didn't know if I could help. If I started to help I would be late for the film.' Talk like that, every day.

*During the workshop period, Meirelles was invited to make a Christmas special for Globo TV.* Palace II *was directed by Meirelles and Katia Lund, and starred the eleven-year-olds Douglas Silva and Darlan Cunha. These boys would make striking impressions in* City of God *as, respectively, the younger Li'l Zé and the corrupted Steak and Fries, whose initiation into a drug gang involves murdering an even younger boy. But in* Palace II *they were to create the much sweeter characters of Laranjinha and Acerola, who would later feature in the TV series and spin-off film* City of Men – *lovable lads who find imaginative ways of surviving without resorting to crime.*

FERNANDO MEIRELLES: I told Globo, 'I have some very interesting boys here, can I create a story with them? They're unknown, they're black, and I want to shoot in a *favela*.' It had never happened in TV before. But I have a good friend in Globo and he agreed to take a chance. So we did *Palace II*.

The name doesn't mean anything outside Brazil. It refers to a controversial story involving a senator who also had a construction company. He built a tower block called Palace II in Rio, and this building collapsed. It was discovered that they had mixed sand from the beach in the cement, so the cement didn't work and it fell apart. In the short film these two boys think of a plan to create a cement that doesn't work, so they can sell a gate to somebody then at night pull the gate off, because the cement hasn't set, and sell it to somebody else.

I shot this short as a rehearsal – for the crew, the photography, the actors, everything for *City of God*. It was shown on television before *City of God* and was very successful. And immedi-

Darlan Cunha and Douglas Silva make their mark in *Palace II* (2000)

ately Globo said, 'Why don't we produce a TV series with those two characters?' I said, 'Well, I have to shoot a feature first.' So we shot the feature. Then we made the series *City of Men*.

KATIA LUND: A really important part of the selection of the two hundred for the *City of God* workshop was improvisations, and what we were looking for was imagination. People who would just go into the story and forget. Live it. The minute that Douglas Silva walked in – skinny arms, big belly, huge eyes – for the first improvisation, everybody's eyes were just glued to him. Of all of them, there's no doubt that he is extraordinary. Pure talent.

FERNANDO MEIRELLES: We had pretty much cast the feature before *Palace II*. In the short the boys I thought could be lead characters in *City of God* are doing small things, but they're all in there – the guy who plays Rocket, the guy who plays Li'l Zé, Bené has two or three lines.

Aside from the guy who plays Li'l Zé, all the boys are very similar in the film to how they are in real life. And some of the stories that are in the film are their stories. The guy who plays Rocket for example – when we shot the film his virginity was the biggest problem in his life. His biggest drama was that he needed to get laid, which is why I put it in there. At the end of the film he wasn't a virgin any more!

*Palace II also provided Meirelles with a 'rehearsal' he had not expected, namely for dealing with the complicated demands and interests of both the drug gangs and the police.*

CÉSAR CHARLONE: It is very dangerous shooting in *favelas*. You are living in a reality that is unthinkable in other cities. It was usual that we would hear gunshots. The production guys would come and say, 'Don't worry, there are going to be some blue things coming overhead, it's the new Israeli arms they are testing, they are just throwing them over to the other *favela*.' And stuff like that. Suddenly there would be a car in the frame. Can we move that car? No, that car is not to be moved. Why? There's going to be a settlement tonight and they have to deposit a body there that they are going to take away afterwards. This car has to remain there.

That reality came closest to us when we were making *Palace II* in the *favela* Cidade de Deus itself – which is why we didn't film the feature there. When we were doing the short we had a shoot-out right in front of us. I had a gun pointed at myself. It was tough.

FERNANDO MEIRELLES: That was a crazy five days of shooting. We had problems, little incidents, every day, leading to the last day, which was the worst. We had promised [the dealers] that there would be no police coming to the set. And we went to the police station and we asked the police not to come. We told them we were gonna be there with actors, and children, please don't go there, we don't want any problems. And they agreed.

But on the last day of the shoot there was one policeman who was disguised as a street sweeper, and he arrested this drug-dealer – because we thought there would be no police, all the drug-dealers were watching the set – and put him in a car. And they stayed there, parked. The other dealers came to us and said, 'OK, you said there would be no police but there are police here so you're responsible. Give us this guy back or you won't leave.' And they blocked our way out.

I knew that we couldn't leave, but I didn't want to tell the rest of the crew we were surrounded. I had a hundred and something people. So we kept shooting. I decided to keep everyone occupied and so shot more and more and more. Our producer went to the police and explained our situation and asked them to release the guy. They said OK, but asked us for 10,000 *reis*, $4,000. We didn't have money, so had to start collecting all the money – pocket money – that everybody had, but all we could raise together was 1,000 *reis*. And we went back and the police said, 'No, that's not enough,' and we went to the drug-dealers and they said, 'No, we want the guy.' We stayed till four in the morning. And after a while, when we had nothing else to shoot, all the make-up artists were crying, and people were saying, 'I'm not going to do the feature, I'm out.' In the end, this producer convinced the police to take the money and let the drug-dealer out.

It was a very interesting experience. We were surrounded by people with guns. But they were really friendly. 'Hey, what are you shooting, what's the story? Give me some lines to say.' You know that you can't leave and he knows that he won't let you, but there's no prejudice, it's a good spirit. Making jokes. Would they have killed us? I don't know. But the first decision the next day was to look for another location for the feature. We couldn't shoot there. I was so glad it happened when it did. It would have been a nightmare.

So for *City of God* we shot in three different *favelas*. It was always the same thing: we would ask the drug-dealers for permission to shoot – of course, you have to ask them – they would ask for money, we would say no, because if you pay drug-dealers you know where this money is going. But we would say, 'Ask us for anything for the community.' Because the drug-dealers protect the community and the community protects them. So they gave us a list of things that they wanted: we gave some computers for the community centre, we built two soccer fields, this kind of thing. In the end, it's like politics.

There's a second part of that story, by the way. Four months later we heard that they caught the same policeman who held their guy, and burned him alive. They call it the microwave.

*Creating a sense of place was particularly imperative to the telling of* City of God.

FERNANDO MEIRELLES: The actual Cidade de Deus in the beginning was exactly like the *favela* you see in the first part of the film: only houses with little roofs, all looking the same. Then little by little people started making walls around their lot, and then built a second floor . . . and so on. That's why as the story develops, and the *favela* developed, we needed different locations.

This is a very interesting subject for an architect. I like very much the metaphor: in the first part of the film, when the drug-dealers are just coming to this place, there is a lot of order, the houses are all organised, you see the horizon, you see perspective. Openness and order. Then little by little it starts to become disorganised, walls are being built, your view is blocked by little buildings, you don't see any horizon any more, it's very confused. And in the third part, the war, I used only telephoto lenses, which have the effect of bringing all the walls in: you lose depth of field, so if you choose a place with a lot of walls, it looks like a maze, a labyrinth – there's no perspective, no order, you really don't understand the space any more. It's just a confusion of walls. It's as if the boys are rotting in their space. If you turn down the sound of the film, and you only see the image, the space tells the whole story. From order to the chaos that the boys put themselves in. They have locked themselves in that place with no perspective.

We had a set designer, but most of the film is on location. And if you think of it in three parts, the set of the three parts is the same place: City of God. And it is so different. The city, the architecture is telling the same story that the characters are.

CÉSAR CHARLONE: Fernando was very concerned that the people would not understand the film because of this back-and-forth storytelling. When we talk about the Latin American movement of films, *City of God* is part of a wave of films that started with *Central Station* and was followed by *Amores perros*. And *Amores perros* had this three-story structure, and in a certain way was a bit of a reference for us. And Fernando was keen that people would follow the stories better than in *Amores perros*, where some people got lost. So we said we should help them with photography. And let's separate the periods very clearly.

FERNANDO MEIRELLES: I had some rules, like a manual, for make-up, wardrobe, art direction, for camera, based on the idea of the three parts of the film. We would call the first, more innocent part of the film the beer part; the second part marijuana – colourful, psychedelic; the third the cocaine part, which is sad and depressing. And you can see that in the colour schemes. The beginning of the film is very monochromatic – it's very bright, and there's no colour: brown, a bit of orange and a bit of white, and that's it. With the second one, the idea was to mix as much as we can – all kinds of colours, people wearing stripes, it was very uncontrolled. And in the third part there are no warm colours any more, just blues, grey, black, some white. That last part is very dark, it's almost night.

The idea of the three phases was really what organised the whole process of the film, everything – the sound, the music, the sets, the palette and also the way we shot. The first part is always with tripod, with dollies, very classical. I wanted it to look like a western. And we used short lenses, so you had the sense of perspective. For the second part we used a bit of handheld, longer lenses, we started to create some confusion. And the third part is mostly handheld, really long lenses, no continuity, we didn't respect the reverse angles, anything like that. So the film starts very organised and in the end is very disorganised. Like the life of the place, like the story.

*Only one of the principal actors in* City of God *was a professional, Matheus Nachtergaele, who plays the drug-dealer Carrot.*

WALTER SALLES, co-producer: Like other directors in Brazil, I am used to working with non-actors, but I still do not know how Meirelles and Lund managed to achieve such a sense of realism.

FERNANDO MEIRELLES: I remember when I was shooting *City of God*, I had a kind of Ken Loach festival for myself. I watched all the films I could get in Brazil. *Ladybird, Ladybird*, *My Name Is Joe* . . . His films are very different from mine, the way he shoots is much more formal. But I love the way he allows real life to enter the frame.

We didn't have much money to shoot, only eight weeks. Therefore I spent eight months improvising, so that I could be there on the day and be fast. We rehearsed from mid-January to May. By this time I had a very well-written script, but the actors never read it. I didn't want them to lose their spontaneity. If I just gave them each specific line, if it came from 'outside', it wouldn't be like they were saying the line. It would not be natural. The interesting thing is if you read the last version of the script and you watch the film, it's almost the same thing; though of course some lines appeared during the shooting.

We rehearsed each scene, over and over again. First in our office, then we took the boys to each location and rehearsed there. So on the day we came to shoot the scene they knew what to do. I always let them go from the top to the end of the scene, to let them really get the energy. With a trained actor you can ask him to do just parts of the scene, but with a non-actor you have to put him in the mood and let him go to the end.

Of course, because they had never read the dialogue, sometimes they would forget the lines. Each take would be different. To edit the film was very complicated, because there was no continuity. This is the film with the biggest number of continuity mistakes ever made. Two or three hundred problems. If you watch the film, in every single scene people are changing places when they shouldn't. It was a disaster. But I told Daniel [editor Daniel Rezende] to forget about continuity, just get the best acting. Who cares?

CÉSAR CHARLONE: I think one of the qualities of *City of God*, in the photography, stems from my documentary background. When we were discussing how we were going to shoot with these kids, who were not actors and could not follow marks, we said, 'Let's just let them do their thing and we will follow them with a camera, as if it is a documentary, as if we're shooting the real thing.'

KATIA LUND: César was literally in the middle of lots of the scenes, almost as if he was an actor himself, but with the camera on his shoulder, filming. I remember one in particular, the scene where Li'l Zé calls Rocket in to take the photograph of the dealers with the guns.

César's filming the guys with the guns, and in the middle of the shot he decides to turn around and shoot Rocket, and the boom and everybody is flying across after him, because nobody knew he was going to do that. That shot is in the film, and the boom is probably there too, but nobody notices. Fernando and I were cracking up, because we had no idea he was going to do it either.

FERNANDO MEIRELLES: César started getting amongst the action with his camera, in the middle section of the film and especially the third part. He has a pretty small 16 mm camera – an Aaton A-minima, small camera, small reel – that he used a lot. During each take I would watch and then go and say, 'César,

I need more of this guy and I need more of that reaction and I need a bit of that.' And we would play it again and he would da-da-da and I'd say, 'OK, give me another look at this guy, and we need a wide angle of that.' And each take he would do a different way. I'm kind of an editor, you know, so I was shooting and editing at the same time. So that's how we worked.

Before we started shooting the film we spent ten days, scene by scene, deciding how we were going to do it. And I think eighty per cent of the visual concept is César's. Something that was his idea, and it became a marvellous part of the film, was the circular movement in the opening, as the camera speeds around. It's very simple, just a circular dolly. Then when he realised that we were going to cut from this scene to Rocket as a goalkeeper eight years before, we decided to do the same movement with the boy, and mix both. It's incredibly effective. Cost to CGI: zero. This is something that amuses me, because the critics would say this is a film from Hollywood, they're doing *The Matrix*, these fancy shots. And the cost of the shot was . . . $20. Just a guy pulling a dolly. Period.

'The cost of the shot was . . . $20.' *City of God*

*The film whip pans, slo-mos, stop-frames. It uses cranes, dollies, strobes. But the effects, like the complicated narrative structure, are always used to serve the drama. Among the stand-out scenes, cinematically, yet one that is never mentioned, is the one that sees Li'l Zé's troops march through the night towards a fateful encounter. It begins with an overhead shot of people moving in darkness. Suddenly the film speeds up, then slows to normal, then speeds again, then slows, making eerie this nocturnal procession of child killers. Then, as the camera shoots from eye level, we see a woman walking against their flow. It brings to mind the forbidding procession of men in Béla Tarr's* Werckmeister Harmonies, *but whereas Tarr takes several minutes to create his effect, Meirelles, Charlone and Daniel Rezende take sixty seconds.* City of God *was Rezende's first feature film as editor. He had previously worked with Meirelles for four years, editing commercials.*

FERNANDO MEIRELLES: Daniel wasn't a risk for me, because I knew he was talented. He didn't have any experience in drama, but he's very good with rhythm, he's very quick, always good at choosing the right interpretation, the right moment for the actor. When he cut my commercials it was amazing, he would always see the little moments. We had the same taste, that's why I knew I could give him two hours of material and he wouldn't miss the good moments. He became an editor by accident. Everything in our lives is a bit like that. But he is now very much an editor. He did *The Motorcycle Diaries* and *Dark Water* with Walter. *Elite Squad*. And now he's editing *Blindness*.

DANIEL REZENDE, editor: It was definitely not an easy film to edit. Literally no two takes were the same. To tell a story so rich in characters, with so many sub-plots, without a loss of rhythm was very challenging.

City of God *was my first full-length feature film, so I started out as part of the generation that uses digital editing. I can't make a fair comparison with the 'classic' editing process as I am unfamiliar with it. What I can say in favour of the non-linear process made possible with digital technology is that, without doubt, it saves a huge amount of time. This allows you to try out a lot more ideas, to experiment.

What we tried to do with the editing was use what we called 'effects' whenever we thought that this could bring something extra to the sensation or emotion that we were aiming to evoke. If the situation is tense, and there's no time to think, we speed it up and make it even tenser. If the character is going to be important later, then we freeze the face to commit it to memory. If two things happen at the same time, then we split the screen, so as to not lose anything.

In the third part of the film, we especially welcomed anything out of the ordinary for the editing style. If a 'badly made' cut could increase levels of discomfort in the viewer, then we incorporated it.

FERNANDO MEIRELLES: There are a lot of critics who think that if you cut fast you give the audience no time to think, and that they need time. Which I think is totally wrong, at least for me. When I'm doing hundreds of things at the same time, that's when I have insights, when I have ideas. Thoughts don't depend on time.

CÉSAR CHARLONE: Fernando thinks as an editor, he's got an editing head. So when he contributes to the script, he's editing. There were sequences in the script that were brilliant which came from him, for example when he tells the story of the drug-dealer's apartment: visually, that was in the script. The scene that opens the film was in the script. It said, 'A knife against a stone'. Very precise. I get lots of scripts, they are very literary, but this script was filmic.

*The contrast between the depictions of violence in* City of God *and the later* Elite Squad *is informative. As Meirelles presented the phenomenon of kids killing kids as a tragic, almost careless consequence of their atrocious environment, he had no desire to show their violence explicitly. In contrast, José Padilha is dealing with a*

*later period, in which premeditated murder and torture – the suf-
focation of suspects by the police, the 'microwaving' of an NGO
worker by the gang – are carried out with a cynical cruelty that he
feels does not deserve to be concealed by being out of shot. There
is one, notable exception to* City of God's *usual approach, however: the murder of another boy by the child Steak and Fries.*

FERNANDO MEIRELLES: I knew it would be the strongest scene
in the film. But it came out harder to watch than I thought. We
included it, first of all, because when reading the book it's one of
the scenes that you really notice. And then Paulo Lins says that
he saw that happen, he was there, he saw the boy shooting the
other boy.

Actually, when we shot it that scene didn't end there. Li'l Zé
tells the boy who's been shot in the foot to stop crying, walk
away and don't look back. So the boy starts walking and just
turns his face, and Li'l Zé shoots him and he dies. It was too brutal, so I cut it. Paulo Lins and I had a little fight about it. He said,
'You have to include that . . . you coward.'

CÉSAR CHARLONE: I'm a big admirer of *The Battle of Algiers*
and what it meant.* And the day we shot that scene, I got the feeling we were doing another *Battle of Algiers*. Because of the way
we were shooting it, very improvised, we were shooting and
shooting, finding the scene; and because it was as though I was
living something I hadn't lived. Tonino Delli Colli, the Italian
cameraman, says that the cameraman is the first audience of the
film. And to me I was seeing something that was shocking, I was
being the first audience of this awful thing, this horror.[†]

*La battaglia di Algeri (The Battle of Algiers, 1966)*, Gillo Pontecorvo's powerful
recreation of the struggle for Algerian independence between 1954 and 1962. The film
demonstrated, to very disturbing effect, the savage tactics employed by both the
Algerians and the French. So real were Pontecorvo and cameraman Marcello Gatti's
dramatic re-enactments that the director felt the need to declare, at the film's outset, the
absence of newsreel footage.
[†] Tonino Delli Colli is a celebrated cinematographer, a frequent collaborator with Pier
Paolo Pasolini and Federico Fellini. He also shot *Once Upon a Time in America* with
Sergio Leone.

Ironically, the kids involved were never traumatised when we were shooting. Perhaps because they would live it and would already know.

FERNANDO MEIRELLES: We were keen not to be exploitative with the violence. The violence was supposed to be in the audience's head. I avoided graphic violence all the time. There are only two moments when you see the bullet – which is very usual in gangster films, bullets hitting people and them falling. We have that kid, just for half a second. And in the end, when you have the confrontation between Li'l Zé and the police, there is one boy who gets shot. Those were the only special effects we used to exploit violence. For all the rest, all the bloody attacks, the war, the camera is always far away, it's very dark, you hear but you don't see.

I just don't like to see graphic violence when I'm watching films. You can watch this film and you don't need to avert your eyes. Even with that scene with the two small boys, when Steak and Fries shoots the other boy you don't see it: the camera is behind him, the focus is on his neck. You just hear the sound. Not showing is much more powerful than showing.

WALTER SALLES: The decision to be part of *City of God* was defined by the trust we had at VideoFilmes in Fernando Meirelles and his co-director, and also because few films could shed more light on the social apartheid of Brazil. *City of God* does not offer the comforting and touristy image of the Brazilian slums that Marcel Camus's *Black Orpheus* sold to the world in 1959. This is about a nation within a nation, about the millions of *olvidados* [forgotten] that are statistically relevant, but scarcely represented on screen.*

FERNANDO MEIRELLES: As a producer on *City of God*, Walter helped me in two different ways. First, he presented me to

---

*Los olvidados* happens to be the title of Luis Buñuel's powerful, atypical film from 1950, which dealt with the poverty and injustice experienced in the shanty towns of Mexico City.

Miramax, he presented me to Canal Plus, he introduced me to the international market. We're the same age, but he's really guided me. Now I know a lot of people, but he helped me in the beginning. That's how I sold the film, through him and through his company. He was really pushing me.

But he also helped with the script. I remember when I was twenty days away from shooting, I sent him the script, and he sent me pages and pages of comments and problems, scene by scene, a lot of work. And then he invited me to go to his house with some friends. Karim [Ainouz] and Katia went, and Bráulio, and we read the script together. And everybody talked. It was really helpful.

When Daniel and I finished the first cut the first person I sent a copy to was Walter. He was in Los Angeles and he wanted to see it, and I remember he called me at four in the morning or something like that – there's five hours' difference with LA, so he probably finished the film and called me straight away – and he was very enthusiastic, saying, 'It's a great film.' He was so positive.

*Despite such support, Meirelles has been famously quoted as saying that he made* City of God *always thinking it was going to be a 'Brazilian film' only, rather than the international hit it became.*

FERNANDO MEIRELLES: I tried to sell the film on the basis of the script, but nobody wanted to buy it. I tried four or five different studios, everybody said no. Then Miramax said they were going to buy the film, so we moved ahead. But two months into pre-production – I was rehearsing the scenes – our partner from Walter's company, Mauricio [Andrade Ramos], called us and said, 'Fernando, stop everything, close the office, the money won't come till next year. You have to break for a few months and next year we'll try again.' I said, 'Mauricio, I can't. We're gathering speed, and there's no way to stop.' And he said we wouldn't have any money. And that's when I said, 'OK, thank you very much, I'm going to go anyway.' That's why I financed the film myself. The budget was 2.9 million *reis*, which is $1.5 million.

What happened was that Walter was going to do a film for Miramax, *Redemption of a Virgin*, with Juliette Binoche. They built the sets and everything. In his contract with Miramax Walter said, 'OK, you give me $22 million to do this film, and $2 million to do *City of God* and *Madame Satã*.' So Miramax said OK. But they weren't interested in my film. Then Walter's actor broke his finger and couldn't shoot *Redemption of the Virgin* for six months. Walter had another commitment, so couldn't wait. And so Miramax pulled the money from ours.

It's funny. When I finished the film and edited the tape and came to New York and showed distributors, Miramax said, 'This is our film!' I said 'No, it was your film because you were going to pay for it. But you didn't. So it's not.' Anyway . . . they bought the film.

I've got to say the deal wasn't the best, but I'm very thankful, especially to Harvey Weinstein, because he believed in *City of God* more than me. He did a very good release. The film wasn't nominated for best foreign-language film – it was picked as the Brazilian entry, but wasn't nominated. This was in 2003. So Harvey re-released the film in the US and paid for an Oscar campaign, and in 2004 the film was nominated for best director, best photographer, editor and screenwriter.

BRÁULIO MANTOVANI: I can only be grateful for Fernando's dedication in getting *City of God* made. That film changed my professional life for good. There were virtually no jobs for film writers in Brazil in the nineties. It wasn't regarded as a real job. And now the film scene in Brazil has changed a lot. We make eighty films per year and screenwriting is starting to be seen as an interesting career. Screenwriters here should thank Fernando for that. He put me in the spotlight; not only by hiring me and paying me decently, but also by mentioning my name in every interview he gave. Then the film people and part of the public started to pay more attention to the work of the writer in the process of film-making. The performance of *City of God* both

Seeing themselves on screen for the first time: *City of God*'s young cast,
on set with Fernando Meirelles and Katia Lund

here and abroad (plus my Oscar nomination) certainly helped to speed up this change.

WALTER SALLES: Rarely has a film created such heated debate in Brazil. The country's current leader, Luiz Inácio Lula da Silva, at the time the socialist presidential candidate, urged the then president to see *City of God* in order to understand the extent of the urban tragedy. And I remember that Arnaldo Jabor, one of Brazil's most important intellectuals, wrote: 'This is not only a film. It is an important fact, a crucial statement, a borehole in our national conscience.' There were some dissonant voices, of course, arguing that the film gave the impression that *favelas* are populated only by drug-dealers. They are not. In fact, an immense part of the Brazilian population has been the victim of this present situation.

FERNANDO MEIRELLES: We had some critics. I think a minority – especially outside of Brazil – said, 'How can you do a film about this kind of subject with this disrespect?' And I said, 'I'm sorry, that's how it is. You see a dead body here, and somebody dancing on the other side of the street. I'm sorry about that. That's only what I saw. I didn't make anything up, I didn't invent this world. If you read the press you read these stories all the time.'

But in the City of God *favela* we had an amazing response. They loved it. We did big screenings, for two thousand people. I think it was the first time they were seeing themselves on film. Nobody had filmed inside *favelas*, using their language, in a way that was so close to their real life. I think that's why they liked it. They saw themselves.

## José Padilha: *Bus 174* and *Elite Squad*

One moment José Padilha was a little-known, if highly respected documentary film-maker. The next, he had made the most talked-about Brazilian film since *City of God*. *Tropa de Elite* (*Elite Squad*, 2008) became a *cause célèbre* from the moment it was stolen from Padilha's Rio office and pirated to eleven million Brazilians, before even reaching Brazilian cinemas.

Concerning the battle between the *favela* drug gangs and the city's nefarious police force, the film was received ecstatically by thousands of *cariocas* for shining a light on the violence that plagues their city. But Padilha's decision to tell his story from the point of view of the police – who are shown to steal, torture and kill with impunity – also opened him to criticism, with a number of commentators at home and abroad accusing the film of glorifying police brutality. Just as it was winning the Berlin Film Festival's coveted Golden Bear (awarded by a jury led by the famed political director Costa-Gavras), one American critic dismissed it as 'a recruitment film for fascist thugs'.

The cops' perspective: José Padilha's *Elite Squad* (2007)

Such contrasting reaction, focused on the winning of such a prestigious award amid such opprobrium, simply meant 'mission accomplished' for the then forty-year-old director, whose aim was to generate debate about his city's severe social problems.

Padilha was born in Rio in 1967. He graduated in business studies and worked for an investment bank in the late nineties, before, he says, his conscience suggested that finance wasn't his *métier*. It was then that he teamed up with stills photographer

Marcos Prado to make documentaries with a social bent (*Elite Squad* was conceived as a documentary, Padilha claims, before he decided the subject might be too dangerous to film for real). The pair first produced *Os carvoeiros* (*The Charcoal People*, 1999), based on Prado's photographic essay and directed by the Academy Award-winning English documentary-maker Nigel Noble, about the exploited migrant workers who produce charcoal from the Brazilian rainforests.

'Nigel directed the movie and while doing so taught us how to direct docs,' Padilha recounts. His first as director, *Ônibus 174* (*Bus 174*, 2002), was a sensational debut, winning a clutch of awards and international distribution. The film also happened to be released in a period when the documentary form was receiving unusual commercial attention, through the diverse works of Michael Moore (*Bowling for Columbine* was released the same year) and Kevin Macdonald (*One Day in September*, 1999). One might argue that Padilha combines the showboating and pamphleteering tendencies of the former, with the skilful use of TV footage and interviewing skills of the latter.

In Brazil, *Bus 174* could be seen as an important companion piece to *News from a Private War*: while Salles and Lund had shown the violence that was being contained within the *favelas*, Padilha was revealing what happens when a different element of Rio's *olvidados* – the street kids begging on the city streets – was made to ignite by years of injustice and despair.

Prompted by the dramatic TV footage of an infamous bus hijacking in Rio, which ended with the death of the hijacker and one of his captives, Padilha set out to do what the news reports had singularly failed to even consider: discover the personality and motivation of the hijacker, Sandro do Nascimento.

The film plays on two synchronous levels: one, a gripping reconstitution of the TV footage to recreate the long day of the siege, the bus surrounded by dozens of police, drawing into night with the tension ratcheting up and no sign of either side giving way; the other an investigation, via interviews with the boy's family, other street kids, police, sociologists and criminals, of the personal, social and political dimensions of the story.

What he found in Sandro was an innocent, five or six years old when his mother was murdered in front of him, who fell into the ranks of what the film identifies as 'invisible' children, 'starved of social existence' by prejudice, bounced between homelessness and incarceration in Rio's inhuman detention centres. 'People get used to coexisting with the Sandros, with the sons and daughters of family tragedies,' a sociologist tells the camera. 'This has become part of our daily lives.'

The documentary also casts ahead to the drama *Elite Squad*, by revealing the internal tensions and shared antipathy of the police and the city's organised criminals: a policeman condemning his superiors' political motivations and competence, a bandit declaiming how he would happily torch a policeman; both men masked, fearful for their lives or reputations.

Padilha demonstrates no such caution. *Elite Squad* presents the world in which Sandro struggled to live but finally died a criminal, from the point of view of the so-called law enforcers – the correspondence between the two films being cutely marked by the director naming his lead character Nascimento, even though he's from the opposite side of the fence. And he doesn't pull his punches.

Set in 1997, the film focuses on the special police unit Batalhão de Operações Policiais Especiais (BOPE), whose role is to tackle the drug gangs running the *favelas*. Captain Nascimento (Wagner Moura) is a respected BOPE officer. With his first child about to be born, he wants to leave the battalion and return to normal, safer police duties. But first, as seems to be the rule in this small and select unit, he must enlist a new BOPE officer to take his place. Meanwhile, he is ordered to make safe the Turano *favela*, close to the location of the Pope's imminent visit. He starts to suffer panic attacks.

Padilha weaves threads of malfeasance and moral ambiguity around the experiences of Nascimento and his two prime candidates, Neto and Matías – one a trigger-happy firebrand, the other an idealist also studying law at college. The result is a world in which no one is innocent: the regular police are portrayed as being corrupt from the top down, supplementing their wages through extortion and theft; the BOPE 'soldiers', whose insignia is a skull crossed with guns and a knife, shoot on sight (as actor Wagner Moura has ruefully remarked, 'They just don't bother with "Hands up. You're under arrest."') and torture whomsoever they please to get information. Middle-class students righteously condemn all cops, while their own drug use keeps the *favela* gangs in business; in order to help the *favela* communities, the NGO workers must liaise – and therefore risk complicity – with the drug lords who cause much of the grief.

The film was co-written with Rodrigo Pimentel, the BOPE officer first seen in *News from a Private War* and who effectively broke ranks through his contribution to *Bus 174*, and Bráulio Mantovani, the writer of *City of God*. As a crime drama, it's very well made, cleverly dressing its dialectic with action, as well as moments of comedy and sentiment. Padilha adeptly arranges his numerous characters and plot strands. And the structure of the film, which opens with a *favela* gunfight that introduces the two young men to BOPE, then loops back to trace their path to that moment, ingeniously fuels the genuine confusion as to who's on whose side in this complicated conflict: second time around, we realise the rookies are spying not on drug-dealers, but bent cops.

Padilha draws comparison with Oliver Stone, who wrote the book on this kind of high-adrenaline, close-to-the-knuckle confrontation. Both men are provocateurs in the best sense of the word. But also, like Stone, Padilha can be guilty of over-egging. Did we really need the thrash-metal music played over the BOPE insignia at the credits? The chief debating point is the decision to have Nascimento narrate the film. This decision was made in the edit, for a number of reasons, including the power of Wagner Moura's performance. Nascimento is shown to be a brute (when the captain feels a pang of guilt, his response is to go and torture someone else), yet the lack of irony in his commentary arguably costs Padilha a degree of distance from the debate. This is a view that generates a fulsome response from the likeably bullish director.

Either way, *Elite Squad* is not fascistic, but thought-provokingly dystopian. And although Padilha has never made such a claim, nor would probably wish to, the attitude of his film-making does recall a comment made by Glauber Rocha in his essay 'The Aesthetics of Hunger': 'Wherever there is a film-maker prepared to film the truth and to oppose the hypocrisy and repression of intellectual censorship, there will be the living spirit of Cinema Novo.'

I met him in Berlin, after the first press screening of *Elite Squad*. Though he was beginning to receive some of the more negative critical views, this was before the balm of the Golden Bear.

*Berlin, 2008*

*Can you say something about your reasons for making* Bus 174? *I understand you watched the drama unfold on television while in your gym.*

What captured my imagination was not only the drama of the hijack, but the statements Sandro do Nascimento was making from inside the bus, the message he was sending to all of us by means of the television cameras. In the middle of all that confusion, Sandro was telling us about the origins of urban violence in Brazil.

In Brazil, people generally equate the high level of urban violence with misery: there is a lot of misery, so there is a lot of violence. But this is not accurate if you read the statistics of other countries. Indeed, there are many cities that have more misery than Rio or São Paulo, but lower levels of violence. So there is something peculiar to Brazilian cities that turns misery into violence. Sandro was telling us what it was. He was telling us that he was angry because the State mistreated him as a street child, in the streets, in institutions for juvenile delinquents and in jail.

He was stating, in short, that the State itself was converting small-time criminals into violent individuals. This is why I decided to tell Sandro's story.

The fact that the State breeds violence in Brazil is also the theme of *Elite Squad*, which aims to explain why so many Brazilian policemen become corrupt and violent. And the answer is, once again, centred in the behaviour of the State. By paying very low wages to cops, by giving them very little training, by forcing them to do very risky jobs, the State creates an environment that generates corrupt and violent cops. Thus both 'characters' – Sandro in *Bus 174* and Captain Nascimento in *Elite Squad* – were 'created' in the same way. This is why, indeed, I chose to give Captain Nascimento the same name Sandro had. It was a way of pointing that out.

And in *Elite Squad* we are basically saying that a society cannot sustain itself if its police believe in the idea that violence is something that you control with violence, which is of course a stupid idea.

*Do you see yourselves in this long tradition of Brazilian film-makers 'revealing' aspects of Brazilian society that are over-looked? Or something more overt, more dynamic?*

Marcos and I produce films with social content. This is our main goal. And we do this for three reasons. First, because Marcos, as a stills photographer, always belonged to a very long tradition of engagement in social issues. Second, because we started to work with Nigel [Noble], who as a *cinéma vérité* documentary film-maker also belonged to a tradition of engagement. And finally, because we thought we could make a difference, albeit a small one, with our films. This is what we have in mind when we choose our projects.

The fact that sometimes we end up making films about hidden aspects of Brazil is a side-effect of that. It's a little bit like this: we are Brazilians, so it is natural for us to make films about Brazil.

Since freedom of opinion is historically recent here, and film production is not so big, by making films about social issues we tend to 'talk' about things people did not talk about before. It's as simple as that.

And in the case of Rio's invisible kids, it's important to note that the 'invisibility' is not a property of the kids themselves, who are quite visible. It's rather a property of the middle and upper classes, who choose not to see them. So what the film is really revealing is not the kids – rather the fact that we largely choose to ignore them.

*Can you explain your thinking behind the structure – the parallel stories?*

Telling Sandro's life in parallel to the bus hijack created interesting heuristic and emotional effects. By understanding Sandro's life before the hijack, one could understand his behaviour in the bus and relate it to social issues. This is the heuristic effect. But Sandro's story is a story of pain, and this makes the audience feel sorry for him: the audience gets angry because he hijacked the bus, but is sorry for what happened to him. This is the emotional effect. From a rational perspective, the parallel structure creates understanding, but from an emotional perspective it creates confusion. It was my way of working this conflict between reason and emotion into the film.

*What was the biggest challenge – editing hours of TV footage into a coherent narrative, or researching and shooting your original material – the investigation of Sandro's life?*

The biggest challenge was the research. The editing of the TV footage basically followed the chronology of the material.

*Did you decide that the interview with the cop killer, for example, or the trip inside the prison, were absolutely essential to the story? Or was their inclusion more about the creation of drama?*

Those sequences were essential to the story, for without them one would not be able to understand Sandro's character. *Bus 174* is character-driven. Even the sequences that apparently have nothing to do with Sandro are there because of him. They aim to establish what he endured in the past, and thus to give the audience a feeling for the social processes that helped to shape his personality and his behaviour in the bus. So the intention was not to create drama, rather to reveal the drama that was going on inside Sandro's head, and which is still going on in the heads of many kids in Brazil.

*Could you talk about the interview with the cop killer. How did you set it up? How dangerous was it – were your lives at risk?*

The cop killer wanted to know the assistant director's address prior to the interview. This, to him, was a guarantee that we would not set him up or edit the interview in a way he did not find appropriate. I told my assistant not to give his address, but he did it. So there was a risk, but mostly for Mr Alex Lima.

*Was the film successful with audiences in Brazil? You have said that the original TV coverage had no interest in Sandro whatso-ever. Were viewers now eager to learn? Or did they simply want to 'relive' the drama?*

The film was seen by forty thousand people in the theatres in Brazil. This is a good figure. But the best to me was the huge debate the film created, and the numerous university theses it brought about. I think that people who went to see the movie to understand the Bus 174 incident left the theatre understanding much more than that. For this reason, I consider the film to be successful.

*Has* Bus 174 *changed anything in the way that society deals with these youngsters? Or the prison service?*

No. I can't say it made any significant difference. It takes much more than one movie, or several movies, to change society.

*How do you and Marcos Prado fit within the Brazilian film industry?*

Marcos and I have our own production company, which is very much outside the mainstream. We have never made commercials, never made television productions, nor co-produced with the big production companies. We produce and direct our own films. For this reason, we have built our own trajectory, with our own personal influences, which are very peculiar. But that does not mean, of course, that we consider ourselves better than the mainstream companies. We simply made a choice.

*The organic relationship between features and documentaries in Brazil seems to exist in a complete state within* Bus 174: *it's not a docu-drama, per se, but your editing, use of music, etc., have turned documentary material into an intense drama. What would you say about this?*

There are many documentary film-makers who think that the use of music, the creation of a dramatic structure, the exclusion of the film-maker from the footage, etc., make a documentary less of a documentary. I do not believe that. As a documentary director, I consider myself free to use all the cinematic techniques available. My only constraint is to be faithful to the facts and to the research, which I take very seriously. So in *Bus 174* I tried to stick to the facts, but also to create a dramatic structure that resembled a fictional movie.

*How did you find the transition to fiction with* Elite Squad?

The way that I moved from doc to fiction was to try to reproduce on the set an environment that would be very, very close to a documentary. So first of all I worked with researchers, and I wrote the screenplay with a BOPE cop. This is a very important thing to understand: there was a BOPE cop writing the script with me. My idea was to give society this point of view as it is, and see how it deals with it. Everything that you see in the movie, even the Pope operation, happened. It's all fact. All the characters came out of the interviews we did off-camera with BOPE cops and police psychiatrists. There was a regular cop who stole money from the colonel, in exactly the same way.

Another thing that I decided was not to give the actors the screenplay. We gave them a preparation period of four months, during which we worked on the situations, but never with a script – they did not have dialogue. It's all improvised.

*What informed the decision to make the central characters policemen?*

Around the time we made *Bus 174*, film-makers and critics across the country began talking about how the theme of urban violence had been overdone. But cinema, so far, had only shown these stories from the point of view of the dealers and marginal characters – they never saw it from the police standpoint. And I don't think you can talk about violence in Brazil without taking that perspective into account. It's not a mere detail, it's one of the most important factors in this issue.

Picture the numbers: two hundred people are killed by cops in one year in the United States, twelve hundred are killed in Rio de Janeiro. It's very violent. It has a lot to do with how our police are structured, and we need to change that. But at the same time, the police are also victims, of a system that we have created. So I wanted to make this very clear to everybody. The film is about the hypocrisy that we are surrounded by in Rio, which is subjacent to the violence.

Also, if you look at American cinema, or French, there are many films with cops as main characters. Until *Elite Squad*, there was never a Brazilian film about a cop. Why is that? So we decided, let's do a film about cops, and let's give the cops' perspective.

*Explain the police system in Rio, and how the BOPE fit in. They look like soldiers.*

There are two police forces in Rio: the one that investigates crime, who are the civil police, and those whose job is to prevent crime from taking place, and they are the military police that you see in the film. They are not part of the army, but they are run as if they were. They have a colonel, they have their own judicial system. So if a military policeman kills someone he is judged by his own peers.

*Which keeps them busy.*

Which keeps them free of being arrested. And so it goes.

*So BOPE is part of the military police?*

Yes.

*There seems to be a complicated dynamic between BOPE and all the other military police. BOPE regard themselves as the only ones who are honest.*

This is the key. If you are an honest cop in Rio, if you don't want to be involved in protection rackets or take bribes or whatever, you are either going to be fighting every day with your own colleagues in this corrupt institution, or you are going to join BOPE – which portrays itself as honest, as above such corruption – and fight the drug-dealers. But then to survive in the *favelas*, in these extremely violent armed confrontations, you have to become violent. It's impossible not to. So we've made a situation in Brazil where you have to choose. If you're honest, you're violent.

I wanted to see a conversion, showing a good kid, who wants to be an honest cop, become violent. Then I wanted this kid to interact with rich kids who hate cops. Because rich kids do hate cops. So Matías's character goes to university. In a way the movie is also about the incompatibility of different social groups in this country.

*Of course, BOPE's idea that they are the white knights, while they torture and kill at leisure, is fatuous.*

And the idea of the film is to get into the minds of these guys, so you understand how fucked up this is. First of all, look at their logo. Look at the way they dress, all in black. There is a book written about this, in which there are stories of BOPE cops killing other BOPE cops, who they have found doing illegal things, like selling car parts or whatever. It's not in my movie; there are many things not in my movie that are much worse than what we show.

*Apparently people who have seen the film in Brazil do regard these guys as heroes.*

Maybe this won't make sense to people who haven't seen *Bus 174*. The final scene of the documentary really got to me. And it was this. When the hijacker came out of the bus, with the hostage and a gun, and he is confronted by the police, there were hundreds of bystanders, regular folks, watching this. A shoot-out began. There was an aerial shot on the TV and I thought, watching in my house, that everybody would run away. But that's not what you see. What you see is everybody running towards the bus – to beat and maybe kill the hijacker. So there is anger in the heart of many Brazilians who face violence on a day-to-day basis, and some of them unfortunately want revenge. This is true, I won't deny it. And it's an understandable fact.

Also, the choice of buying drugs implicitly includes another choice, which is, 'Am I going to finance the drug-dealers, or not?' Now when I put this economic fact in *Elite Squad*, giving voice to the cops, who accuse the middle-class kids buying drugs in the *favela* of financing the drug-dealers – then beat them up – a small percentage of the population got behind that idea. They thought that Nascimento was a hero, like an avenger. And why is the movie like this? Because this is what reality is like in Rio.

*Who from these worlds, of the police or the criminals, did you have advising?*

I had former drug-dealers coaching actors and non-actors who would play the drug-dealers; former regular cops coaching actors who would play regular cops; and former BOPE cops coaching actors who would play BOPE cops. I didn't need any-one to coach the students, because I was a student myself.

*How did the actors feel about liaising with former drug-dealers?*

I think they loved it, because you get to know another world on its own terms. And furthermore they didn't have a screenplay, so that's all they had to go on.

*What was the motivation of the police to help you?*

The average age of a BOPE cop is twenty. So these very young guys go into a war, every day. Most soldiers, in Vietnam, in Iraq, wage a war, come back, and cannot readjust. But in Brazil you go to war at night and then you have to adjust in the morning. Every day. How do you do that? This gets to your mind. And by the time they reach thirty they want to leave. Exactly like Nascimento in the film.

Rodrigo Pimentel left BOPE and he wanted to say why, he wanted to say, 'This is what's going on.' We had eight ex-cops helping us, and they all had the same feeling. They were all about thirty.

*Is there any extent to which Nascimento is Pimentel?*

To some extent. Pimentel wanted out. He had a kid.

*And he contributed to* Bus 174. *Did that get him into trouble?*

Yeah, it got him expelled from the police. He was just like Nascimento and he found a way out.

Some existing BOPE cops tried to prevent the film from being screened. They entered a legal action saying that we had to take the torture out, because it didn't correspond with reality. Fortunately the judge said, 'No, this is exactly how Rio is and the film should be allowed to be screened.'

*Why 1997?*

Good question. I wanted to say up front to an audience that the whole thing is absurd. So I searched for the most absurd Elite Squad operation in the history of the police, and I found that it happened in 1997, when they killed about thirty people so that the Pope could sleep one night without hearing a gunshot, close to a *favela* called Turano. So this guy who wants out is forced to take part in the most stupid police operation ever, in which people will die so that the Pope can have an undisturbed sleep.

*The logic being that if they killed a lot of people, there would be no activity for a few days afterwards.*

No. They actually occupied the place. But in order to occupy it, they had to kill people. The governor, instead of telling the Pope to move to, say, Copacabana, where there is no *favela* – instead of admitting the situation is all fucked up – thought it was better to send BOPE in to kill everybody.

*Can you say something about the ending, when Matías effectively joins the dark side? There's no semblance of hope here.*

With a film like *Bus 174* that question is not asked. It's OK not to solve the problems in a documentary because it's reality, and reality is not 'solved'. In fictional movies there is a lot of pressure on the film-maker to solve the problem, to have a 'happy ending'. What that means if your subject is based on real life is that you solve the problems of reality in the movie, and everybody can go home happy, while reality remains the same. Matías would get the gun and say, 'No, I don't want to shoot,' and he would overcome his anger and I wouldn't be a right-winger and stuff like this. But this is not what goes on. BOPE goes on. It gets bigger, not smaller. So what is my responsibility in this? I'm not going to pretend.

So our research had two purposes: first of all it told me what reality was, so that I end the movie in the way that I do; and it also, kind of, directed me not to fool around with reality. When somebody is bad in a movie, it's usually completely bad. But while Nascimento kills, he also loves his kid; he tortures, but he loves his wife. It becomes ambiguous, because life is ambiguous. I bet I could introduce you to a BOPE cop who has killed and tortured and not tell you this, and you would get along very well with him.

*Can we talk about the reception the film has had?*

There are many things in life you can't control, and one of them is the reception of your movie. And it's a good thing. In Brazil the movie generated a huge debate, because those things are very close to us. One of the debates was over the film's commentary on middle-class drug use. The movie said for the first time, 'Listen, the fact that we can use drugs and go home is not tolerable, when kids are dying in the *favelas*.' We have a responsibility – if we are buying these drugs, we are financing the drug-dealers. There are a lot of people who would smoke a little joint and then sit down to write about the movie.

It's going to be different outside Brazil, because the cultural background is different. The movie is going to be seen more like a movie, more like a story.

*Apparently you decided to have Nascimento as your narrator during the editing.*

We had several treatments of the script. Some of them were narrated by Matías, others by Nascimento, another by the two of them, and because the dialogue was not set it was always open. In the end we went with Nascimento for two reasons. First of all I realised that only an experienced cop could talk about all the ideology, and so if I made Matías the narrator it would basically give the game away that he becomes one of them. And secondly, because of Wagner Moura's extraordinary performance.

*It's a bold decision, especially since there is no irony or regret in his commentary. Do you think the film would be better – or more acceptable for some people – without it?*

I stand by my film, because I stand by the Brazilian audience. No one questioned the ability of the American audience to deal with such issues in films like *Platoon* and *Goodfellas*. Why should we question the Brazilian audience? I see a little downplaying of the intelligence of a developing country's audiences in such considerations. Furthermore, I do not think that movies are like medicine, that they should be accompanied by 'directions for taking'. Should I tell the audience that torture and killing are bad things?

*We haven't spoken about* City of God, *which foregrounds the drug-dealers.*

I don't know if people remember that when it was released in Brazil it was accused of glorifying drug-dealers. What's happened with me and *Elite Squad* is exactly the same thing that happened with Fernando [Meirelles], which was the critics jumped down his throat.

This is one thing the two movies have in common. There is a film ideology that says that films about social issues should give the audience critical distance, in order to evaluate what's going on. Therefore you have an intense scene, then you have a slow one in which nothing happens, so that somebody can sit back and be distanced and therefore criticise.

I think the great thing Fernando did was say, 'Let's make a movie that has social content, but it's gonna grab you by the balls.' It's gonna be emotive, and we're going to run with it and you won't have time to think while it goes on. Which means that you are going to emotionally engage with a drug-dealer and you're going to like him. And by the end of the movie you're going to feel fucking guilty for having done that. And this is what we do with *Elite Squad*. Engage with Nascimento, my friend, and you're going to like the fucking torturer, and you're going to be emotionally in there. And at the end of it what happens is that *City of God* has generated fifty Ph.D. theses, *Elite Squad* is generating several Ph.D. theses, *Bus 174* I can't even tell you how many Ph.D. theses, in Brazil and the US. So lo and behold, you can think after the film is over.

*Elite* Squad *was the biggest film at the Brazilian box office in 2007, with 2.4 million, I think. Have you contemplated what might have happened if it hadn't been pirated?*

I don't know what would have happened without the piracy. Don't have a clue. The distribution company hired a poll company which came up with the figure of 11.5 million people who had seen the movie in a pirate copy. And two thirds of these people were not going to see the movie in the theatres. So we began by losing seven million people altogether.

*Even so, the piracy sort of fuelled the instant myth of the film. My gut feeling is that you might be secretly pleased about it.*

Yes, I punish myself when I'm asleep for being pleased that the piracy was a success.

# Another Brazil

Now, as ever, Rio de Janeiro and São Paulo, the Cariocas and the Paulistas, dominate film production. The commercial companies and television stations that fund films are based in the two cities, as are the independent production houses O2 Filmes in São Paulo, and VideoFilmes and Conspiração Filmes in Rio. The majority of the directors and stars are also to be found in the two cities.

It's a truism, too, that most films that gain worldwide distribution are from these commercial centres, and are those that focus on urban problems. It's a pity. For as important as the problems of the *favelas*, say, may be, and excellent as some of the films are, they are only a part of the story.

There has always been a parallel filmic universe in Brazil, which, if looked to, would redress the balance. It is located in the north-east of the country, and particularly in the *sertão*, the dry region that covers part of the states of Bahia, Pernambuco and Ceará, among others: this is the Brazilian backwater traditionally ignored by the country's politicians and economy, and the socio-political battleground of the Cinema Novo provocateurs.

Cinema Novo did not represent merely an ideological dissension, but a geographical shift, the movement's directors locating in the *sertão* both real and metaphorical meat for their analysis of Brazil's woes. Glauber Rocha, the chief polemicist for the movement, was himself from Bahia.

'Some people say that the north-east of Brazil is what's left of the real Brazil,' says director Marcelo Gomes, who is from Recife, the capital of Pernambuco. 'Because it's much more poor, much more isolated, the culture is actually much stronger. It's less industrial, less cosmopolitan, and in a way it's peculiar –

Portuguese mixed up with Indian. The people are very hospitable, very aware of their culture and traditions. And they are very human.'

In the years since the *retomada*, the north-east has slowly returned to the frame – in front of and behind the camera, with Gomes one of a number of emerging local directors and actors making a name for themselves. In some cases these film-makers, mirroring the patterns of migration within the country, have relocated to the capital, including the two directors I have interviewed here: Karim Ainouz, from Fortaleza in Ceará state, and Sérgio Machado, from Salvador, the capital of Bahia.

The characters of these men reflect the diversity within the region, and the country. Karim Ainouz, for example, tiptoed into film via architecture and visual arts, inspired by his experiences in New York in the eighties to return home and make films. Sérgio Machado is someone who lives and breathes his native Salvador and was first noticed, fittingly, by the great Bahian writer Jorge Amado. As for Gomes, such is the dearth of film schools anywhere in Brazil that he attended the Radio, Film and Television School in Bristol, in the UK, for his training. Whatever their wanderings, their roots remain manifest on screen, enriching to an enormous degree the reflection of what it is to be Brazilian in the twenty-first century.

It's interesting that when Rio directors travel to the north-east for their subjects, it is to find an optimistic antidote to the city in the 'real Brazil' that Gomes mentions (Salles' *Central Station*), or in pursuit of the extraordinary stories that are offered up by a region whose physical character varies from beach via desert to Amazonian rainforest (Andrucha Waddington's *House of Sand*). From the local directors, however, the overriding impression is that you don't need to be in the midst of drug wars to be suffering.

Cláudio Assis' *Amarelo manga* (*Mango Yellow*, 2002) is a dark, pessimistic portrait of the Recife working classes which involves crime, misery, sexual perversion and religious delusion, with yellow as the colour of disease and death; Ainouz's *O céu de Suely* (*Suely in the Sky*, 2006), a poetic, even feminist film, centres on his heroine's desire for self-determination, restlessly moving about the country; Machado's *Cidade baixa* (*Lower City*, 2005) is a visceral and vibrant portrait of street hustlers and prostitutes in Salvador's waterfront; Paulo Caldas' edgy, dream-like and disquieting *Deserto feliz* (*Happy Desert*, 2007) concerns a young woman's yearning – several years on from the exodus described by Salles' *Foreign Land* – for a European escape route.

Gomes' own first feature is a different animal, a homage to cinema as well as the underlying spirit of the north-east. *Cinema, aspirinas e urubus* (*Cinema, Aspirin and Vultures*, 2005) revisits and reconfigures the territory of Nelson Pereira dos Santos's neo-realist depiction of dust-driven impoverishment, *Barren Lives*. Set in 1942, Gomes's film features a German conscientious objector who has found himself selling aspirin in the hinterland, swapping war for a world of drought, poverty and refugees. When his local companion bemoans that 'Not even bombs come to the backwater,' the film trumpets an age-old discontent and desire for escape. The film's mood is a lighter one, however, not least because Gomes identifies a balm to each man's woes, in friendship. *Cinema, Aspirin and Vultures* is as stripped of colour as *Mango Yellow* is steeped in it, but it is a much warmer film.

There are, of course, other Brazils, even in the cities that seem so familiar. São Paulo-based director Beto Brant is building an incredible body of work, often collaborating with the novelist Marçal Aquino, their subjects ranging from São Paulo crime (*O invasor*; *The Trespasser*, 2002), to art criticism, disability and sexual obsession (*Crime delicado*; *Delicate Crime*, 2005), to tragic love story (*Cão sem dono*; *Stray Dog*, 2007). Brant's works are dark, provocative, intellectual and – even when they deal with a familiar subject, as does *The Trespasser* – with a point of view that is extremely original. Incidentally, *Stray Dog* was filmed in Porto Alegre in the south, another emerging centre of film production, where Jorge Furtado is a prolific and respected director.

But the north-east has a symbolism that still resonates strongly, allied to a unifying camaraderie. Machado and Ainouz met and first joined forces writing scripts for Walter Salles; Ainouz and Gomes learned of each other while making short films in their home towns and finally met at a film festival; all three, with Caldas, have collaborated on each other's scripts. This bond seems to speak through the movies, along with the tenacious character of the region they depict. 'They have a sort of melancholy happiness, the people in the north-east,' says Gomes, jovially. 'And we don't know why they are so happy, because their lives are so fucked up.'

## Karim Ainouz

Karim Ainouz's two features to date are, at face value, quite different: one a period piece, set in the bohemian Lapa district of Rio in the thirties, the other a contemporary story set in a culturally and economically under-nourished town in the north-east. What *Madame Satã* (2002) and *Suely in the Sky* (2006) have in common is an empathy with individuals who are determined to define themselves and their own way of living, with or without society's consent. Whether it is because Ainouz's father is Algerian, because he himself is gay in a predominantly macho society, because he spent formative years in New York, because he arrived at film having already thought of himself in the context of other disciplines – or all of these together – he offers a quite unique view of the outsider in Brazilian society.

Ainouz talks of a 'permanent feeling of displacement' in the Brazilian people. In *Madame Satã*, this is expressed with volcanic anger by the eponymous criminal-cum-female impersonator and nightclub singer, the real life João Francisco dos Santos; in *Suely in the Sky*, more serenely, as a young woman makes what might seem like dramatic decisions, not least involving parenthood and her sexuality, with calm self-assurance.

The films themselves display their own confidence. Ainouz, as he describes below, cut his teeth working with directors of the New Queer Cinema, on films such as Todd Haynes's *Poison* and Tom Kalin's *Swoon*. One can see in his own work not just an openness to subject, but also experimentalism in form, which puts plot secondary to tone, allowing the spirit of the character and environment to carry the audience. *Madame Satã* plays as one might imagine a gaudy opium dream, evoking a world of pimps and prostitutes, samba composers and bohemians, in which João Francisco – black, homosexual, stubbornly determined to assert himself – struts and rages, at turns bloodied and bejewelled.

© David Prichard

'Intoxicating and dangerous': Lázaro Ramos as *Madame Sãta* (2002)

While the world of *Madame Satã* is intoxicating and dangerous – and very alien – the world of *Suely in the Sky* is that of so many desert backwaters, yet one that Ainouz shoots not with an eye in search of grime or misery, but with a bold use of colour, framing and motion, and a sense of enigma in the landscape.

Ainouz made two quite brilliant short films in the early nineties, before the *retomada* had transformed feature production. *Seams* (1993) is about the five sisters, his great-aunts, among whom he grew up in Brazil. These women reflect with a mixture of disappontment, pragmatism and independence on a life without men, while instructing the young Ainouz not to trust the macho paradigm in 'the state of knives'. *Paixão nacional* (1996) is a bitter account of the contradiction between Brazil's happy-go-lucky tourist image and its sexual prejudice, centred on a true story of a gay man who hid in the hold of an aeroplane in an attempt to leave the country, but died while still over Brazilian airspace.

Having met Walter Salles during the screenwriters' programme at Sundance, Ainouz co-wrote Salles' *Behind the Sun* with Sérgio Machado, and has since been produced by Video-Filmes and the numerous European co-producers that Salles can bring to the table. The older director's influence and friendship was evidenced when he introduced *Suely in the Sky* at the Rio Film Festival in 2006. I spoke with Ainouz the day after he was awarded the best film prize.

*Rio de Janeiro, September 2006*

*It was quite amusing seeing you standing alone outside your screening. You looked quite dazed.*

Yeah. I don't see my films with audiences. And I find screenings quite nerve-racking. When *Madame Satã* premiered in Cannes it was a traumatic experience. My father was at the screening: he is a Berber, very conservative, very proud, and he did not know I was gay. So he comes to watch the movie, and I'm sitting next to him, worried that he's going to think that I'm this sick fuck. And, on top of that, the Cannes situation is really kind of annoying –

people there are always chatting through the film – and I was paralysed. I felt horrible. I have never watched that film again with an audience.

*And you couldn't make yourself watch* Suely?

But for the first time I thought, 'Ah, this is something that is supposed to be communicating with a lot of people.'

*That never occurred to you before?*

You have to understand that for me the act of film-making has been so consuming that I never thought that it was something that had to do with the public. It's not because I don't care about the audience, but because making films was something that I wanted to do, as a way of artistic expression, and of expressing things that I believe about the world. And for me it was hard to do, financially, it was always a hassle, so the audience has never been an issue. But I do think that the more films you make, the more evident it becomes that, 'OK, we have to communicate here.'

*Thinking of Walter Salles' introduction to your film, and what he said about the dumbing-down influence of television, it's a good time to be communicating ideas to cinema-goers.*

Just look at this place. This country is absolutely crazy to everyone. It's like a cross between Tel Aviv and Shanghai. You can't figure it out. There's a sort of fictional quality to it; if you look at Brazil, it doesn't make any sense, physically, sexually, politically, socially. It's really mad.

Take São Paulo. There are no underground electricity wires, so everything is above ground: the city looks like a spider's nest. A wire comes from an exchange that is supposed to go to one house, but goes to fifty houses. You think it's a miracle that this thing doesn't blow up. There's something wrong and really interesting about Brazil and I think that when you open the newspaper every day and read the daily section, it's almost fiction. I feel there's a mirroring of that in our cinema, the cinema that looks at reality, but a reality that doesn't seem real.

*So in front of the camera Brazilian reality looks as though someone's made it up?*

There's definitely a curiosity here about reality, about people's desire just to try to make sense of it. There is an out-of-control quality here and it leaks into the films. And I think that's why in fiction and documentary even the mode of address, the grammar, is trying to make sense of itself – what is fiction, what is documentary?

I remember when we were shooting *Suely*, 7 September, Independence Day in Brazil. My production editor comes to me and says, 'We have to change the shooting schedule because there's going to be a parade here.' And I said, 'Let's shoot the parade. Let's put the character in the parade and let's shoot it.' In the end the material didn't work, but you can't do that in many places. There is a freaky and yet exciting sort of freedom here.

I think also that there are certain conditions of production that allow us to be more playful. There is no completion bond, for example, so no need to send progress reports all the time. There's no industry here, it's a bullshit industry. It doesn't exist. And thank God, you know. How can you have an industry when the biggest success this year, *The Three Sons of Francisco*, had five million attendances – out of a population of 180 million? It's nothing. But that's 'record-breaking'. And how can you have an industry when so many cinemas are in shopping malls, showing American films? Come on.

I think it could be more organised, more planned, more professional. But as I said, thank God there is no industry, because if there were it would lead to a certain homogenisation of the films. You want good economic activity, but at the end of the day I think it's so important to keep a terrain of experimentation.

*There is a difference between having a self-sustaining industry and an interesting national cinema.*

I agree. Brazilian cinema began again, after Collor, just eleven years ago. Now, in this Rio Film Festival, I think that of the ten Brazilian films in competition, nine were second films. So first there was this explosion, and then a certain consolidation. At the same time, our work is very diverse, there are all kinds of cinemas. Brazilian cinema has no specific visage, it's all over the place. And I think that's interesting.

*Tell me how you ventured into film.*

I left Brazil in 1987 to go to New York. I was going to do a masters in visual arts. Then I quit and did a masters in cinema studies instead. I stayed in New York until 2001. In Brazil at the start of the nineties there was no cinema. It was dead. But in New York I had the chance to work on a lot of features, often as an editor. Basically, my film training was in editing.

*Why did you quit visual arts?*

The school I went to was very traditional and really boring. Next door to it was the film school, and I could see people studying structuralism, feminism, psychoanalysis and film history and I was completely thirsty for that kind of stuff. So I did not go to cinema studies, originally, because of film.

*But then you met Todd Haynes.*

It was 1988, and I was flirting with making films. I was taking a workshop in Super-8, and there was a film theatre workshop called Millennium Film Workshop, a sort of experimental hardcore seventies film theatre. And one day I went there and saw Haynes's film about Karen Carpenter [*Superstar: The Karen Carpenter Story*, 1997]. And it just blew my mind. Here was a way to talk about pop culture and be political. And here was a way to make a film that cost no money, because it was made with dolls and VHS cameras. It was just really exciting, mad.

I left the theatre, thinking that, one, maybe I can make films and, two, I really want to know this guy. So I went to his office and offered to intern for free. And I worked with him for about four years. I was really lucky because they were beginning to do *Poison* [1991], his first feature. At the time the company was called Apparatus. I became the office manager – meaning I cleaned the trash cans and organised the phone calls. Then I was promoted to assistant casting director, because there was nobody there to do the job. Then I was promoted to second assistant director, which I didn't like at all, so I started working in the camera electrical department, as a gaffer. And then I went to editing, and I spent a year being the assistant editor of that film. *Poison* was like a film school for me.

*Can you say more about why Haynes's film-making appealed to you?*

Firstly, it was this desire to make films that complicated the idea of narrative. That really fascinated me, because I've always had a very conflicted relationship with narrative; I'm not interested in storytelling. There was something about the script of *Poison* which was questioning – academic, very precise, theoretical questions. And the whole question of fiction and documentary was very present in one of the stories. So it was an incredible opportunity to be working on a film that had a very strong theoretical background, yet also was so sensual, and so complex.

I think the fact that Todd came from an academic background – he went to school at Brown and was in the semiotics department – gave me the opportunity to think I could be a theorist and make films, I could navigate between both worlds.

*It was also a very emotional and political period. This was the time of AIDS, and of the New Queer Cinema.*

It was a moment of a war, really, in New York at that time. In 1989–90 most of my American friends died, you know. I remember just crossing people's names off. There was this political feeling: we're queer, get used to it. And there was a feeling that we were changing something, that we were making a political difference by making films. It was all identity politics, at the end of the day. What mattered was this desire to be present, be visible, and to make work that had to do with identity. It was about reinventing ourselves – or inventing yourself, if you want. For me it was very exciting.

There was a whole gang of people: Todd, Tom Kalin, whom I worked with afterwards on *Swoon* [1992], Ira Sachs, Rose Troche making *Go Fish* [1994]. It was a gang of people making films that were not only about film-making; it was about being in the world and going to clubs and going to demonstrations and making films. There was something happening in New York at the time, and it was sad to be there, but also energising.

*You made your shorts*, Seams *and* Paixão nacional, *during your time in New York. Was either infused with the spirit of that time?*

Totally. At the time I was working with Todd I was also attending the Whitney Museum's independent study programme, which was a sort of breeding ground for a lot of ideas that were airing in America at that point. And my masters thesis was about Black British Cinema, particularly about John Akomfrah's *Handsworth Songs* [1986]. My shorts definitely came out of all those things: *Paixão nacional* is very much informed by ideas about sexual identity and post-colonial identity. At the time, I *needed* to make those films. And *Madame Satã* also. I don't want to sound like a romantic, but those were things that seemed necessary.

Seams *is an overtly personal film, about this extraordinary family of women with whom you grew up.*

I thought, 'OK, maybe I want to make a film.' So I saved some money, bought this camera, and went to Brazil with the thought that if I made a film it had to be about something I love. And I love those women. I was brought up in a family in which there was barely one man who had not left. I was brought up by those who were left behind, in other words by strong, yet gentle, good-natured women. So I went to Brazil for two months and I shot my aunts. I knew they were old, so it was really an essential document for me.

*You speak of the 'necessity' to make films. What compelled you to make* Madame Satã?

I needed to make a film about an assertive, aggressive gay character, I needed to make a film about a character who was not a *cordial* character. I was really sick of the Brazilian daily politics of cordiality. There was never a place for confrontation. I think *Madame Satã* is very inspired, if anything, by the civil rights movement of the sixties, in the sense that there was something about the African-American, identity-based political movement that was very confrontational, very in-your-face.

And when I read João Francisco dos Santos's biography, *Satã on Satã*, he seemed such a strong and unique character, first and foremost because he was a survivor of a society that had no place for black people or gay people at the time – or now, actually. He had a certain stubbornness, a will to be alive against all the odds, he wanted to derive pleasure from life, despite life hitting him all the time.

I was fascinated, and thought he would be a great character for a film – a mix of Josephine Baker, Jean Genet and a 'tropical' Robin Hood. I wanted to do his portrait because it would enable me to address things that I needed to talk about in my life, and it seemed to be a great way to look at Brazil and its contradictions.

*You had been back to Brazil to make your shorts, of course, but* Madame Satã *signalled a permanent return.*

And having been away for ten years, I felt anxious to understand this country that I had left behind. Ironically, to try to understand the so-called Brazilian culture, I had to understand the *carioca*, the Rio de Janeiro culture. You have to understand that the 'country' I come from is not Rio. I was born in Ceará, in the north-east, my mother was from the region, and it is very different from here. But when I was growing up in the seventies, because of television the cultural reference was always Rio: we had to dress like people dressed in Rio, had to talk like people talked in Rio, we had to be *malandros* like people in Rio, a little sleazy. For me it was a culture that I always loathed, and never understood.

So I came here to understand what was so interesting about this place, why the fuck the cultural reference, where I came from, was always Rio.

*João Francisco lived to seventy-four years of age, and spent twenty-seven years in prison. Why did you choose to focus on his life in the thirties?*

Because at that time two rites of passage took place: he became known as a star, fulfilling his dream of being loved on stage, and soon after he committed a serious offence and became a criminal. And these two facts are topped with the creation of 'Madame Satã', a name that summarises the duality of his character: 'Madame' – feminine, sophisticated, delicate, imported from France; and 'Satã' – masculine, violent, destructive. I was not interested in telling how the myth was born, or explaining it. I wanted to portray the character prior to the creation of the myth. I wanted to share his intimacy.

*You mentioned cordiality. He is the complete opposite.*

This is a guy who doesn't take shit. I'm sick of Brazilians being nice.

*It seems an odd complaint.*

I think it's fine that we are nice and joyful people, but at the same time it's a problem. It creates the sort of quiet, peaceful apartheid that has existed in this country; though it's becoming less quiet, less peaceful. But *Madame Satã* was not about making an ideological statement. I think that's how identity politics was productive for me: the film was more about subjective standpoints, the character's experience, trying to talk about things that were politically relevant to me from that standpoint; instead of a plot-based issue film, it was really about the intestines of a character.

*How did you get the project started?*

In 1994 I received an award from the Hubert Bals Fund in the Netherlands to develop the script, and started thorough research: the National Archives, legal sources, I interviewed people who knew him from Lapa and from the Ilha Grande prison. I also went to where he was born, in the backlands of Pernambuco. The Brazilian popular music of the twenties and thirties was also an important source for understanding the period – it seems that Noel Rosa's song 'Mulato bamba' was composed for him. After lengthy research, I realised João Francisco was a mythomaniac: the myth about him came out of his inventing and reinventing himself.

*You've suggested that the social scenario that made João Francisco an outcast still exists today.*

Yes, no question about it. Unfortunately, many of the problems of the thirties still exist. And one way of speaking about the present time is to recall history. During my research, I found a 1928 picture of a black woman with her children seated on the kerb of a downtown street. This picture could well have been taken today. Much has changed since that time, but much has not changed, and social exclusion as a barrier to affirmation as an individual, as a community and as a cultural presence is one of them. Brazilian society lacks permeability, and even though there appears to be some integration among the different sectors, the social abyss seems to keep on broadening.

But I am not pessimistic, just the opposite. I think this is an optimistic, redeeming film. After all, João Francisco never considered himself a victim.

*You really evoke the period, and particularly the seedy allure of this bohemian district. How did you achieve that?*

The film was almost entirely shot on location. Locations have smells, history, life, and I wanted to convey this fetid, musty aspect, which is hard to get in a studio.

*Lázaro Ramos has since become one of the most popular actors in Brazil – and a rarity as a successful black actor. But this was his first major role. How did you come to cast him?*

It was an all-or-nothing issue. After all, the character is in ninety-nine per cent of the scenes. In a way, the film *is* the character. I wanted a fully intuitive actor – I even flirted with the idea of not employing an actor at all. But I also wanted someone theatrical. Lázaro could fulfil these two opposing features. He is very talented, very intuitive, and has a visceral, physical quality that is crucial for the character; at the same time as he offered a naturalistic register, he could invent the characters Madame Satã invented.

*Having such an anti-hero, who is all the things you describe – aggressive, morally suspect, angry – is very daring. Did you consider the risk of alienating the audience?*

I didn't know about the risk. It was a first film. I think there are people who hate Madame Satã, because they don't understand why he's so angry. But that was something that I started to realise only after the film was ready. When I was making it, those were not questions. The questions were: How can I translate his energy? How can I translate his rage? How can I translate some of his flamboyance? When I made the film, the fact that he could be regarded as an unsympathetic character never crossed my mind.

*For* Suely *you returned to your home state, Ceará.*

As much as *Madame Satã* was an excuse to spend time in Brazil, this film was an excuse to spend time in Ceará. So again there was a personal impetus to making the film.

*It seems to me there are some neat through-lines between the shorts and the features. Just as the diatribe against macho Brazilian heterosexuality in* Paixão nacional *feeds into* Madame Satã, *so the study of women in* Seams *leads us to* Suely in the Sky.

That does make sense. *Madame Satã* was a way of addressing questions of sexuality in *Paixão nacional*, but with a different vibe, a more violent, daring vibe, and with a black hero. Then, after *Madame Satã*, I wanted to go back home to the north-east and talk about something that was very familiar to me, which was a female universe. I felt that since *The Hour of the Star*,* the Brazilian film from the eighties, there had been a lack in Brazilian cinema of strong, subjective narratives with female protagonists. The north-east of Brazil is by its nature a region of emigration. *Seams* was about the women left behind. So I went

*A hora da estrela (Hour of the Star, 1985), directed by Suzana Amaral. A young, badly educated woman from the north-east moves to São Paulo to work as a secretary. Her struggles in the city are only made worse when she starts a relationship with a man also from the north-east.

about thinking how this pattern could be altered. What if the women had left, instead of the men?

© Kirsten Johnson

'A permanent feeling of displacement.' Hermila Guedes in *Suely in the Sky*

*Walter Salles calls Suely's act, of leaving her home and child in search of a better life, a 'micro-revolution'.*

In Brazil today the idea of utopia is usually linked to God, to religion. There is a widespread epidemic of religion in Brazil these days, not Catholic, but evangelical, which is very fucked up. But when I interviewed a lot of kids, teenagers and twenty-year-olds, before making the film, it was very clear that their idea of utopia was 'tomorrow' – to get the house, or go to school, it was very concrete.

So for me Suely does something revolutionary, in that she pursues a sense of a concrete utopia, rather than a religious or supernatural utopia. And she does so – and this could be another small revolution – by breaking rules, but not breaking the main rule, which is the rule of ethics. She doesn't rob anything to get where she wants to get, she doesn't steal from anybody, she doesn't hurt anybody but herself. So there was a question, also, of how can you talk about transformation within a certain code of ethics, which I think is lacking in the country in general, culturally.

*You talk of a concrete utopia, yet she doesn't really know where she's going.*

But she's going *somewhere*. She is seeking change. The 'sky' in the movie is not paradise, it's a place in her; it's a concrete place of freedom – but here, now, not after you die. There is a dictionary definition of '*ceu*' that is 'anywhere you can find happiness'. The place she's headed for on the bus is Porto Alegre, 'happy port'.

*And she's taking control of her life.*

She's also, you know, a female terrorist, using her body in the raffle to challenge social convention. It's very high-brain and low-tech, reacting to abandonment, to desperation, with forward, positive attitudes.

*Isn't there an ethical decision in leaving her baby?*

Yeah, she leaves the baby. I think if this woman went away, with no job, no specific goals, and with the baby, that's what would be very irresponsible. It's interesting to think of certain cultures where the concept of family is more fluid. So maybe the neighbour would take care of the baby, in *Suely's* case, it's the mother

I was very inspired by *Wanda*, the Barbara Loden film from the seventies. When I saw *Wanda* I thought it would be very liberating to have a female character with the freedom of a male and not be deemed irresponsible. Men also leave kids behind. Why is it right for men to do, and not for women?

*It's interesting you mention* Hour of the Star, *because that female protagonist also leaves the north-east for a better life in*

*the city. But Suely doesn't keep still. She has left once, for São Paulo, returns, and leaves again at the end of the film. And there's every chance that she will return again. What's to be read into this coming and going?*

First, Suely returns because she had run away from home with her boyfriend and now has a child, and it's hard to raise that child in the big city, for economic reasons. But I was really looking to do a film not about a one-way migration movement, but a circular movement. This is a very contemporary situation, a sort of schizophrenia: you're torn between where you come from, where you are, and where you want to be.

Before making this movie I did a trip with Marcelo [Gomes] to the north-east, to make a documentary, and we found a constant repetition of people who left and came back and left and came back again. So for me the idea was more about this circulation than the departing. I think that's how migration is structured these days: the migration of people who leave their home and never come back occurs less and less.

*How does this relate to the period of* Foreign Land, *the early nineties, when people were leaving Brazil entirely, perhaps never to return?*

It's good that you bring this up, because I think on an international level this circularity is less frequent, though it is quite common. A friend of mine has just made a documentary about a Brazilian who went to California in the eighties, when she was fifteen, and her whole family followed, and they have moved between San Francisco and São Paulo eight times, with all their belongings. Everything.

*When I asked José Carlos Avellar about the lack of genre film-making in Brazil, he said that directors are finding their language for each film that they make. That seems to apply to you.*

Yesterday I saw the Tsai Ming-liang movie, *I Don't Want to Sleep Alone* [2006], and I've seen almost all his films. And it seems to me there's a very clear film grammar there. When I was making *Suely in the Sky* I was watching a lot of his work, and a lot of Hou Hsaio-Hsien's work, and I was very seduced by how rigorous they were, in their formal approach to film-making, dramaturgy and all that. But I realised I'm just not that way. I'm *messier*, and I'm just gonna take that on, as a trace of my own film-making. Maybe when I grow up I might be like them.

It's not only that. I think that in Brazil every film has to have a different form. Living in a country where reality is such a turmoil, and also very different from place to place – the geography, the smells, everything is so different – I think it would be absurd to impose one fixed grammar on the films.

*You could say the process, generally in Brazilian films, and certainly yours, is more rigorous than the form itself. I'm thinking, for example, of the fact that on* Suely *you did not allow the cast to mix with the crew during the shoot, and none of them could leave the town.*

Absolutely. And then you can be more fluid with the form. There was a review of the film in a Brazilian magazine, it was a good review but basically said that *Suely* was a great realist film. And I don't think that the film is realist at all. But when you talk about the process, there is a reality that I impose on people they have to live that reality, and after three months they are going to believe that that is their reality. So for example, by having the actresses [who play a family] live in the same house together and wash their clothes and make their food together, I basically induced the crew and the cast to believe that that was reality. So when you go to shoot, you can be a lot more playful if you want, because the parameters are set.

*There's an interesting contrast between the contemporary Brazilian attitude to real life and cinema 'realism', and that in Europe. The Dardenne brothers, for example, and Bruno Dumont approach realism in that extremely rigid, minimalist, austere way. But if you take* Suely *and, say,* City of God, *two films dealing with real subjects, using non-actors . . .*

They couldn't be less 'realist'. The interesting question is, how is Brazilian reality translated into fiction? Because it's not like the Dardenne brothers. I would say that in our films the raw material is the real, but the grammar is not.

*You've spoken of identity a great deal. But my feeling is that you're less interested in a national identity than Walter Salles.*

Actually, I am interested in that. And there is a genuine desire to create that mirror that he talks about. It's very present. But I just think I phrase it differently from Walter. An 's' is the difference. Because I think he thinks about the national identity and I think about the national identities. For me, it's a question of reinvention, which for me is the essence of – and the beauty of – Brazilian identity. And that's the problem: when you reinvent, sometimes you suffer from amnesia.

*I've had a number of conversations here, in which young Brazilians declare that Argentines can't get over the mistakes of the past, whereas Brazilians get over the past too easily. They say that you're strolling into the future with chins held high – and that's fucking you up.*

I agree. In Argentina the dictatorship is serious, you have the Madres de Plaza de Mayo,* for example, and the controversy over the arrested *junta*. But if there's a Latin American country

---

*The Mothers of the Plaza de Mayo, an association of mothers whose children disappeared during the Dirty War. They still congregate in the Buenos Aires square, every Thursday, to protest against the unknown fate of their children.

that never did *mea culpa* in regards of dictatorship, that would be us. No one really cares about our dictatorship. We don't talk about it. 'OK. OK. Next?'

On one hand, that's great, because we are sort of more colourful, there's a different sense of humour. But there's a problem in not dealing with certain aspects of history. Look. We had a governor of the state of São Paulo, who had been proven to be a robber, he was in jail, then had the biggest number of votes in the state. That's very interesting, to say the least, if not tragic. But that goes with the contradictions that make the country fascinating.

I think there's something relevant here, also, about the black religion in Brazil, Candomble. The great thing about Candomble is that it's not based on guilt, it's based on pleasure; it's the only religion where you go to a ritual and people are drinking and dancing. Candomble is so emblematic of certain Brazilian attitudes: it's almost like we have to go forward, let's not blame ourselves, let's not dwell on guilt, because it's not going to take us anywhere. At the same time it's problematic.

*It's interesting, too, to see how film-makers in the different countries respond to those broadly similar experiences, in ways that perhaps reflect their national temperament. A number of Argentine directors have referred to their dictatorship, overtly, in features and documentaries. In Brazil, much less so.*

Absolutely. And you could say our cinema is fresher for it; yet also more superficial

*Would you say there is any significance in the fact that we have you, Sérgio Machado, Marcelo Gomes and other directors coming from the north?*

Yes. People are very shy about this, but I think there is. There is one significance, which is that we are not in the north, we are displaced: I'm living in Rio and I've lived around the world, Sérgio is living in Rio, Marcelo is living in São Paulo. There is something to be said for this alliance of displaced people. And I think there is something quite interesting in being from there and not being there, talking about the north-east but not living in the north-east, not actually being part of it. When I think of all the other film-makers that I'm close to in Brazil, they share this experience.

There are other groups in Brazilian cinema, very clear groups: the Conspiração Filmes group, the group of film-makers from São Paulo including Tata [Amaral], Roberto Moreira, all those people who came out of the São Paulo film school in the eighties and nineties. What's different about us, and perhaps a bit more vibrant about what we're doing, is that there is a certain discomfort in ourselves, and I think it's there in the movies. I think the same discomfort sort of fuelled Cinema Novo. A number of those people in the sixties were from the north-east: Glauber Rocha from Bahia, Barreto from Ceará. I think it's about making films from the periphery.

*There does seem to be a collective spirit at work.*

That's true. Walter introduced me to Sérgio after *Central Station* in 1998, and we became two of the young generation of directors who started working with VideoFilmes. We wrote *Behind the Sun* together, for Walter; Sérgio helped me with *Madame Satã*, and I helped him with *Lower City*. I co-wrote a film with Marcelo. But there are many more connections. There is a real feeling of collaboration in film-making here. It's not an artificial situation. We have things in common. We are friends, and it's great to have friends at every stage of making our films, to react to you, and to confront you.

# Sérgio Machado

There is a neat, fated feeling about the early career of the young *soteropolitano* – such is how people from Salvador refer to themselves – Sérgio Machado. In his early twenties, Machado was given a significant shove into the film world when the Bahian author Jorge Amado recommended a short film he had made to Walter Salles. A few years later, when casting the young woman at the heart of the steamy love triangle of his feature debut *Lower City*, he chose newcomer Alice Braga. Braga's aunt, Sonia Braga, once starred in her own love triangle, the strangest in cinema perhaps, between a real-life bore and the ghost of a rogue, in *Dona Flor and Her Two Husbands*, which was based on the novel by Jorge Amado.

Did the elderly author, whose life had been dedicated to chronicling his state, Bahia, sense something of himself in the self-possessed cinephile? Who knows. But though, in our interview, Machado plays down the Braga connection, there's no doubt it would have tickled him.

There is a flavoursome *vérité* feel to *Lower City*, at the heart of which are three charismatic and vital performances. The film helped to make an international star of Alice Braga, while consolidating the local fame of her screen lovers, Lázaro Ramos and Wagner Moura. And it marked Machado out as one of the most talented young Brazilian directors, one whose devoted representation of his milieu could have a strong appeal for the world outside Brazil.

Set in a distinct, far from salubrious stretch of the actual *cidade baixa* in Salvador, Machado's story centres on childhood friends Naldinho and Deco, who make a living transporting cargo on their boat, and Karinna, a pole dancer and prostitute. One night the boys give Karinna a lift, with sex as payment (something we later recognise as a quite casual form of currency). What otherwise would have been a fleeting exchange is prolonged after the men are engaged in a near-fatal fight; Karinna becomes nurse to one, comforter to the other, then lover to both.

The amorous merry-go-round is merely the seductive surface of a film whose chief ambition is to bring to life a place: both viscerally, allowing us almost to smell the sweat, blood and sex (while the illegal cock fight that opens the film reminds one of the frightening dog fight in *Amores perros*), and also in terms of its particular moral compass.

Apparently, if you ask a *soteropolitano* about his where-abouts, he might say, '*Estavo na lutta*' (I was in a fight), meaning that he was at work, or trying to find work, or maybe even that he was in a fight. Machado conveys this fine line between honest work and dishonest, through characters who travel a long way down a crooked road before being troubled by guilt or reflec-tion. Far more important than guilt is necessity, a fact of life that lends an interesting, amoral patina to proceedings.

Machado's camera is as comfortable as it is mobile amid the hustlers, criminals, boxers and prostitutes. Though a fiction, there is a keen awareness that the people colouring the back-ground of *Lower City* are the real deal.

The film won, most notably, the Prix de la Jeunesse in Cannes, and the best film and actress awards in Rio. It bodes well for Machado's future. And that future involves, in the first instance, his adaptation of *A morte e a morte de Quincas Berro d'Agua*, a novel by Jorge Amado.


*Rio de Janeiro, 2006*

Lower City *offers such an evocative depiction of this part of Salvador. What was the inspiration for the story?*

It's something that I have always felt, since I was very small, which is this idea that when you see somebody from a distance, the first things you notice are the differences – you're from England, or the United States, or Japan, I'm from Brazil. But when we are sitting together and talking, there's not so much dif-ference. You could be my best friend. If you look at people very closely, if you break your prejudices, you will see similarities, not stereotypes.

In Brazil there are two parallel societies, the rich and poor, and they just don't cross, unless you really want it. In Rio de Janeiro seventy per cent of the population is black. How many black people have you met in Rio? Probably very few. So it's really important to me to show people that you don't normally look at, and don't want to look at – including prostitutes, smugglers, transvestites – and say to the audience, 'These people are not that different from yourself.' Everybody has fears, desires, dreams and nightmares.

The people in my film live in such a hard environment. They have to find a way to survive and be happy. But this story is not an exposé of the living conditions among waterfront prostitutes and hustlers. It's a story about people like us who desire, love, suffer, weep, get horny, get pissed, have orgasms. It's good and it's bad, it's violent and it's peaceful.

*In Salvador you do actually have the 'lower city'.*

I've had some trouble explaining this, even to other Brazilians. I remember before shooting I was telling the crew that in Salvador we have the upper city and the lower city, and an elevator that links the two. And if you travel down there, especially at the waterfront, it's really amazing, it's like a different city. 'Let's just go down the elevator,' I would say, 'and I won't need to explain anything.'

*Your male leads, Lázaro and Wagner, are locals.*

Yes, the two actors are from Bahia, so they understood the city. Salvador is the third largest city in Brazil, after Sao Paulo and Rio. In fact, it was the first capital of Brazil. It was a very rich city. Then, when the capital moved to Rio, it lost importance, became poorer. But it has also become very cosmopolitan.

*You say that this is not an exposé of living conditions. But it's pretty revelatory, hard-hitting material. This isn't the Brazil of the tourist brochures.*

© Christian Cravo

Set for stardom: Lázaro Ramos, Alice Braga and Wagner Moura
in *Lower City* (2005)

I think most of the best films made in Brazil in the last ten years
are mainly about survival. The situation for many people in this
country is so difficult. Also, it's not a coincidence that some of us
have lost belief in the 'big solutions' from the politicians. Some
very representative Brazilian films are about people joining
together, creating different kinds of family, and surviving.
*Central Station* is about that: two drifting people, the old lady
and the boy, join together to survive. My film is about that, of
course. *Madame Sãta* and Karim's new film are about that. And
*Cinema, Aspirin and Vultures* also.

Another thing I really wanted to do with the story was look at
young people from the lower classes in Brazil and ask, 'What
moves them? What do they do to make their lives better?' Here
you have a young prostitute in Bahia. She is not stupid, she
knows that life is not going to be great for her, ever; she's sort of
been forced into prostitution, so now she's going to find it hard
to get married because she's a prostitute. What can she do? It
doesn't matter whether the three are going to stay together for
the rest of their lives, or for a few seconds. What interests me is
the insistence on not giving up, the will to improvise, to experiment.

I have travelled all around with this film, to at least eighteen different countries in six or seven months – and when you go to Florence or Paris or London, you wonder to yourself, 'What does Brazil have that is special, compared to those cities?' And I think that what we have, what really impresses me in Brazilian society, is this ability to survive.

Salvador is possibly the most African city outside Africa. And what the black people in Bahia – where you have had so much slavery – have learned, is how to survive in the worst environment: without regret or nostalgia, making jokes about everything, laughing. Of course, this culture of parties and making light is also a culture of acceptance. It's hard to say what's best.

People in Bahia are, at least, very proud, much like in Cuba. Also like Cubans, Bahian people are sexy. There is a very peculiar, open approach to sex here. If you walk around Bahia you can see it clearly.

*You've said you were influenced by the book* Laróyè, *by Bahian photographer Mario Cravo Neto. The depiction of sexuality in his images is incredibly strong.*

I wanted to portray the city the way it really is. And when I saw this book I thought, this is the same feeling I have when I'm walking around. You can smell the city just by looking at the photos. The great thing that people from Bahia said about *Lower City* is that they could smell Salvador in the film: the smell of sweat and piss and oil.

*Usually if a film has two characters fucking in the street, or in an alley, as they do in* Lower City, *you tend to think, 'Oh yeah, here's some more wish-fulfilment.' But such behaviour is there in the photographs Neto has taken on the streets and in the carnivals.*

It would be faking reality if I *didn't* show it. It's such a peculiar attitude, without the guilt that you have in a Christian society. There is a very important influence here of the African religion

Candomble. It is a religion that accepts everybody the way they are. Most of the priests are gay and nobody cares. You worship through dancing and singing, and again it's very sexy. It's an experience of a lifetime to see a ceremony. It's so beautiful, the way the elderly, black ladies dance, most of them dressed in white.

One particular memory I have. There are always huge parties going on in Bahia. Carnival is the biggest party, of course – half a million people dancing in the streets – and leading up to it you have a party in a different section of Salvador every week. I was writing the script, on an island, and I took a boat to one of those parties. On the boat I had to pee. I didn't notice there was a lady peeing right next to me. And she said, very naturally, 'You like what you see?' That's the way it is.

*You're from Salvador.*

Yes. From the upper city.

*I understand that the waterfront is a very specific section of the lower city. To what extent did you know and understand it when you made the film?*

While I was writing on the island I was not happy with what I was doing. I was romanticising it, it was not as powerful as I thought it should be. So I decided to spend three months living on the waterfront. Every night I would go to the street bars, past the whorehouses, to the harbour. I made some very good friends, so that when I went back for the shooting everybody knew me, and some of the people I met in this process are working in the film as actors.

One day one of these friends I had made came to the set with a group of his friends and I put them all into a scene. There was one guy who was the worst actor of all, and I kept complaining to him. Then my friend said, 'Hey, slow down with this guy. He's just come of jail this week.'

*Was Karim with you when you were living on the waterfront?*

No, but he went with me to the island. We spent fifteen days working together. Then I spent some time alone and he came again.

*His and your films are very different. How, or why, do you think you and Karim complement each other?*

First, just to talk about the similarities, I think we share the same interest in human beings. I'm really interested in listening to people, seeing them in the street; I'm more interested in people than providing the perfect movement of the camera, or something formally perfect. I think he also shares with me, somehow, an admiration for this capacity of people to survive. And as I said, that is a connection between our films.

There are differences. I am a lot more of a cinephile than he is. Karim has travelled all around the world and has plural interests. The film-makers I love are Eisenstein, Kurosawa, John Ford, completely different from his references, which would be avant-garde. Maybe I'm more interested in storytelling than Karim.

*Eisenstein has had a strong influence on Brazilian film-makers over the years. What do you like about him?*

I like the energy he could achieve, by the way he shot, the way he cut. The cockfight scene in my film is completely inspired by him, specifically by *The General Line*.

*Did you go to university?*

Yes. I did journalism because there was no film course in Bahia – I started in the worst years in Brazilian film-making history, the time of Collor. I call it 'the time of cholera'. But my background has always been about being a cinephile. Ever since I can remember I've watched a film a day, at least. Being from a city that is far away from the centre, I was just watching as many films as I could on VHS first, then DVD, and reading about film-making. When VHS was invented it changed my life. I could see everything. Right now, it's like a problem. I can't sleep at all if I don't see a film every night.

But as an actual film-maker I started late. I visited a film set for the first time on *Central Station*. I was assistant director and that was my first time on a set.

*So are you unusual, these days, as a film-maker from Bahia?*

Yeah. In the last twenty years very few films have been produced in Bahia. That was one really amazing thing for me, that the film was a hit in Salvador itself. One third of the Brazilian audience was in the city.

*Tell me about the short.*

It was called *Troca de cabeças* (*Changing Heads*), and was about a tradition in African religion where you can avoid your own death by saving somebody else. It's a suspense film, with a very important Brazilian black actor, Grande Otelo. He was very old at the time and died just a few months after shooting. His last appearance was in my film, and that's one reason why Amado was curious to see it.

*And what was your reaction when Amado put you in touch with Salles?*

At the time I didn't know he was such a talented guy, because I hadn't seen anything he had made. Then I saw *Foreign Land* and was astonished. He was the only person in the film-making business I had contact with – he was my only chance – and besides that he was the best around. It was such a lucky thing. A little later I started working with him on *Central Station* and we became very good friends. Walter is the godfather of my son, and my son's name is Jorge, after Jorge Amado.

*What does an assistant director do for Walter?*

On *Central Station*, he was looking for the kid to play Josué and suggested I give him a hand. I started directing screen tests in São Paulo and he liked the way I directed, so sent me all around Brazil doing the tests. Then during the filming I worked with the actors, preparing them. In his next film, *Midnight* [1998], I did the things a first assistant director traditionally does – organising the shooting schedule, which was very difficult, because I had no experience at all. On *Behind the Sun* I didn't sign as an assistant director but as director's assistant: I was just discussing scenes with him, filming second unit and working with actors. Once I met Walter everything happened very fast. It was all an amazing experience.

*When making* Lower City *you used the legendary acting coach Fatima Toledo. She also worked on* Pixote, *of course, and* City of God.

And *Central Station*. I think she has raised acting in Brazilian films to a different standard. The performances by non-actors in *City of God*, the way they portrayed the lower classes is, to me, very important. If you get somebody from the *favela* to portray someone from the *favela*, it's not easy at all. They will tend to play the stereotypes of themselves. In my film there was a guy, a smuggler. He was playing a character like himself, but he wanted to play it – play himself – as a B-movie gangster.

*What is so unusual about Toledo's approach?*

She developed her method of working on *Pixote*; she was an actress and started coaching the young guy who played Pixote. It's a very peculiar technique, because she does everything based on physical exercise – not on memories or emotions – repeating them to awaken true sensations in the actors, related to the situations experienced by the characters. In our film, if they had to film a sex scene, they performed a physical exercise called *kundalini*, which seeks to liberate the sexuality through pelvic movements; if they were shooting a scene in which the character is desperate, they did something physically that would make them feel desperate. It's common for actors who have done Fatima's technique, two minutes before shooting, to vomit; not on my film, but *City of God* and Karim's.

*I've heard about the* kundalini. *It sounds extraordinary.*

They would do the exercise for half an hour, just moving the pelvis. Once, it was incredible, after a while both the guys just had an orgasm. On their own, no contact with anyone. It really works. Then there is an entirely different example. For scenes where Alice Braga's character was in distress, Alice would lie face down on the floor, and we had a very strong guy in the crew, a ju-jitsu fighter, pin her down. He would not let her move, not a finger. Then after 15 minutes of not being able to move she was really agitated, and totally primed for the scene.

*Did they use these exercises in rehearsal or immediately before shooting?*

Immediately before shooting. They prepared the scene during the rehearsal. And then fifteen minutes before the take they would do the exercise. What was different in my film, is that I let them do the exercise in the middle of the set, with all the crew watching. Somehow it made sacred the act of shooting, because the whole crew would feel the way they were feeling.

*It sounds unnatural. Almost like a religious trance.*

It does have something religious about it. But on the other hand Fatima controls it very well. At the beginning I was scared, because it did seem crazy, we were just doing a film after all. But she would say, 'Trust me, I know what I'm doing.' Then I asked the actors what they thought, and they just loved it. They saw it as a once-in-a-lifetime experience.

*Presumably they did not need the technique for every scene, just particular ones?*

Actually, in my film almost every scene is very dramatic, very tense – there is either sex or violence. So we used it often. The only scenes that were acted without it were the fights, because they were choreographed. The boxing scene was rehearsed like a ballet.

*Would you call this approach to performance naturalistic?*

I have never thought about it really. I just want something that feels real, not acted. And that's exactly what Fatima achieves. I'm touched by films by Ken Loach or Mike Leigh, because I believe that I'm seeing something that is really going on in the world. I want people to have the impression that they are seeing something that is real, somehow, life the way it is. I'm really upset when I'm directing a scene and I can see the actor is using a trick, a mannerism, when I can see that they are acting.

When we were shooting I wanted my actors to feel, after these exercises, very spontaneous. 'You know the feeling,' I would say, 'now do it in your own way.'

*In films like* Pixote *and* City of God *Toledo was working with non actors, who would not have any other technique or training of their own. Professionals do. So do they react differently?*

I think there was more confrontation at the beginning from the actors, because the non-actors see the whole experience as so new, they just said, 'Let's do it.' Fatima expected Wagner and Lázaro to react against it, and they did. But after fifteen days they jumped in, more radically than the non-actors.

*Would you use Fatima in every film?*

I think I would like to do a comedy with this technique. It would be interesting.

*Since you, Lázaro and Wagner are from Bahia, and Alice Braga is from São Paulo – and of course the only woman of the principal players – I guess she was the wild card.*

And she joined us very late. At first I did many tests but could not find the girl. Then I cast one, and Fatima started working with her, but it was not really working. Two or three weeks before shooting we decided we had to replace her. I brought Alice in and she was really scared, because she was the least prepared person, but I was happy with that. I said, 'Let's have one element that's not prepared.' And the two boys were very generous. They took care of her.

*Her aunt is Sonia Braga, who starred in the film version of Amado's* Dona Flor. *Is that why you thought of her?*

No. Walter knew her. She had a role in *City of God*, and had done some commercials. But this was her first leading role. The great thing about Alice is that she trusted everybody. And she did it. It wasn't easy for someone who was twenty years old, with not that much experience. She was very brave. The film won perhaps thirty, thirty-five prizes internationally, and she got ten of them.

*In real life Lázaro and Wagner are best friends. But they seem like quite an odd couple.*

It's true. Lázaro is more introspective, sweet and elegant. Wagner is more outgoing, crazy, hot-blooded. They are two equally talented actors, but totally different. Those two guys are very special. Sometimes they complained that I was only focused on Alice, but I knew that she was more fragile – and that they never make a mistake. They are among the best actors of their generation. And they have gone the opposite way of most actors. They became successful in cinema, then went to TV. You can't walk in the street with Lázaro, these days.

*You were filming in the locations. I presume many of the people in the background are authentic.*

And sometimes they don't know there is a shoot going on. The actors were also prepared for that aspect: they were already quite well-known, so if somebody said, 'Hi, how are you?' they would interact with them as if they were good friends.

*And you were using a handheld camera.*

In 16 mm. And with very few lights, so that we could always follow them very closely. All the technical decisions were based on this desire to show people intimately. When we were editing, I tried to think about their heartbeat: if they are anxious I will cut it more, if they are calm, let's let them be.

I am obsessive about preparing every shot. I storyboard. And I spent a few months collecting things, objects, images from classic films, anything I thought related to the scene, then made a big book with four hundred pages, with everything that I thought about the film during those two years of preparation. I remember when João Salles came to visit me, three days before shooting. He said he had never seen anything so prepared, but that I should be really careful, because it could tie me. But I have to do that, because otherwise I would feel insecure. Then once we started I forgot all this preparation. I could just film it very freely and spontaneously.

*What was most important to you as a first film-maker: to have large audiences in Brazil, or have the film released in other countries?*

The first ambition I had was to make a film that people from Bahia would recognise as the way their lives are. So it was amazing for me that the film was such a success in Bahia. But then the film was accepted in Cannes. The party there was huge. There were lots of people interested in what I had to say. I was not expecting that at all. And I thought, 'This movie business is bigger than I thought.'

I've received many invitations to film abroad, in England, the US. Some of these offers come from the belief that because Latin American directors such as Walter and Fernando Meirelles, but also Iñárritu and Cuarón, have been so successful, they should search for more. But I think I should make more films in Brazil first.

The best thing about this experience is that I feel that, after having some success with *Lower City*, I can do more films. It's the thing I enjoy more than anything. There was one guy, an extra in the film, who said, 'It's really amazing, as soon as the camera turns on, you just change.' It's true. I am more comfortable on a set, in an editing room, than anywhere else.

# Football stories

Andrés Wood's Chilean portmanteau, *Football Stories* (1997)

At the start of the Brazilian film *O ano em que meus pais saíram de férias* (*The Year My Parents Went on Vacation*, 2006), a young boy is playing a makeshift form of Subbuteo in his living room, while his mother packs their bags. The air is thick with tension. When his father arrives, the parents are eager to leave. We soon learn that this is 1970, in the middle of the *anos de chumbo*, the 'Years of Lead' of the Brazilian dictatorship: Mauro's parents, who are dissidents, are about to go on the run, which they euphemistically describe as 'vacation'. And yet Dad can't resist one last play: 'Wait, let me position the goalkeeper.' He drops his bags, places the matchbox in front of the goal, the boy shoots. Father and son together yell, 'Great goal!' It could be the last time they ever play together.

Cao Hamburger's debut feature, a coming-of-age movie in which the World Cup and dictatorship (and, with lesser impact, girls) vie for the boy's attention, is one of a number of contemporary films that reflect the essential role that football plays in South American life. Soccer on the continent is shown to be not merely 'the beautiful game', but life itself – an admittedly romantic phrase that variously alludes to football's role as singular distraction from the grim realities of repression, its position as a source of quasi-religious obsession, and its function in providing the only means by which young boys might transcend poverty, through becoming players themselves. As the Argentine director Carlos Sorín says when discussing his own, typically offbeat football film, *El camino de San Diego* (*The Road to San Diego*, 2006), his eponymous saint – a certain Maradona – 'belongs to a world of gods'. To the English, that will only conjure the infamous 'Hand of God'; to Maradona's followers, it may represent unattainable wealth and glory, but also a source of hope and meaning.

'Not just the beautiful game, but life itself.' Cao Hamburger's *The Year My Parents Went on Vacation* (2006)

While the population takes its game very seriously indeed, South American directors stay at one remove: they don't make soccer films per se (the portmanteau that lends this chapter its title is an exception), but use the sport as context, sometimes serving a social-realist purpose, often a symbolic one. Joy vs Repression, over ninety minutes.

Hamburger, a Paulista who cut his teeth on children's TV – as did his co-producer Fernando Meirelles, in part – says that he conceived his film while in London:

I was very annoyed with the perception that British people have about Brazil, which was very stereotypical: beach, sex, football; then the rainforests and the *favelas*. Nothing else. At the same time, the taxi drivers, the ones over fifty, knew the 1970 Brazilian soccer team by heart, from the goalkeeper to the striker and everyone in between. They could say the names: Carlos Roberto, Rivelino, Jairzinho, Pelé of course. It was a different perspective: they loved this team, as we do.

So I wanted to talk about the multicultural history of Brazilian people – we come from a lot of countries, with immigrants from Asia, from Africa, as well as Europe – and how we can live peaceably with each other. We have social problems, but not a cultural problem. And 1970 was particularly remarkable in Brazil, because we won the World Cup for the third time, with the best team of all time; there was a very interesting cultural melting pot; and, at the same time, it was the height of a military dictatorship. It was a meeting of very different forces.

Hamburger's own experience had some similarities to that of his young hero: aged around ten in that World Cup year, growing up in São Paulo, his parents – father German, mother Brazilian/Italian – themselves jailed for a few days for hiding political activists in their home. 'Both of them are university professors. Many teachers had problems.'

All of these influences are subtly combined as the boy Maura, made ignorant by political parents of his Jewish roots, suddenly finds himself in the care of strangers in the Jewish community of the city's Bom Retiro district. When the Jews and Italians of the district play each other at football, the secret weapon is an athletic black goalkeeper, a person looked on with envy and awe by the opposing side, not disdain. Football is seen in its most positive social manifestation, bringing the disparate factions of the community together on the field, uniting them as supporters in front of the televisions in bars, homes and student unions. (Comically, the only dissent from the Brazilian support, by an Italian communist, is not for his own country, whom Brazil beat in the final, but for communist Czechoslovakia.) But as passions rise during the televised championships, so too does tension on the streets; the police raid the university and start making arrests.

The result is an astute film, evocative of its period, and of the delicate balance that existed in Brazil under a dictatorship that was careful not to let its repression be too evident in day-to-day life. And, of course, the boy still doesn't understand why his parents are not back from holiday: his life, even his mood, is dictated by forces of which he is only dimly aware. Relating, in his occasional voice-over, a vociferous debate as to whether Tostão and Pelé should play in the same side, the boy tells us that he is convinced, like his dad, that they should; before adding, 'but everything was so weird, even I started to have doubts'.

A new World Cup, different despot. Chilean Andrés Wood deals with the confluence of repression and sport more obliquely, but just as powerfully, in *Machuca* (2004). Another coming-of-age tale, it involves the friendship in Santiago between an upper-class boy, Gonzalo, and the indigenous Machuca from the slum on the edge of the city, in the days leading to Pinochet's coup. Whereas Hamburger's film has football squarely as its context, Wood focuses more on the political volatility of the last weeks of Allende's government. However, after the peripheral community is overrun by Pinochet's soldiers, soccer weighs in to show how the country is to fare under the new regime. In a piquant epilogue, Gonzalo sits on the back seat of his reactionary guardian's car (liberal dad now out of the picture), the old man reading a newspaper with the headline, '*FIFA Informo al Mundo que la vida en Chile es Normal*'.

Explains Wood:

Chile was playing qualification games for the World Cup of 1974. Before the coup we played the Soviet Union for a place in the finals and tied 0–0. A famous tie. After the coup the Soviet Union said it would not play the return match in the Estadio Nacional in Santiago, because the government was holding thousands of political prisoners there, torturing and murdering them.

So FIFA went to visit the stadium. And during the visit the regime hid the prisoners beneath the field – it was a big stadium. And so FIFA told the world that everything in Chile was normal. Russia, to its credit, still refused to play, Chile played the game without an opposition on the pitch, scored in the empty net and went to Germany '74.

Wood, a young boy at the time of the coup, has invested a large part of his own memories into his story, among them the image of the soccer field that borders the slum: an outline in the dust, empty as Gonzalo gazes over it at the end of the film. 'I am a football fan,' the director declares. 'But more than that I realise that football is the only issue that will cross all Chilean society. For me this field of dust was the door, the place that belonged to both sides.'

Hamburger's and Wood's films, both told through the eyes of children, are excellent examples of the way in which the new generation of South American directors prefers to deal with the dictatorship years through 'filters', rather than directly and polemically. A rare exception is *Crónica de una fuga* (*Buenos Aires 1977*, 2006), by the Argentina-based Uruguayan Adrián Caetano, which is a full-frontal account of one of the continent's most violent dictatorships. Based on a true story, it recounts the horrors that took place in an Argentine detention centre in the seventies, where left-wing dissenters were tortured and interrogated, before often joining the growing number of the disappeared.

Though it feels very much like a genre exercise, and is a little obvious, the film is nonetheless gripping, with a compelling performance by Rodrigo de la Serna (of *The Motorcycle Diaries*). And, once he has established the hermetic world of the detention centre, Caetano takes the brave step of denying us, as these captives were denied, any sense of the outside world – with one exception, through soccer.

Briefly, before he is abducted, we see de la Serna's character in his everyday world, as a goalkeeper. The image of the gleaming-eyed and healthy man out on the field stays in our minds as, physically and spiritually, he is reduced before us. Then, in the midst of his torture, we glimpse his captors watching the national team on television, their chants of 'Ar–gen–tina' making even a casual onlooker gag with rage.

Fittingly, there can also be lightness derived from the subject. Back in Chile, Andrés Wood actually kick-started his film-making career with *Historias de fútbol* (*Football Stories*, 1997), an extremely jolly triptych that offers fond social observations of his country in the eighties, without any direct reference to the dictatorship or politics.

'First Half', set in Santiago, involves a narcissistic centre-forward for a local team whose ambitions to play in a better league lead him to accept an offer from the local hoodlum to throw a game, by firing blanks in front of the goal – the question being whether the man who loves the adulation afforded by hitting the net can give up the rush, even once. 'Second Half', set in the city of Calama in the Atacama desert, follows a group of poor boys denied entry to a big game because they have no money for a ticket, but who inadvertently find themselves in possession of the match ball, suddenly the most prized item in town. In the hilarious 'Extra Time', the supporter's nightmare segues into the supporter's fantasy, as a young man finds himself stranded on the remote island of Chiloe, just as Chile are playing West Germany for qualification to the 1982 World Cup – with a couple of sex-starved sisters in possession of the only, barely functioning television set on the island.

The film could hardly be described as state of the nation. Yet it speaks with insight and humour of very diverse communities. Where there is corruption, it is accompanied by enjoyably hubristic folly; where poverty, also decency and good grace; where loneliness and lust, a sort of romance.

Wood says:

I always thought that the links between Chileans in those years were to be found more in social areas, like football, than in anything else. I asked myself: what is the relation between a person who lives in the city, in the desert and in the south? Why do we call them Chileans? Football was one of the few things where the social, political or intellectual backgrounds were not relevant. And that, in a country like Chile, with all its divisions, is important.

Corruption in football is also lent comic spin in *Chicha tu madre*, a big hit in its native Peru in 2006. Directed by first-timer Gianfranco Quattrini, the film is rough around the edges, but nevertheless offers a ribald tour of Lima through the experiences of a ducking-and-diving taxi driver, Julio César.

Julio wants to change career and become a tarot reader. Ironically, everyone involved with his local football team has already decided that he himself is bad luck – to the extent that he's barred from matches, lest his presence affect the result. 'Were you there for the entire game?' asks one player who spots him in the dressing room after another defeat. 'Just the second half.' 'Unlucky bastard.' The team has a way, though, of making its own bad luck. Having lost their star player to injury (the minute Julio entered the stadium, of course), the management conspires to send out the player's twin brother, in order to frighten the opposition with the original player's apparent powers of recovery.

Football has no symbolic value in the film, though the characters involved in the game do add to the unfortunate impression that no one in Lima is all that honourable. As if to underline that point, the film ends with Julio's decision to leave the country altogether, for a new life in Argentina.

And undoubtedly the funniest football-themed film from the continent is from Argentina, Sorín's *The Road to San Diego*. This is typical of Sorín's output: a cast of non-actors, seemingly playing personalities close to their own; a road-movie format rarely touching the city; droll, situation-driven humour that never patronises the hard-up characters, and protagonists with a goal that will, temporarily at least, give them a new lease of life. In *Historias minimas* (*Small Stories*, 2002) it was the chance to win a TV game show, in *El perro* (2004) a new, albeit brief career on the dog-show circuit, and in *El camino* a pilgrimage to meet Argentina's football superstar.

Tati Benítez is an out-of-work lumberjack in the north-eastern province of Misiones whose friends have to remind him that he is married to his wife, not Maradona, with whom he is so obsessed that he has 'No. 10' tattooed on his back and a parrot trained, with moderate success, to squawk the footballer's name. Tati is the proud owner of a tree root that, he is convinced, bears the visage of Maradona. When he hears that his hero has had a heart attack and is lying in a Buenos Aires hospital, he decides to make the long trek south to present the tree, in person, to 'San Diego'.

Prompted by Maradona's actual heart attack in 2004 and the massive crowds that camped outside his hospital, Sorín fondly constructs Tati's pilgrimage to the then overweight and drug-addled sportsman, the highlight of which is a hitched ride with a Brazilian who riles at the idea of the Maradona effigy in his truck. Meanwhile, as Tati, a black marketeer and a priest make their way to the city, Maradona checks himself out of the hospital for a round of golf.

Sorín is a smart, crafty chap, with a genuine feel for the ordinary working (and often not-working) people of his country. His eccentric road movie brings Argentina alive, giving a sense of the locations outside the Eurocentric capital, and suggesting, alongside naivety, a sort of purity of spirit that the director manifestly admires.

Meanwhile, in Rio de Janeiro, the Salles brothers, operating their collaborative exchange between documentary and fiction, are again in the thick of things. In 1998, João Moreira Salles directed (with Arthur Fontes) the three-part television documentary *Futebol*, which highlighted not only the Brazilians' passion for football, but their dependency on it as a route out of poverty; in 2008, Walter Salles (with Daniela Thomas) drew directly on his brother's work in introducing this theme into the fiction-

© Daniela Thomas

Walter Salles and Daniela Thomas' *Linha de Passe* (2008)

al story, *Linha de passe*. If anyone wants to know what football really means to Brazilians, they need look no further than these two works.

The documentary-makers talk to the stars of former Brazilian national sides (the aforementioned Pelé and Tostão among them, as articulate in front of the camera as they were with the ball), while following the attempts by a handful of youngsters to get onto the professional-soccer ladder, with mixed success. Once a year, fifteen hundred boys from all over the country flock to Rio and the single day of open trials for the country's biggest team, Flamengo. Almost all are unbelievably poor. And for some, success on the pitch is a question of survival: says the father of one such boy, who lives in a *favela* where twenty-five people a month are killed in the drug wars, 'I hope he makes enough money to get us out of here.'

Following the tribulations and frustrations of four brothers in a São Paulo slum, *Linha de passe* considers a number of forces in their lives, including evangelism, the lure of crime, chronic unemployment, and the pain of not knowing your father (a common Salles theme, of course). Soccer was added, he says, 'because we wanted to look at the role it serves as one of the few means to transcend the social barriers in Brazil. There is no place for romanticism here: every year, two million kids, aged fifteen to seventeen, try to make the cut in second- and third-division teams. Only a few thousand make it.'

The taking of the baton from the documentary is an uncanny and worthwhile exercise. For all those who would not have seen *Futebol* and witnessed the tragedy of boys, blessed with incredible skill, buffeted between hope and disappointment, the older Salles recreates their story through the character of Dario (Vinícius de Oliveira, first seen as the young boy in *Central Station*), who at eighteen realises that he is almost out of time; and for whom it could all rest – as it often does in life – on a penalty kick. In keeping with Salles' determinedly non-melodramatic approach (and in contrast to the climaxes of most British or American sporting films), we're denied the closure of actually seeing the ball hit the net.

Hollywood, at its best, understands how sport can tap into and represent the national psyche. But whereas US movies, like the culture in general, are also founded on the idea of achievable ambition, South American films are more often than not about resignation to the hand one's been dealt – which adds a certain poignancy to these tales of the beautiful game, played in the dust by barefoot kids, better than anyone else in the world.

On a personal note, having spent one of the most extraordinary nights of my life at the Maracanã, home of Brazilian football – at a thumping match in which Flamengo came from behind to win 4–2 – I can testify to a level of collective euphoria that defies description. But I was disappointed at not seeing one of the luckless chickens that are habitually thrown through the air when a goal is scored.

# Letter from Buenos Aires

*Buenos Aires, April 2007*

You've got to credit the Argentines: they don't muck about. While almost every film festival in the world, whatever its pretensions, gets sucked into the celebrity circuit, in Buenos Aires there's only one thing on people's lips, and it isn't which A-lister is in town. At this year's Buenos Aires Internacional De Cine Independiente – blessedly shortened to BAFICI – the topic is nothing less than the decline of *el nuevo cine argentino*.

Apparently this is an ongoing debate, which BAFICI actively addresses in its selection and commentaries. However, two things should be noted immediately: the festival's participation is entirely benign, for the very reason that its own history, founded in 1999 with a mission to promote independent cinema, is inextricably bound up with that wonderful creative revolution sparked in the nineties; and such musings are in any case premature, if not erroneous, when New Argentine Cinema is such an amorphous concept to begin with.

Nevertheless, it reveals how seriously the Buenos Aires cinephile community takes film, and itself. And the buzz of café and screening room conversations, and wry onscreen provocations is so enthralling that I almost forget that I'm here during the twenty-fifth anniversary of the Falklands War. I shouldn't, for the war is the reason we can have this discussion in the first place.

The 1982 defeat in Las Malvinas hastened the exit of the country's military dictators, after which Argentine culture slowly started to rediscover its voice; or, in the case of the independent cinema that flowered in the late nineties, *voices*. Unlike their

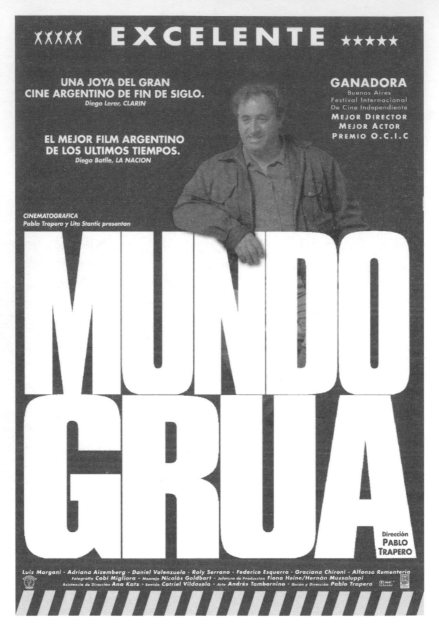

*Excelente*: Pablo Trapero's *Crane World* (1999)

contemporaries in Brazil, the generation that includes Martín Rejtman, Pablo Trapero, Daniel Burman, Lucrecia Martel and Lisandro Alonso is not allied by shared themes, politics or style, but by something less tangible: the desire to pull away from what preceded it, to eschew film as political soapbox (the sixties/ seventies) or psychiatrist's couch (the eighties), for something more personal, and more rigorously cinematic.

Trapero's *Mundo grúa* (*Crane World*, 1999), Burman's *Esparando al mesias* (*Waiting for the Messiah*, 2000), Martel's *La ciénaga* (*The Swamp*, 2001), Alonso's *Los muertos* (*The Dead*, 2004) and Rejtman's *Los guantes mágicos* (*The Magic Gloves*, 2004), along with the late Fabián Bielinsky's *Nueve reinas* (*Nine Queens*, 2000), to name a few, speak eloquently about a society's peculiarities and disorders, while offering a diversity of form of which most national cinemas can only dream.

Thus, New Argentine Cinema was never a movement as such, more a generational shift, during which talented directors with a dogged desire to make films put their country's cinema back on the map. More than that, Argentine cinema has actually reinvigorated world cinema. Eduardo Antín, the Argentine critic and former BAFICI director (commonly, and rather cutely, known as Quintin), has spoken of films that 'display great confidence in cinema and its unrestrained searching'. That's well put, for while much cinematic output, worldwide, is mired in join-the-dots genre exercises and narrative hand-holding, many of the films produced here over the past decade do exactly the opposite: not leading us, but walking with us, inquisitively and thrillingly, into uncharted territories of everyday life, where there are no perceived answers.

Argentina is a rarity among developing-world countries in having had some sort of continuous state support for film for fifty years. As Manuel Antín, the veteran director, former head of the state film institute and current director of Buenos Aires' illustrious film school, the Universidad del Cine, tells me: 'All the governments, democratic and not, have respected that support. In fact, cinema was the only thing they all respected.'

That said, Argentina is also a country where every aspect of cultural life is influenced, mostly for the worst, by party politics and manoeuvring. Since the return to democracy there have been innumerable changes of leadership at the film institute, for political reasons, with Antín himself losing his job when Carlos Menem became president. It would be difficult to argue that the corrupt and market-driven Menem respected cinema.

Moreover, for years after the Falklands the state subsidy was affected by the very real problem of the *junta*'s wretched economic legacy, which led to hyper-inflation in the eighties reaching almost five thousand per cent and ultimately to the country's worst ever economic crisis, in 2001–2. The government not only froze personal savings accounts that year, but appropriated the production funds of the film institute, as it also did in 1989 through the Emergency Film Law – an ironically named measure, since the emergency for film was imposed, not solved, by the politicians.

Add to this the dramatic fall in the number of cinemas around the continent, and the likewise universal dominance of Hollywood fare in those screens that remain, and Argentine cinema has had a topsy-turvy fate over the past twenty-five years.

Back to the eighties. Under Raúl Alfonsín's post-*junta* democratic government, and Antín's stewardship of the film institute, then called the Instituto Nacional de Cine (INC), film production rose from the annual fifteen films of the dictatorship years to around twenty-five in 1989. During this transitional, liberalising period of the new democracy, known as the *destape*, Antín presided over largely highbrow fare, which he described at the time as 'psychoanalytic sessions on film'. Epitomised by the Oscar-winning *La historia oficial* (*The Official Story*, 1985), the aim of these films seemed to have been not just to engage with subjects that earlier censorship had prohibited, but also to offer catharsis, a full-blown raking over of the sins of the past, for those who suffered, facilitated or turned the other cheek to the crimes of the Dirty War.

With the advent of Menem's neo-liberal and philistine presidency, film production first ground to a halt, then was steered towards increasing commercialisation. In thrall to the market, INC encouraged big-budget films aping both Hollywood genre pictures and the country's popular television, with financing from multimedia conglomerates. The massive Argentine box-office hits of 1997 were *Comodines* (*Cops*), an action movie using actors from a successful television cops-and-robbers show, and *Dibu: The Movie*, an animated TV spin-off.

But if *Dibu*, or the following year's *Dibu 2: La venganza de Nasty* did not bode well, it was during Menem's reign – ironically, and as the result of pressure from the film-making community – that the industry was to be financially strengthened and given at least the possibility of supporting a wider range of cinema. The 1994 New Cinema Law finalised moves to broaden the revenue stream – hence the production funds available – to the newly named Instituto Nacional de Cine y Artes Audiovisuales (INCAA), adding to the existing tax on box-office receipts further levies on advertising revenue from television and cable broadcast, and on rental in video stores.\*

Two other initiatives sowed the seeds for New Argentine Cinema. One was the funding of state-run film schools, in the regions as well as the capital. The other was the sponsorship in 1995 of a short-film competition, *Historias breves*, which finally directed monies towards the young directors waiting in the wings. A number of these, Daniel Burman among them, were to become synonymous with the new independent cinema.

---

\*INCAA estimates that it finances between sixty and eighty films per year. A director must win an INCAA contest (there are two a year) or be approved by its selection committee. The institute awards a subsidy (a maximum, in 2008, of around US$833,000), which is received by the producer when the film is finished (the amount is linked to the film's box-office receipts). There is also a credit system (maximum US $330,000), which is given during the film production and is deducted from the final subsidy.

Burman recalls:

Two hundred young film-makers took part in the contest, and I was one of ten who won this award. They gave us $40,000 each to make a ten-minute short film, which was a huge amount of money at that time. This was a generation of new film-makers – Lucrecia Martel, Adrián Caetano, Bruno Stagnaro – some who are now well-known. And when we finished our shorts, we started to meet together, to share our experiences. Then someone said, 'Why not put these shorts together to make a feature film?' So we proposed the idea to INCAA and they supported us with some money for promotion. And we released *Historias breves* [*Short Stories*] in the theatres.

'It was a little success,' he reports modestly of an impressive three-month-run, which the young directors had produced themselves. 'We were twenty-one, twenty-two, twenty-four years old. And so we had our first experience with audiences at a very early age.'

I'm speaking with Burman in his modern production building, in Colegiales, a quiet district of the city and an address that belies the director's energy. Of all the Argentine directors I'm to meet, he's the one whom you could most imagine talking the talk in LA or New York: it's something about the rat-a-tat patter, the urgency, and the fact that thirty minutes in Burman's world really does mean thirty minutes, allied to a punctuality that in Latin circles is positively alien. That said, he shares with his peers a certain Argentine contrariness, which refutes any notion of a movement and even chides at the entirely justified mention of thematic strands through his own films.

But Burman understands exactly just what these young directors have collectively achieved:

The special thing was not the shorts themselves, but the spirit. There is nothing more egocentric in the world than students of cinema. But, and I don't know why, this group of young people understood that we could work together to improve our chances of reaching the audience. So we broke with the history of Argentine cinema as something very tough to get into, structured around the union rules, with things you can and can't do, where there is supposed to be this distance between the director and the rest of the crew. And we broke with this tradition of [serious] cinema as something heavy and solemn and formal. Almost every one of this group, after the competition, had a new way of presenting cinema.

The style that first comes to mind when thinking of this period is epitomised by Adrián Caetano and Bruno Stagnaro's *Pizza, birra, faso* (*Pizza, Booze, Smokes*, 1998) and Trapero's *Mundo grúa* from the following year, the break-out films of New Argentine Cinema. These introduced a startlingly immediate, fully immersed form of cinematic realism which captured the disenfranchisement of the youth and working class of Buenos Aires. Shooting in black and white on the streets, in long single takes that often breathe with the veracity of documentary, and including non-actors in the cast (in Trapero's case, certainly, family and friends), these directors employed the cheapest and most available means of making films; yet what they fashioned with those means was a variation on neo-realism that shook up the Argentine film scene.

If there was a key difference between those early films, and their directors, it would be one of tone. Caetano's debut, which follows a group of teenagers whose casual life of crime escalates out of control, and his even more impressive solo second film, *Bolivia* (2001), about a Bolivian immigrant struggling to forge a new life in Buenos Aires, are raw, angry films, whose characters are constantly on edge. Set mostly in a working-class cafe, *Bolivia* depicts all the rage and despair of that class, inflected by racism and a language resounding with hostile poetry. 'There are arseholes everywhere. But the ones who are fucking with me are Uruguayan.'

In contrast, Trapero's calling-card film established the mood for the subsequent prolific career ahead, the same authentic connection with a hitherto unseen strand of Argentine society, punch-drunk between crises, but given a different – fresher, breezier – presentation, and the sort of defiant humanism that is evident in Walter Salles' work.

Voicing a country's disenchantment: Adrián Caetano's *Bolivia* (2001)

This tonal divergence between directors using many of the same tools typifies New Argentine Cinema at the outset. In that first rush of activity, a panoply of approaches and areas of concern were in evidence: Burman's interest in Jewish identity and father–son relationships, expressed in a trilogy of *Waiting for the Messiah*, *El abrazo partido* (*Lost Embrace*, 2004) and *Derecho de familia* (*Family Law*, 2006), quippy, quirky comedies with professional actors and a busy, pragmatic cinematography that mirrors the director's personality; Martel's dissections of the provincial bourgeoisie, floating dreamily between drama and satire, her bigger-budgeted production values giving free rein to a *mise en scène* that is richly textured and sensuous; Lisandro Alonso's near-existential interest in marginal loners, articulated through meticulous minimalism, which started with *La libertad* (*Freedom*, 2001); Carlos Sorín celebrating the spirit of lower-class people in the country's regions, notably Patagonia, in exuberant, comic road movies such as *Historias mínimas* (2002) and *El perro* (*Bombón: El perro*, 2004).

The pool of directorial talent in the country is so deep that the roster above could equally well have contained a quite different set of names and titles. For example: *Garage Olimpo* (1999), Marco Bechis's dictatorship drama, which follows a young female teacher's fate in a government torture centre; Ariel Rotter's engaging, slightly more European look at youthful indecision in *Solo por hoy* (*Just for Today*, 2001); Diego Lerman's mercurial *Tan de repente* (*Suddenly*, 2002), which segues from off-beat drama to touching, comedic character study, about two Marxist, lesbian kidnappers and their overweight hostage; Celina Murga's expertly understated *Ana y los otros* (*Ana and the Others*, 2003), in which a young woman returns from the capital to her childhood home, searching for an ex-boyfriend and mulling over her old life.

And then there was Bielinsky's *Nine Queens*, the most mainstream of those early trailblazers for the national cinema, and the film that had a considerable crossover impact at the international box office. It also enjoyed that particular mixed blessing from Hollywood: the American remake. Typically, *Criminal*, directed by Gregory Jacobs in 2004, was a misguided affair that couldn't come close to the panache of the original.

*Nine Queens* was a rare foray into genre by these new filmmakers, and a consummate one – a con movie with the brewing economic crisis providing its *pièce de résistance*, and a classic anti-hero performance by the weasel-like, deliciously bad Ricardo Darín at its heart. *Nine Queens* reached a local cinema audience of more than 1.2 million people – figures normally reserved for a studio product. Indeed, the film was produced (after Bielinsky won a script competition) by the Disney-backed Patagonik Film Group, the biggest producer in Latin America. And of all the films that have broken out internationally in the past decade, this was one of the few made with a commercial eye on the domestic box office.

Yet one feels the need to link Bielinsky, spiritually, to the independent auteurs of New Argentine Cinema: taking life from the streets of the capital, and commenting shrewdly on the disintegration of Argentine society, his film displayed not one ounce of rote or audience manipulation. The academic Tamara L. Falicov suggests that Bielinsky is an 'industrial auteur', along with Juan José Campanella, the director of another Argentine hit, *El hijo de la novia* (*The Son of the Bride*, 2001), again starring Darín. It's a neat distinction, but one that Bielinsky's next and last film soundly undermines: while Campanella went on to direct US TV shows such as *Law and Order*, Bielinsky (who died of a heart attack, aged forty-seven, in June 2006) made *El aura* (2005), an existential thriller as oblique and challenging as *Nine Queens* was populist.

All these films provide a marvellous cross-section of Argentine society. As Burman puts it:

> If you chose one movie per year, over the past decade, through the window of each one you would see how the crisis of the country has developed, and also how the identity of the country has developed. So *Pizza, birra, faso* gives you the marginality of the nineties, and the sense of abandonment of those excluded from the neo-liberal system. *Mundo grúa* the same, but with the conflict of older, unemployed people. *Garage Olimpo*, the terrible mark of the dictatorship, and an understanding of how that consequently tore our society. And so on.

Being Burman, of course, he hasn't time to complete his list, but it's a salient observation.

With a few exceptions, a common denominator of these directors is that they are products of the new film schools. And the most influential of those is the private school founded by the indefatigable Antín, whose original title, Fundación Universidad del Cine, has left it with the happy acronym, the FUC. The school opened in 1991, and by 1995 was not only teaching and training, but producing student feature films for theatrical release – an otherwise rare, if not unheard-of-exercise. Trapero was in the first year here, Bruno Stagnaro was here, Lisandro Alonso and Celina Murga. Two others have won Silver Bears in Berlin in the last two years: Rodrigo Moreno for *El custodio* (*The Custodian*, 2006), and this year Ariel Rotter for a film light years from his youthful, angst-driven *Solo por hoy*, the existential midlife crisis drama *El otro* (*The Other*, 2007).

I meet Antín in the school itself, a gorgeous mansion in the cobbled, characterful San Telmo *barrio*. 'When I was at the film institute, there were perhaps forty students in the whole of the country. So when I started this school I thought it would be a very little school for a small group,' recalls this charming, ebullient eighty-year-old.

But today we have a thousand students at FUC. Now there is a film school in each state in Argentina – in Buenos Aires, there are ten. And we have fifteen thousand students in all the country.

The main reason, I think, is that to be a film student in Argentina is the only way you have to enter the world of cinema. Of our thousand students, two hundred and fifty come because they love culture – the school has a very strong humanistic tradition here, we teach philosophy, literature, theatre. And the others come because we have all the technical resources to make films.

Not surprisingly, Antín characterises contemporary Argentine film-making as 'a student cinema. Of every ten films made in Argentina, nine of them are from former film students. This marks the movies of the nineties, and now.'

I wonder how their content is distinguishable from, say, those films he helped finance while at the film institute in the eighties?

This generation has no hope. In the eighties they had a lot of hope. Even under the military government you had the hope of another life. But when that other thing, democracy, comes, there's nothing else you can hope for. I don't know if I'm too old, but my view is that the world now is not very good for this generation, politically, environmentally. We have more money, but we also have more poor people. And we have more rain.

These films show a bleak picture of reality. Argentine movies today are like post-war Italian films, in content. They are pessimistic. But they are better made.

Antín takes me along to a party for a student competition that coincides with the BAFICI, where one of the star presenters

Ariel Rotter's Berlin Silver Bear winner, *The Other* (2007)

is the alumnus Ariel Rotter, whose debut feature was one of the first films made under the auspices of the school. 'It's not a question of how useful the FUC was in making *Solo por hoy*,' he tells me. 'The FUC *is* the film. It exists because of the existence of the FUC. The whole crew was made from students of the university, every process of production was done between the FUC walls.'

The next day I visit Lita Stantic, the veteran producer who has been instrumental in the early careers of some of the most celebrated of the new directors. It was she to whom Trapero turned when he ran out of money to finish *Mundo grúa*, and Stantic who produced Martel's first two films, *La ciénaga* and *La niña santa*, Caetano's *Bolivia* and Lerman's *Tan de repente*. But she also produced films during the dictatorship and the *destape*, directing her own dictatorship-themed drama, *Un muro de silencio* (*A Wall of Silence*), in 1993.

'I think that my generation had the need to make a very overt social critique,' she says.

However, this generation doesn't seem to have this intention. They want to tell a story, they all say, and the social critique just happens to come with it. Trapero would always insist that he only wanted to make a film about a crane, but of course his film touches on the *Menemismo* and the unemployment that has taken place from the nineties.

Somehow these films are unwittingly political; although maybe not in Lucrecia's case, as I think her intention has grown political. But I think that so many things have happened lately in Argentina, from a social and political point of view, there has been such significant social change, such a big crisis, that when any sensitive person tells a story, reality infiltrates this story.

And here she echoes Antín. 'It's like in post-war Italy, with neo-realism. By putting the camera on the street you are immediately making a social critique.'

But while Antín has posited a 'student cinema', Stantic suggests an alternative way of considering this current work: as that of a *junta* generation.

These directors have maybe a different emotional perspective. Somehow they are influenced by the fact that they were kids during the dictatorship, which I think is something very strong in this generation. Diego Lerman was born on 24 March 1976, the day of the military coup. The first sentence of his biography is, 'I was born on a very sad day.'

Stantic's remark reminds me of something Lucrecia Martel said to me when I first met her during the London Film Festival in 2004, as she was presenting *La niña santa*: 'This deepening of the crisis, which lays bare the system, unmasks it, also generates the need to express oneself. For some people the situation is like a death, but for film-makers the effect is very motivating.'

And so it continues to prove. So why, at BAFICI 2006, the gloom and doom?

On one level, there is a critical concern that the shadows of the New Argentine Cinema directors perhaps loom too heavily over those following behind, that the 'homage' is too strong. One film here, otherwise highly impressive, does bear that out to some degree. *La león*, by the French-based Argentine Santiago Otheguy, is a story of gay isolation in a delta community in northern Argentina. It's exquisitely lensed, in black and white, using local people fronted by two professional actors, and it has the eerie feel of a man who has looked across the water, at Trapero and Alonso and others, and made his 'Argentine' film.

So perhaps this might be a warning sign, not because *La Léon* doesn't stand up in its own right, but because the essence of, say, Trapero's films – an irrefutable, innate connection to his characters – can't be facsimiled.

That said, in light of some of the impressive new work I am seeing here, the charge of copycat-ism feels like a quibble. And there is a more pressing concern. In a town not characterised by sentimentality, the hard realities are beginning to bite: that the vibrant new cinema, just like art-house or auteur cinema worldwide, is struggling to maintain its audience; and while a good return for an independent movie here would be around a hundred thousand tickets, that's not enough to help its makers recoup their investment. For someone like Martel, who uses production values and budgets more commensurate with a commercial film, it could be disastrous if she did not sell her films overseas.

'If you only screen your film in Argentina, you will lose money. Even if the film is a success,' laments Óscar Kramer, a producer whose last film, Caetano's *Crónica de una fuga* (*Buenos Aires 1977*, 2006), actually achieved a very respectable four hundred thousand tickets domestically.

But Kramer's collaboration with Hector Babenco, on the Argentine-born, Brazilian-domiciled director's hit *Carandiru*, is revealing:

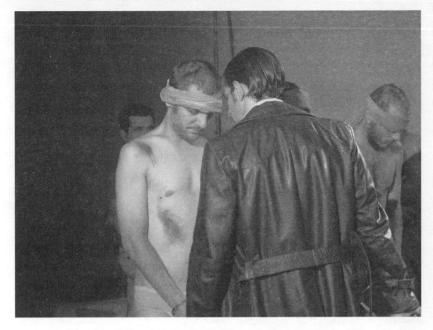

New Argentine Cinema takes a rare look at the Dirty War:
Caetano's *Buenos Aires 1977* (2006)

The difference in Brazil is the size of its population and the potential audience. *Carandiru* was a success in Brazil, where it sold five million tickets. That's huge compared to what we can achieve here. So you can make a movie only for Brazil and have an economic success. We don't have that market in Argentina, so we have to sell our movies abroad. The good thing is that some Argentine directors can write and direct stories that do have that appeal.

We are trying to be both artistic and commercial. In a way, I'm trying to be realistic, looking for scripts with the 'wow factor' for audiences; at the same time, I am trying to find the new Lucrecia Martel.

Meanwhile, despite its estimation that it funds as many as eighty films a year, INCAA's system of subsidies (the maximum is less than a million dollars) and loans is no panacea – certainly not for the hundreds of young film-makers graduating each year, without the track record or established producer to woo the selection committees.

*

It's extraordinary, really, the way in which such issues of self-reflection are mirrored in the films programmed at BAFICI. Indeed, the features that generate the most attention are those that actively address the legacy and problems of the new independent cinema.

*Estrellas* (*Stars*, 2006), which wins the international jury prize, is rather fabulous. It is co-directed by Federico León and Marcos Martínez, who surpass Christopher Guest's 'mockumentary' style by satirising Latin American film-makers' deployment of ordinary, often poor people as non-professional actors. 'I used to be a worker from the shanties,' says the film's protagonist, a wily fellow who decides to represent a community of non-actors. 'Now I talk about works in progress.' It's very funny, and smart, recognising the thin line between authenticity and exploitation.

*UPA! Una película argentina* (Tamae Garateguy, Santiago Giralt, Camila Toker), on the other hand, gives full, painful expression to the frustrations of a younger generation intimidated by their forebears, and struggling with exactly the sort of marriage between art and commerce that Óscar Kramer is talking about. A micro-budget film about the making of a micro-budget film whose twenty-something makers self-destruct under the pressure, *UPA!* wins the prize for best Argentine film.

Meanwhile, the two films that particularly resonate for me do not lament or reflect, but soldier on with the business of film-making. *Copacabana* is the first documentary by the accomplished feature director Martín Rejtman. A reflection on the Bolivian community in Buenos Aires, through the prism of its dance-dominated Festival of Our Lady of Copacabana, it's an ebullient film with a cunning undercurrent, as Rejtman hints at the complex response to immigrant Latin Americans in his country.

And with his spare, taut, claustrophobic day-in-the-life of a very intriguing criminal, *El asaltante* (*The Mugger*, 2007), Pablo Fendrik presents himself as a possible heir to the late Fabián Bielinsky, as a director of genre film-making with bells on.

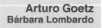

The great Arturo Goetz, in Pablo Fendrik's thriller *The Mugger* (2007)

Fendrik's style, glueing his camera to the face of his ageing protagonist (Arturo Goetz) as he races around town robbing school
offices, raises the adrenalin so considerably that the film needs
no more than its seventy minutes. I've seen nothing quite like
this. The plot, and the sting in its tale, acquire huge resonance
during the festival, when local schoolteachers go on strike –
again highlighting the social relevance of even the most generic
of this country's films. The mesmerising Goetz, a sweet-faced
favourite of Argentine cinema given a nasty new lease of life
under Fendrik, wins best actor.

As I'm watching the awards, with the talismanic Pablo
Trapero among the jurors on stage, I think of a cute moment in
*Estrellas*, when a director announces his next film, called
*Treading Water*. That could well be the feeling in Buenos Aires.
But with such an exciting new director as Fendrik joining the
party, and the likes of Trapero, Martel and Alonso all working
on their next films while I'm in town (see 'Cannes, 2008'), there
is so much to be enthusiastic about.

Before I leave, I get to speak to Martín Rejtman, whose first
film in 1992, *Rapado* (*Shaved*), represented a lone, original voice
in the desert. He's still a fighter, still an individualist, and a man
seemingly unable not to call a spade a spade. So I'm keen to hear
what he thinks.

'Everybody wanted to be the first one to say that there was a
*nuevo cine argentino*, and now somebody had to be the first one
to say that it's over,' he notes, deadpan. 'But how can you talk
like that about something that's still before us? Every year there
are one or two interesting films coming out from new directors,
as well as the established directors. For me it's a miracle. I know
what the story was before. I've been there. And I tell you, this is
paradise.'

# The droll revolution of Martín Rejtman

Martín Rejtman recalls that when he was making his first feature, *Rapado* (*Shaved*), in Buenos Aires in 1991, 'I felt totally alone in that moment. I felt there were no other movies I could really relate to. For me *Rapado* was starting from zero.'

In many respects, it was. At that time Argentina was in a post-dictatorship hangover, its emotional and psychological bruises still purple, its economy labouring under the billions of debt also left by the generals. Cinema, too, was in the doldrums, with the Oscar success of *The Official Story* in 1985 something of a mixed blessing: an explicit attempt to excite middle-class guilt over the *junta*, it arguably represented the high point for a period of over-earnest political film-making.

'In the eighties everybody wanted to make a political film,' suggests Rejtman.

Maybe there were political statements to make, but I don't know if they were made in an interesting way in terms of cinema, or if they were telling the right story. Films became a vehicle for the political ideas of the directors, and nothing else. When you make melodramas – soap operas – with the subject of the disappeared, it is a little dubious, I think.

Rejtman is the unofficial godfather of New Argentine Cinema, which was not even given a name until six years after *Rapado* appeared, in 1992. A little older than the likes of Trapero, Burman and Caetano, he is not the best known, the most commercially successful or the most prolific of them. Yet it was Rejtman, as a writer, director and producer, who led the breakaway from stuffy soapboxing or inane commercialisation towards the independent film-making – born of film students and cinephiles, with their own, diverse stories to tell and new

'I felt totally alone in that moment.' Martín Rejtman on making
*Rapado* in 1991

ways of telling them – that has characterised the best Argentine
cinema since the late nineties.

His three features to date – *Rapado*, *Sylvia Prieto* (1999) and
*Los guantes mágicos* (*The Magic Gloves*, 2003) – could be seen
as a trilogy about young Argentines struggling, albeit noncha-
lantly, to establish an identity for themselves in a country itself
unsettled, inchoate, in which even making a living is difficult. In
*Rapado* this effort is at the most basic, materialist level: a teenager has his motorbike stolen, so sets out to steal another – to re-
establish, in lieu of a job, vocation or any apparent ambition, the
one object that defines him. *Rapado* is the leanest and meanest
of the three films, as epitomised by its opening sequence: the
young Lucio rides through night-time streets, a seeming friend
behind him on the bike, only for us to realise that the other man
has a knife to Lucio's throat and is about to rob him of bike, wallet and shoes.

While Lucio's middle-class parents conduct a life on auto-pilot
in their comfortable apartment, paying only offhand or quizzical

interest in their child, Lucio's world is one of young people wandering aimlessly in the streets at night, streets where robbery, theft and forged banknotes are commonplace, and where there are intimations – in the form of the ever-increasing cost of tokens in the video-game arcade – of the inflation that will soon lead the country to recession. (Incidentally, the choice of the arcade as a key location is loaded with its own meaning, since this was one of the common uses to which many of the country's cinemas were converted around this time.)

In *Sylvia Prieto*, the eponymous heroine starts the film with the declaration, 'The day I turned twenty-seven I decided to change my life' – though beyond separating from her husband, giving up marijuana and buying a canary that can't sing, she has no idea how. Sylvia is at the heart of an impromptu coterie of old schoolfriends and criss-crossing lovers who float around Buenos Aires with dead-end jobs, or no work at all, forever scrounging, and aspiring to family without being able to express the slightest passion for each other; young people variously listless, clueless or, in Sylvia's case – horrified by the discovery of another 'Sylvia Prieto' in the phone book – eventually eschewing all semblance of a character.

The protagonists of *The Magic Gloves* are older again, now in their thirties, and still aspiring to a better life. Chief among them is Alejandro, who sells his car, with which he works as a taxi driver, in order to fund the import of one-size-fits-all 'magic gloves' from Canada, with a business partner who declares, optimistically, 'We must become capitalists.' When their venture, almost inevitably, fails – their cargo ship misses an unusually bitter winter by a matter of days – the taciturn Alejandro returns to the road, but a step further down the food chain, behind the wheel of a bus.

No one complains; people rarely do in Rejtman's films. Nor, as a rule, does anyone in these films display guilt or apologise for their behaviour. For his part, the director merely observes, refusing to impose melodrama or comment, allowing captured

moments in his characters' lives to speak about their environment and time. *Rapado* ends with one shimmer of a tear, in the
eyes of a young woman who may have experienced the same
sort of robbery as Lucio. But the gorgeous gamine could have
been plucked from a frame of Godard or Truffaut, Jim
Jarmusch or Hal Hartley: this is more a nod to cinema than to
social outrage.

The rejection of polemic and matter-of-fact rendition of everyday life run through the work of many of the directors who have
followed Rejtman. *Rapado*, with its evident empathy with the
morally ambivalent young hero, the immediacy with which
Rejtman shoots in the streets (it is a very evocative portrayal of
Buenos Aires) and the naturalistic performance of the non-actor
chosen to play Lucio, Ezequiel Cavia, clearly casts ahead to
Caetano and Stagnaro's *Pizza, birra, faso* and any number of
Trapero's films.

Yet there is a strikingly individual quality to Rejtman's work,
epitomised by a line in *The Magic Gloves*, as Alejandro's ex-
girlfriend is told, 'All that melancholy has plunged you into
depression.' Rejtman's treatment of his dour scenarios, particularly in the latter two films, is very, very funny. When the pill-
popping depressives of *The Magic Gloves* congregate in a bar for
Happy Hour, the director is basically saying, 'You've gotta
laugh' – even if his characters can't.

While the deadbeat protagonists and deadpan dialogue
remind one of Aki Kaurismäki's films, there is a peculiar, indefinable quality, a 'cuddliness' to Rejtman's absurdist comedy. It's
there in the casual way that improbable friendships are struck,
often between a character's new and former lovers (Alejandro
doesn't register an iota of the anticipated male jealousy when his
ex-girlfriend hooks up with a strapping foreign porn star); in the
obsession with objects – Lucio's bike, Alejandro's car, an Armani
jacket that gets passed around the ensemble in *Sylvia Prieto*, the
free washing-powder samples in the same film, which are enthusiastically collected by people who never seem to wash their

'All the melancholy has plunged you into depression.'
*The Magic Gloves* (2003)

clothes; in the final revelation of an apparently real-life association of Sylvia Prietos, filmed documentary-style; and in
Alejandro's indefatigable love of disco. *The Magic Gloves* ends
with its inexpressive hero, alone on his long distance bus route,
stepping onto a dance floor for New Order's 'Vanishing Point' –
just in time for Bernard Sumner to sing 'My life ain't no holiday'.
Hardly a feelgood denouement, but a fabulous insight that
leaves a broad smile on one's face.

'For me, the comedy is really what makes the films,' says
Rejtman. 'There is not enough humour in Argentine movies. For
me, comedy is a fantastic genre, because everything is allowed,
as it is in science fiction. Of course, you need to have a logic, but
you can go anywhere, you can get away with almost everything.'

Rejtman was born in Buenos Aires in 1961. In his twenties, and
with only one small film course available in Argentina at the
time, he chose to study cinema in New York. In between two
stints in America, he worked as an assistant director on thrillers
in Argentina and made his own short films. When he returned
to Buenos Aires to make *Rapado*, he says, 'I didn't find any

tradition to relate to, in terms of camerawork, editing, the way the actors speak.'

My feeling was that the films made here at the time were not dealing with contemporary issues; not just that, there was no real knowledge of, or real pleasure in making movies.

I was coming from New York, my education was in watching movies, and I was more interested in foreign movies than in Argentine ones. I loved classic American movies from the forties. Not Capra, I don't understand why people like him, maybe he's too sweet for me. But Howard Hawks, for his energy and the point of view, so simple and direct. And I love Preston Sturges, the way he can move the scenes so quickly, and anything can happen in them. That's a good example of real freedom in cinema.

Perhaps surprisingly, given the period of his sojourn in New York, he does not cite the American independent directors of that time – at least not directly.

I was influenced more by New York, by the city itself. It's funny, I did not see Jim Jarmusch till the second time I was in New York, 1986–7, but by that time I had made short films which were very much in the same style. So I think it was more something that was in the air: in the city, in the time.

Also the school – NYU, the same film school that Jarmusch attended – and the way they taught film had something to do with it. Basically, they made us make a short movie every week. They gave us a hundred feet, small three-minute rolls of 16 mm black-and-white film, and a camera, and we were divided into groups of four people. And since you were supposed to make a film every week, you really had to deal with whatever material was available to you: you had to write and make low-budget movies. That is definitely my main influence, more than any actual movies.

Back home, he has experienced an erratic relationship with the state film institute, INCAA. For *Rapado* he received a first screenplay award from the institute, but when he tried to cash the prize, inflation had reduced the value, in dollars, of the pesos he received from fifty thousand to only a couple of hundred. 'I had to fight for a long time in order to make them admit the inflation factor,' he recalls wryly. 'I even had to threaten to sue the institute director. In the end I got the money.'

His subsequent films also received INCAA cash, although on *Sylvia Prieto* it was a loan that came near the end of a two-year shoot. It is unlikely that Rejtman, a director without a commercial film company behind him and seeking to make small, personal films, would have succeeded without the help of overseas film funds: *Rapado* was the first Argentine film to receive assistance from the Hubert Bals Fund, which also supported *The Magic Gloves*, while the French fund Fonds Sud backed *The Magic Gloves* and *Sylvia Prieto*.

This perennial problem of money is drip-fed into the stories themselves. Rejtman is uncomfortable talking about the themes in his work, insisting that characters are not conduits for his own views, that audiences can read the films as they please. Nevertheless, embedded in the films, like tiny jewels, are character statements or observations that between them build a shrewd social commentary. And obsession with money, or the lack of it, is one constant – with the endless bartering, borrowing, appropriating and stealing providing a major source of comedy.

The fact that he wrote *Sylvia Prieto*, a film in which everyone is skint, before Argentina's financial crash is less prescient than it seems, Rejtman says, for the simple reason that 'the crisis started before the crisis. In Argentina there has always been a crisis. It's really been like that ever since I can remember. Things have always been going downhill.

'I don't think there is a sense of progress in any of my films,' he adds. 'Rather, there is the idea of something that goes round and around, but doesn't change; just small changes – which usually make things a little worse.'

The fragility of personal identity (which I will discuss in the chapter *Quien soy?*) also comes up frequently in Rejtman's work, sometimes expressed formally through the presence, or absence, of an identity card. The bike-jacker of *Rapado* takes everything from Lucio, even his shoes, but leaves him his ID card: Lucio's response is to be entirely underwhelmed, the card being of little use to him in getting home, or indeed in getting through a life that involves next to no social interaction. When Sylvia Prieto loses her card in a club, she grabs the opportunity to abandon her identity altogether – reporting the loss to police, she gives her name as Louise Ciccone: Madonna. And though there is a very friendly club of Sylvia Prietos, she wants no part of it. It's in such elliptical ways that Rejtman was among the first to capture the mood of contemporary disenchantment in his country.

Since New Argentine Cinema is more a spirit than a movement, so Rejtman is a 'godfather' in the same way as Cassavetes was to American avant-garde directors: not by providing a style to imitate (his no-nonsense fixed camera and short, mostly static scenes have not been copied), but a spirit of independence. He has also helped other film-makers, acting as a producer or associate producer on first films by Lisandro Alonso, Albertina Carri and Federico León, all directors whose careers have since blossomed.

'I think everything has changed, a lot, since when I started,' he says. 'I feel much more comfortable now. I feel that I can meet with my colleagues and speak about movies – their movies and my movies – in the same terms. We speak the same language. Before I felt they spoke a different language.' He pauses. 'That's exactly how I felt.'

# Poet of the everyday: Pablo Trapero

Pablo Trapero was not the first person to cut creative ties with Argentina's film-making past; that was Martín Rejtman. And as far as Trapero himself recalls, the first time he saw the words *nuevo cine argentino* was on the poster for *Pizza, birra, faso*, directed by Adrián Caetano and Bruno Stagnaro in 1998, a year before his own first feature was released. Yet if one director most completely represents New Argentine Cinema, in all its aspects, it would be Trapero himself.

It was Trapero's debut, *Mundo grúa* (*Crane World*, 1999), completed when he was twenty-seven, that won the best director prize at the inaugural Buenos Aires International Festival of Independent Cinema (BAFICI), a festival that quickly became a champion of New Argentine Cinema. It was *Mundo grúa*, with further prizes in Rotterdam and Venice, that alerted the wider film community that Argentina might have something to offer the Latin American party that was only then turning up the amps. And it was Trapero, in the first year of graduates from the Universidad del Cine, who has become most synonymous with the generation of entrepreneurial, cinephile, film school-trained directors.

And when the banks closed their doors in Argentina in 2001, in a financial crisis that was to cripple the country, Trapero was making his second film, *El bonaerense*. His response – to implore his family, friends and crew to withdraw their tiny cash limits from ATMs before they, too, closed, then shooting with whatever he had managed to raise – epitomises the resourceful spirit of this generation.

There's something else. A favourite word of Trapero's is '*cotidiano*': 'quotidian'. With his early films, including the short film *Negocios* (1995), *Mundo grúa* and *Familia rodante* (*Rolling Family*, 2004), Trapero's immediate, unadorned shooting style, his willingness to draw on the ordinary stories of his working-class family and friends, and to cast them in front of the camera, gave fresh legs to the neo-realism that had been influencing the continent in one way or another since the forties. Though Argentine cinema is remarkably diverse, these characteristics of Trapero's films, rightly or wrongly, are those most readily associated with the period in which he has worked.

Having tested the waters with *Negocios*, an ambling story based on his father's auto-parts shop, whose good-natured characters and presentation belied its underlying tragedy – the inevitable demise of the shop, within a struggling community – Trapero made, in *Mundo grúa*, one of the unsung classics of contemporary world cinema. Shot, like the short, in black and white, with a style whose immediacy almost defies description – we feel that we are eavesdropping on its characters in a way that documentary cannot even approach – the film follows a character from *Negocios*, Rulo, as he tries to recreate himself in unhealthy middle age as a crane operator. Meanwhile, his former (comparative) glory as a bass player in a band hangs over him: sometimes usefully, as when he is courting a woman, sometimes bitterly.

Trapero observes his hero and his son, himself in a band, through Buenos Aires' building sites, pool halls, underground nightclubs, or as they sit and talk to each other in the dead of night. There is no mockery or condescension: Rulo may be horribly overweight and a bit slow, but he is also a hard worker and serious. His friends are honourable, doing their best to help each other. His son, though a slacker, is fond of his family. Like his hero, Trapero refuses to confront the tough times directly; yet the economic environment very much exists as the context of the story, notably as Rulo heads to the south of Argentina in pursuit of work, only to find life in Patagonia, amid poor working conditions, even tougher.

The only occasion on which Rulo voices his pessimism, at the end of the film, is also the only overt allusion to the country's problems. 'With the mess we are all in. Work, and all that . . .' he says, not willing to articulate further. To which his companion tells him, 'The thing is, we make friends in these situations.' Such camaraderie is a constant in Trapero's films, indicative of a genuine warmth towards, and empathy with, his working-class characters. This is nowhere more apparent than in *Familia rodante*, his third film. Following the tougher (though no less naturalistic, and fabulously original) police story *El bonaerense* (2002), this rollicking road movie drew on childhood stories for material, his father's old camper van as a chief prop and his terrifically amusing grandmother, Graciana Chironi – for a fourth time – as the materfamilias of an extended, warring family on the road to a wedding.

There is a stubborn optimism in Trapero's movies (buoyed by soundtracks of diverse, often upbeat Argentine music) and, as I've suggested elsewhere, a humanity that he shares with Walter Salles. These two directors have something much more important than technical tropes in common with the Italian neorealists: namely, a belief in the people in front of their cameras, however dire their circumstances.

Trapero's last two films have shown him developing his modes of expression. *Nacido y criado* (*Born and Bred*, 2006) concerns Santiago (Guillermo Pfening), a middle-class Buenos Aires family man who, after a terrible accident, exiles himself in a desolate Patagonian hinterland. While Santiago succumbs to the dire routines of a menial job at a small airport, hunting and drinking with his workmates, troubled by night-time sickness and day-time fears, the extent of the loss he is struggling to overcome is left tantalisingly vague.

The film is informed by Trapero's customarily *simpatico* work with a mixture of professional and non-professional actors, and by his focus on the minutiae of everyday life, particularly that of the workplace. But here he takes his inclination towards narrative restraint to another level entirely, turning Santiago's situation into an existential mystery, for which he taps – in the wind-lashed, snowbound landscape – a marvellous metaphor for what is going on inside his protagonist's tortured head. The understatement (reflected in Pfening's nuanced performance) also leaves space for the viewer, inviting introspection as to how we ourselves would deal with such depths of grief and guilt.

The opening of the film saw Trapero viewing a middle-class and notably chic milieu, for the first time – perhaps an indication of how the director's own life had changed. Such a departure, along with the obliqueness of the emotional terrain, may explain why there were some naysayers when *Born and Bred* was released in Argentina. But this would be no more than an indication of just how much his early approach and his refreshing gaze on the working class had swayed his countrymen. For this is an accomplished, complex and involving film, which was greeted ecstatically by overseas critics – not least in London, where the film prompted a retrospective of Trapero's work at the National Film Theatre.

*Leonera* (*Lion's Den*, 2008) won back those wayward locals, while garnering fulsome praise on its Cannes premiere. Starring his wife and producer Martina Gusman as a woman who gives birth in prison, then struggles with the authorities for the right to keep her child, it shows Trapero maintaining his working practices (the non-actors here include prison inmates) and his fundamental interest in human stories and social issues, while moving his cinematic language forward several notches (see 'Cannes, 2008').

In 2002 Trapero and Gusman formed Matanza Cine, dedicated to independent film production. The company has shown a predilection for documentaries, and a willingness to engage in South American co-production; among the directors Trapero has championed is Albertina Carri, two of whose features, *Géminis* (2005) and *La rabia* (*Rage*, 2008), the company has produced.

Trapero was in pre-production for *Leonera* when I met him in the Matanza production offices in Buenos Aires.

*Buenos Aires, April 2007*

*The high-profile films at this year's BAFICI – UPA!* and Estrellas *– are commenting on New Argentine Cinema itself.* Estrellas *is a comedy derived wholly from the way that Argentine cinema uses non-actors;* UPA! *is about the stresses and strains of trying to make independent films. Why such self-conscious discussion at this moment?*

I think because a lot of things have happened in the last ten years, so people are just beginning to reflect. BAFICI is the ideal place to do that. *Mundo grúa* was released at BAFICI in 1999, the first year of the festival. Actually it was the platform for the film. We presented it on Friday at 11 p.m., direct from the lab. A real wet print – we were receiving the final prints, reel by reel, during the screening.

Because I did not have time to go to other screenings, I discovered the festival at the same moment that I brought my first film to the screen. So it was very moving: my first film, my first print, my first festival, in the first edition of BAFICI. And in a couple of hours everybody went crazy about the film. It took the director and actor prizes – and giving the prize to a non-professional actor was also something important at that time. And a lot of international film makers were at the screening, a lot of international press. After BAFICI we were invited to Venice, so a lot of things happened very quickly.

You know, at that moment, for me and my colleagues everything was new. The first time I was in Venice, with *Mundo grúa* I was by myself – just me and my luggage. No other Argentines. Then I won a prize, and I wasn't believing what I was living. And it continued like that: it was a big moment in terms of critics and the public here in Argentina.

When *Mundo grúa* was released, it made around a hundred thousand spectators, which at that moment – for a black-and-white film, with no professional actors, a first-time director – was really moving for all of us. Then my second film, *El bonaerense, Un oso rojo* [*The Red Bear*; Adrián Caetano, 2002] and [Carlos Sorín's] *Historias mínimas* were attracting between two and three hundred thousand spectators, which for those kinds of film is really more than enough, at least here. A positive mood started to form around films that were quite different from the Argentine films that had been on screen before.

*So you were making your own films, personal films, and the surprise was that they actually worked?*

Yeah, because for me it was satisfying enough just to make my first film. That's what I was aiming for. I wasn't looking for critical recognition, or the box office. Everyone was surprised, especially when the films started to work outside Argentina. Between 1999 and 2004 I went to Cannes with *El bonaerense*, then Venice, and three or four directors – Lucrecia, Daniel Burman, Adrián Caetano, Carlos Sorín – were living the same strange moment. It became like a normal thing, everybody was going to Berlin, Venice, Cannes, and Argentine films were taking prizes.

Of course I had hoped that we would one day achieve something, but I didn't know that it would happen as fast as it did. In three years it became normal that this new group of young directors was making films. It was really exciting. But I was also distrustful of all the people looking after us, who were saying, 'Oh, what wonderful films you are doing.' I think something like that happened with other directors: not refusing this label New Argentine Cinema, but not assuming that was our destination. What is clear in these films is that all of us were looking for a personal style of talking about things. Often it works, but you never know that until the films are finished. That's my belief: a film is what you have on the screen; all that happens before that is just talk.

So back to your first question: why this backlash? I think the situation we find ourselves in now is more realistic. For a time we were the trend, the fad, but we can't win prizes in Cannes or Berlin every year. I assume the rest of the world is making good films also. What we do have now is a wide range of people trying to make films: you have the old, old generation, the people whose ideas we learn from or reject; my generation, and now we have all the young people coming from film school – we have fifteen thousand film students.

We had a revolution of sorts. You can't ask this new generation for another U-turn already. It's not reasonable.

*If New Argentine Cinema wasn't a movement, you admit there was something fresh about the work. You, Caetano, Martel, Rejtman, Alonso, Ariel Rotter: you are very different film-makers, not conspicuously held by a shared aesthetic, yet you are connected – by the post-dictatorship period in which you started making films. You are connected not by what you do, but by what you don't do. None of you, apart from Caetano with* Crónica de una fuga, *talks overtly about the country's problems, about the dictatorship or the economic crisis.*

This is what I feel about what happened. We come from a very powerful film history in Argentina. We had a big industrial era of Spanish-speaking films around the fifties, we had a very interesting, *nouvelle vague* movement in the sixties. In the seventies there was a mix of these sorts of films, with directors coming from different worlds and different ways of making films. And of course we had Cine Liberación,* militant film-makers – Solanas, Vallejo,

*Fernando Solanas and Octavio Getino were at the forefront of the Grupo Cine Liberación, which reflected a nationalist mood in the sixties among Argentine intellectuals who challenged the country's economic and cultural dependency. This was reflected both in the pair's epic documentary *La hora de los hornos* (*The Hour of the Furnaces,* 1968) and in their manifesto 'Toward a Third Cinema', which proposed a militant cinema opposed to both Hollywood and European auteur cinema.

even Cedrún – for at that moment films were part of the *militancia* with a kind of manifesto to help the idea of revolution. Che and all that stuff. But in the seventies the dictatorship arrived, and with it *los desaparecidos.** A whole generation in terms of ideas, in terms of a theoretical movement – not only in films – either left Argentina or disappeared. We lost a generation.

Then in the eighties, when democracy returned, we had a kind of spring, with the film law, the film institute, *The Official Story* winning an Oscar. A lot of stuff was happening, but not with a new generation: it was the generation that was stopped in the seventies who were coming back. And after the history they had experienced it was normal, a kind of therapy, to deal with that, to throw out all the hell – because Argentina in the seventies was really hell. Remember, we had thirty thousand *desaparecidos*. People were coming back with the need to talk about what was hidden before.

But also in the eighties a new generation started going to film schools, for it was a free country again. And finally in the nineties we came of age, we came out of the film schools, we had a different approach, a different perspective. I didn't want to make the sort of films that were made at the time. I was comparing world film history with our film history. And as a first step, I wanted to work in the spaces between what I saw and what I would like to see as a spectator.

*So it was a conscious decision not to make political films or, let's say, films with overtly political subjects?*

From my point of view, films have the chance to change things, by offering a place, room where you can think. But as film-

---

*Los desaparecidos*, the disappeared, is the term used for those people – sometimes activists, just as often not – abducted by repressive state forces across the continent. Many were held in clandestine torture centres, before being killed. In Argentina thirty thousand people disappeared, a number thrown alive out of airplanes over the Atlantic. The newborn children of mothers who were disappeared were given to families who supported the government.

makers you don't have the power to push people to think what you want them to think. I believe the kind of militant films we had in the seventies did not help, because the message became the style. But the style must be in terms of cinema: the political ideas will be always there, because you are already doing a political job, which is making films.

*You do think it's a political job?*

Absolutely, because you are giving people your point of view about life, even when you are making comedies. I feel that as a director you have a role in society, you are not just working for a living, you are an agent in this strange chain of society. I assumed that position from before I went to film school. However, if you have already chosen a political job, for me it makes no sense to do a 'political film'. And at that moment, in the early nineties, my generation had a chance to consider what had been made in the past – the political films, the commercial films, the avant-garde of the sixties – and decide what we wanted to do in the future. Some people say that New Argentine Cinema came from heaven – like *boom*, suddenly – but it was a consequence of all this very long history.

*Let's talk about your first feature,* Mundo grúa.

Actually, *Familia rodante* should have been my first film. It was my first feature screenplay. But when I was twenty-four, twenty-five years old I went through the normal channels for production – the producers, INCAA – and they all said, 'What is this? It's a story about a family on the road. OK, but are you sure? You know this film is really big.' 'No, it's a small film, some people travelling around, fourteen hundred kilometres, it's nothing really.' But these people looked at me as if to say, this guy is really crazy. I had to accept that I couldn't make that film at that time.

So I started to think about a new film to do. It was important to me to be *a director with his own film*, not just a guy trying to do any film. So what could be done with what I had at that moment? I had no money, nothing. But I had made a short film, when I was a student, called *Negocios*, which I thought could be the start of something.

*Negocios* was a story about my father's car supplies shop, outside Buenos Aires, where I come from. I had decided to make a film in this border between fiction and documentary. I used to see films, social histories about workers, ordinary people leading their lives, and I always thought, 'Life is not like that. People don't talk like that.' The fact that they are poor or normal people does not mean that they are stupid, or deserve to be made the subject of the fables of directors, of 'good-thinking' people. I decided when I made that short film to do a film about daily life, nothing about social causes, or big movements, just about people going to work. So I wrote a script about my father's shop, where the problem was that they had rats, which were eating the boxes. That was the main problem in the film, and it was the only excuse to talk about that world.

And in that film all my family were performing. Not because I did not have the chance to ask actors to play those characters – if you are a film student in Buenos Aires you can ask the big actors from TV to work with you, it's not impossible – but because all the actors I knew came from the same kind of social class. In a short film you don't have the money to put the actors through the training that will transform them, that will train them in the way of speaking of the working class. And with *Negocios* I wanted to present these people on an equal level with you, the spectator, and with me as the director. I did not want to be analysing them, or patronising them, doing them the favour of putting them on the big screen.

So I decided to do this film with non-actors. When I made that film I was thinking about this idea of turning the reality of my family and friends into a fiction. Things could appear natural, real, but it's not that, exactly, it's fiction. So you have to follow fiction rules and not documentary rules. I made this short in

1994–5 and I realised that I really liked this direction. Not because of the social environment on the screen, but because of the theoretical direction I was taking, this dialogue between what is on the street and what is on the screen.

*This is not far removed from neo-realism. Do you agree?*

Yes. It absolutely connects with neo-realism. But a difference is that neo-realism was clearly part of a social movement in Italy. Rossellini and all those were saying, 'What can we do about this political situation? We need to talk about this.' It was a particular moment.

*I must say* Negocios *plays like a very sincere, unpretentious view of a small community. A real slice of life. But tell me, were the rats a real problem, or invention?*

An invention. The short is telling the story about a shop that is, in real life, going nowhere and will close soon. In fact, it closed soon after. In a way the rats symbolise that fate.

So, when *Familia rodante* went into the – how do you say? – bottom drawer, I decided to go back to *Negocios*. *Mundo grúa* was a kind of second part of the short film. My father was the real owner of the shop, but his employee in the film, Rulo, was actually a close friend of his, and a client of the shop for some thirty-five years, a car mechanic, Luis Margani. And Luis, as Rulo, is the main character in *Mundo grúa*.

I discovered him because I felt that he was really *histriónico*, which means that he is somebody who has the condition, in him, to act. The one in the party who is always telling jokes, and is the centre of attention. *That* guy. I asked him to play the employee because I felt that he was the best equipped to compose the character. Then I made the next chapter of Rulo's life, after the shop is closed, when he must look for a new job. And that takes him to the construction site, in order to get that crane-operator job. It was like a new chapter of *Negocios*, with

Luis playing the main character and my grandmother still playing Rulo's mother.

'I liked the idea of someone with no future operating this
symbol of progress.' *Crane World*

*The title is incredibly apt. For the first part of the film we're constantly on the building site. On a literal level, you have totally captured that work environment.*

From my apartment in Buenos Aires I was looking at one of those sites, which are so busy with construction that they seem to be building as many cranes as buildings – cranes are building cranes. The whole area becomes a mess, dominated by cranes. That was the starting point. Before film school I studied architecture, just for one year. I loved the construction environment. So I decided to make a film about this guy trying to find work in this world. The crane is also a symbol of progress: any time you see cranes, something is happening. And I liked the idea of someone with no future operating this symbol of progress. I started to realise that I loved that environment and the metaphor. And I was really sure that in terms of image it would be interesting.

*At that point the country's own future was very uncertain.*

Yes, of course. And Rulo's experience reflects that. He does not have an easy time at all. Here is somebody in his fifties, who is starting life again like a teenager.

   After I wrote it, I asked some friends for help, and we started to shoot the film at weekends, because that was the only time we had after working in our 'real life'. At that time I had finished film school and was teaching in the same school, FUC, and I was working as an editor, for commercials, clips, whatever. So with the money I earned from those jobs I started to film *Mundo grúa*. And with the first images, I started to put together a work in progress and I sent this everywhere. Finally I got the money from different places, and after a year and a half I could finish the film – as I told you, some hours before BAFICI.

*Why did you give Rulo this back story as a former musician?*

First, it's because I thought that he was not a worker as such, certainly not a construction worker. And we were talking about somebody who at an early age had looked after himself. What is important is that he has had this bright moment in the past, you know, not really successful, but his fifteen minutes of fame. It was important to have this contrast between what he is trying to do and where's he's coming from.

   But you know what, in real life Luis Margani was also a rock-and-roll bass player. The bar in the film is the real bar he played at when he was younger. When I was making *Negocios* and discovered Luis was a musician, it was shocking. 'You were a rock-and-roll musician? What are you doing here?' He just said, 'Things change.'

*Was everyone else in the film a non-professional actor?*

No, although at the time many people thought that. But, for example, Adriana Aizemberg, who plays Rulo's girlfriend, is an actress – maybe you have seen her in Burman's films – who was in a very famous TV programme at the time. Different actors were professional, but not famous, and after that film you could see them in *La ciénaga*, *Un oso rojo*, you could follow them. But some of the workers, especially when the story moves to the south, were normal people from the area.

*What's the benefit of combining the two?*

For the professional actors, it helps them to step out of the structure of acting, the technique, the habits, and it helps them to be less heavy. With the unprofessional actors, you have people with no idea about technique, but some ability to create moments: if they don't have someone to organise them, most of the time those actors are going nowhere.

So for a professional actor it's a way to be not safe on the set, to be uncomfortable, and for the non-professional it's the opposite, it's having someone in front of them who can conduct them, to remind them of the line, remind them of the mood of the scene, and the objective of the scene. What you get from this mix is good actors performing with no tricks or shortcuts, and non-professionals with a fresh and organic way of playing.

*What you, or Carlos Sorín or any of your colleagues who like to use non-professionals, don't want is for the approach to be adopted as a fad by others, a device used for its own sake, which is the point* Estrellas *is making.*

Absolutely. For me, what is in front of the camera must be what is in my mind. I feel a little like Bresson does about actors: for me an actor is the one who's in front of the camera, it is as simple as that. But that does not mean that you are asking a non-professional to play themselves – if you are just registering who they are, it is not a film. You must direct that person and you, with them, must still create a character.

In the same way, you have to be true about the professional actors you cast. For example, in *El bonaerense* it makes no sense to cast a great Spanish actor as Zapa – that anonymous character, living in a sort of underground environment – just because it will help with selling the film after the release. That is also something else about New Argentine Cinema: it refuses the classical ways of production. The directors organise around what the film needs, rather than what the producers are offering you. 'OK, if you use an actor from France, you will have some French funding. If you use a sound designer from Germany, you can get some German money . . .' If you go down that path, your film becomes the consequence of this production parcel and is no longer true to itself.* A film is its own universe, so you have to find the conditions of production which help this universe to be authentic.

*Why did you decide to shoot in black and white?*

When I decided to do *Mundo grúa* I went to different construction sites to learn about the work. I wanted to make a kind of timeless piece, where you don't know if it's the seventies, eighties or nineties. So we made some videos, looking for images for the film, and we felt that colour would make it contemporary, and I did not want to do that. I wanted something in some place, some time, somewhere. So we shot in black and white, in Standard 16, giving to the negative more grain, more contrast, always looking for this kind of old-fashioned image. It was a nightmare for the

*It is often a condition of Spanish production companies, in particular, that investment be met with the casting of a Spanish actor, usually in the lead role; all the better for them to attract their own audience, but far from ideal for the Latin Americans. 'A Spanish actor destroys the essence of the movie,' says Chilean director Andrés Wood. 'In *Machuca* we got around it by using a Chilean who happened to have a Spanish passport. But now they are demanding an actor from Spanish soil.'

lab, because nobody was really working in black-and-white negative at that time.

*You talked of working in the border between fiction and docu-
mentary. It's quite common with directors in South America. Any
ideas why?*

One reason is that when you don't have the budget, or the conditions, to do genre films, or big films like *Harry Potter*, you
have to define your own style. There are producers making
commercial films here, but not as much, of course, as in
Hollywood. Maybe when you're making a film in Latin America
it's easier just to go outside onto the streets to film. In that sense
you inevitably investigate your history. Academically, formally,
for me this edge is interesting: it defines the films.

   You always have this conflict between the dream of making
films and the reality. Here in South America we are particularly
used to that conflict. In our daily life you have a dictatorship followed by a democracy, then another government, and another,
you have the currency up here, then down there; our reality is as
volatile as any fiction can be. That for us is also a reason why we
have good directors here, because they must be resourceful, and
they must be open to change. They must be very adaptable in
order to make their films.

*You said you made* Mundo grúa *on your own with your friends.
So you produced it yourself?*

What I'm saying is that it was with no INCAA help, no TV
producer, no money coming from those normal channels. I had
a company, with two friends from film school,* called
Cinematográfica Sargentina, which produced the film. It was
like a continuation of film school, a place where you could go to
hang out and work and think and be involved in a film environ-

---

*Ulises Rosell and Andrés Tambornino.

ment. At the time of *Mundo grúa* we were working from that place. And I was also living there.

We bought some editing equipment and started to think about doing our own films, but also helping or giving services to other films. Actually, we were co-producers of *Pizza, birra, faso*. Later, I formed Matanza, which aimed to focus more on production and not on these post-production services.

*Your second film,* El bonaerense, *seems much less personal.*

Actually, the starting point is very personal, because the setting is where I lived for the first twenty years of my life. I come from the Provincia Buenos Aires, which is on the outskirts of the city. You have the city of Buenos Aires, where the people are called *porteños*; then beyond Avenida General Paz you have the Provincia, where the people are called *bonaerense*. It is not a suburb, and it is not the interior of Argentina, the countryside, but it's not the main city either; it's somewhere in between. It's where all the people coming from the interior of Argentina are waiting, before they enter the city; and where all the people who have been unlucky in the city go on their way out. It is still a big political and economic area, but not a place that has a strong personality, or deep history, because the history is of people who are passing through.

*And were your family coming in, or going out?*

My family were coming in. They were from the interior. But they just stopped there. Of course it's full of life, but there is a tension there, between the city where there is more money, more opportunities, and the provinces.

Also, in Argentine film history, most of the films are about people from Buenos Aires, or about people in the countryside – Patagonia is often on screen, for example. But I couldn't remember a film about this periphery. So I was wondering about a film about somebody who is working inside Buenos Aires, but is living outside, travelling from one place to the other, but not really existing in either. When I started writing, it was a story based on my own history, travelling from the outside to attend the university – for a couple of years my life was like that, coming and going every day. Then I realised that that film would not be very exciting. But it was the seed to talk about that area, the Provincia Buenos Aires, to talk about the different way of life we have there, the different architecture, all the differences between being in the capital of Argentina and living in the periphery. Then I thought of the police. It's not just the people who are called *bonaerense*. It's also the name of the police of that area.

'Let's shoot the bank manager!' *El bonaerense* (2002)

*The result is a tough film, which touches on police corruption. It's interesting: we don't tend to think of New Argentine Cinema as being interested in genre, but this comes close to being a cop drama.*

The film is not really about the policemen, it's about a guy who is trying to build a life. In a way I'm working with a genre, but not really making a genre film. If you think about *Mundo grúa*, you could see it as social realism; *El bonaerense* could be a cop film; *Familia rodante* could be a family comedy. My new film *Leonera* will be a prison movie. But in every film I make I try to redefine what, for that film, could be the genre. And I am trying to find for each film its particularity, its special touch.

For me films are not a matter of new ideas, but language. We are always talking about the same histories, we are always talking about the same themes. The point is how to deal with all these things that we know, have heard, or seen, in order to create something else. As a spectator, as a cinephile, I am always thinking, 'OK, what's next?' Of course, when you go to the video store, your film is always defined by genre. When *El bonaerense* was released in Europe it was described as a cop film.

With regards to the police corruption, it could have been stronger. At that moment – we were shooting during the economic crash in 2001 – the police were at the centre of the storm. All kinds of amazing stories about real policemen were coming to light; there was a lot of controversy. We just touched the surface.

But it's not a history about the institution, it's a focus on this guy and his daily life, his relationship with his past, his ghosts, his loneliness. What I like the most in that film is that at the beginning you feel sorry for Zapa, coming from the countryside, an innocent. But he's not like that; he's a dangerous person, he's the kind of person I'm afraid of in life, always giving the impression that they are suffering, but actually being self-indulgent. He is always saying, 'What can I do? I have to be friends with my corrupt police chief, this is my only way to survive . . .' And he never changes.

*You'd just had a big success with your first film, then suddenly the crash happens. Did it feel as if you'd made the breakthrough, only to have the opportunities taken away from you?*

277

It was quite strange, because after *Mundo grúa* the world was more or less open to me. I even had offers to go to Hollywood. I had the option to choose a different way of making films, with amazing budgets. It was like a kid's dream, like football, the one who has come from nowhere and is becoming a star. But I had made just one film, I did not have enough experience to expose myself to all that. I was just learning. I still feel as though I am a director who is learning; not learning in terms of technical stuff, but in terms of what it means to be a film-maker.

So when I decided to do *El bonaerense* it was a way to do a slightly bigger film in terms of budgeting, in terms of platform, recognition, but it was still something very close to me: not an autobiographical film – nobody from my family has anything to do with the police – but coming from my personal world, my birthplace.

But yes, the timing was a nightmare. We started to shoot in November. Then in December the crash happened. I was already with some of the crew in the countryside, where the Zapa character comes from – the DP, the actors, some production people, we were preparing the shoot there. And we were in front of the TV hearing our economic minister explaining what was going to happen in the next few days, which for us was something incomprehensible. Nobody understood what he was saying. So we had to decide at that moment what to do: do we stay, or do we go back home and get depressed about how bad our life was going to be? And we decided no, we had to start at least this part of the film, just in order to stay here, safe in our film-making bubble, and not in Buenos Aires, where everything was going down.

*Funnily enough, this period is really well predicted in Fabián Bielinsky's* Nine Queens *– when the banks closed and no one could withdraw their money. How did that affect you?*

The problem was that the money was in the bank and we'd lost the chance to take it all out. And you cannot make a film without money. So we asked the people who decided to stay with us, and all my friends and family, to hand over whatever money they could, in terms of cash. And I put it all in a box. And then I paid the money back via bank transfers – because you couldn't take the paper, but you could move it around. Every individual could take out 300 pesos, which was worth $300 at first, but soon 100. It was crazy, just terrible.

After that, the real crash happened, when the president resigned, and there was an amazing moment when all of us were thinking this was the end of Argentina, this is becoming a civil war. Of course at that moment I lost some people from the crew, because they were distraught; some of them left Argentina, it was really a mess. And we had to stop the shooting for a couple of months.

I had to think about how I was going to finish the film. I had three times less than the budget I started with. I started to call friends. Walter Salles helped me to talk with other producers, for example. Finally I started shooting again. This was two or three months later, in February.

Then on 1 March my first son was born, one month prematurely. The funny thing is that Martina, my wife, is my partner here in the company. She was the producer, so we had to stop the film again for two weeks, with two more weeks shooting still to do. I went home to be a father and started to edit my film with my baby on my lap. And in the middle of this we sent a rough cut to Cannes and we were invited to be in the festival. So it was an unbelievable story, coming from hell, with no idea about how the production could be finished, and in a couple more months we were in Cannes presenting the film.

I have a sort of blackout about that period. I can't remember exactly how we made that film. When I try to explain to my friends how I finished it, I can barely remember. It's hard to explain. You are just there, working and working.

*There's a similarity here with Brazil a few years earlier: just as you think the country is in a better place – dictatorship behind you, democracy in place – the ground is again taken from under you.*

Of course. And that began with this hell of neo-liberalism in the nineties, with Menem; maybe before, when democracy came back. But it was a powerful platform for all of us as film-makers. I was really trying to say something about what was happening. And not only me; even when it's not obvious in the stories, you are saying something.

Another point of view is very clear to me. When I was a kid I always heard that you had to decide on the traditional careers – doctor, lawyer, architect – if you wanted a future. But when you have experienced that crash, that economic instability, when you have such a crisis that nothing is clear, you realise that you might study to be a doctor but end up driving a taxi. So I think that situation made many young people feel, 'I might as well do something I love.' It encouraged them to just go for it – be a musician or a painter, an actor or a film-maker – because it was no riskier than following a traditional profession.

*Then you finally made* Familia rodante.

I wrote that script for my grandmother, because I liked the work she did in *Negocios*. At that time – and if you remember I wanted to make *Familia rodante* straight away – she was seventy-five. When I finally shot the film she was eighty-something! So the idea was that my grandmother would be the main actress and the screenplay would be based on family histories, real stories.

*But the family in the film is quite fractious.*

No, no. I was trying to convey something like memories, ambience, colours. We used to take holidays in motor homes. Actually, one of the caravans that passes by, in the film, is my father's caravan. We experienced that moment when my father

A family affair: *Rolling Family* (2004)

had to fix the car and the caravan on the roadside. So that sort of influence, things from my memories, allegorical maybe, but not autobiographical.

*You presumably didn't shoot in your father's camper van?*

No. We built a caravan, on a track, in order to have all of us – the crew, cameraman, the sound and the actors – all together moving in the same time and space. The vehicle was a moving set: those are real landscapes outside the window, not blue screen.

*I love the soundtrack. It feels very traditional.*

You can see in all my films there is not a main composer or musician writing a score for the film. In *Familia rodante* I used a number of performers. For example, you have [recordings of] Hugo Díaz, a legendary harmonica player coming from the tango, and the tango singer Carlos Gardel. Then we had León Gieco, a very well-known contemporary musician in Argentina, a bit like Bob Dylan, between folk and rock, and the kind of musician who is always involved in social issues. He made the *Familia rodante* song, in different versions over the same melody – Zamba, Chacarera, Chamamé – to create different moods throughout the film.

But I usually try to work with original songs, which I already know, and where I feel there would be a good match between the film and the original meaning of the music.

Born and Bred *seems like a departure.*

I made it, in a way, in layers. The main story, of course, is a drama about this dreamy family that descends into hell. But underneath that is a story about the *desaparecidos*, which is a part of our shared history in Argentina. The process of accepting that a loved one has disappeared, for those who survived, was a nightmare. And for me it's also a kind of western. This guy is fighting with his past; trying to build his life in the middle of nowhere, where no one knows where he's come from.

The film also came from my experience of being a father. I was crazy with worry over my son in the first month of his life. I would often wake in the night, in a panic, and go to check that he was OK. It made me think about what I would feel if one day my child wasn't there.

*Actually, there is this thread, of family, running through almost all your films.*

In fact, the original idea for *Leonera*, before I thought of making a film in a prison, was to make a film about motherhood; in particular that early stage of motherhood, from pregnancy until breastfeeding. Martina and myself have a kid, we share parenthood, and it was something we were talking about for a long time. *Rolling Family* is about a big, extended family. Then *Born and Bred* is about a father. And I was thinking that that film was missing the element of motherhood. I'm not saying there is a trilogy, but the three films could work, differently, at this level: first family, then fatherhood, now motherhood. That was part of the thinking.

Also, in *Born and Bred* the man has lost his family, in *Leonera* she is afraid of losing her child. In a way it's a kind of mirror, even in terms of structure: *Born and Bred* moves from happiness to hell, *Leonera* moves from hell to . . . somewhere else. We'll see!

*I know that you and Walter Salles share an optimistic view about South American cinema, from a collaborative point of view and in terms of a collective, marketable strength. But it seems that a main problem, still, is that one of actually seeing each other's films, in your own countries. Opening those distribution doors.*

Yeah. But if you have more people going to the cinema in Argentina to see, say, Brazilian films, or Bolivian films, and likewise in those countries, it won't be a problem for long. Maybe it's a utopia. Meanwhile, me and Andrés [Wood], who co-produced *Born and Bred*, people like us are still making films, and some of our films are shown in Brazil when five years ago that couldn't happen. And this is helping to build a language of films across the continent, to build up this idea of what it means to live in Latin America.

I feel we have a lot of things in common. Maybe the bloody history of Latin America: all our countries were built over blood, and through colonisation. At the same time, South America is more or less just leaving adolescence, and right now is starting to write that new part of its history. I trust that in that sense, of determining our identity, Latin America and Latin American cinema have something in reserve: something that is going to be more alive, more forceful in the future.

Pablo Trapero

# Maverick: Lisandro Alonso

Lisandro Alonso is the most maverick of the many mavericks of the New Argentine Cinema; not only because as a young man he started making films totally under his own steam, with his family's money and on his family's farm outside Buenos Aires, but because his style is so utterly uncompromising. Focusing on people who exist on the furthest margins of Argentine society, his chief fascination seems to be for the solitary psyche, his *modus operandi* a pronounced, realist minimalism that makes Europeans such as the Dardenne brothers and Bruno Dumont seem positively exuberant.

Born in Buenos Aires in 1975, he studied at the influential Universidad del Cine (FUC), where his fellow alumni included Pablo Trapero, on whose *Mundo grúa* he worked as a sound engineer. Trapero, along with Martín Rejtman, supported him on his own first feature, *La libertad* (*Freedom*, 2001), while Lucrecia Martel is among many other fervent admirers. And if, as he suggests below, the near absence of script material makes it difficult for Alonso to acquire seed funding from the Argentine film body, INCAA, the quality of his vision has earned him near constant support outside his country, notably from the Hubert Bals Fund associated with the Rotterdam Film Festival, which seems to have become a home from home.

Like all his films, *La libertad* opens with a bang – a loud crash of electronic music, a storm, the image of a man eating a strange-looking creature (which turns out to be an armadillo) in the lightning strokes across the darkness. It is a brilliantly thrilling introduction to someone's film career. Surprisingly, what follows is quite different, as the film immediately settles into an observational routine that not only never strives for the same drama again, but is often strikingly mundane.

This is a common pattern in Alonso's work, with the theatrical opening both a monumental tease and a device that achieves something quite cunning: it puts the audience on full alert. *La libertad* is, by its close, no more than the day in the life of a lumberjack: we watch this young man, Misael, cook, eat, wash, cut trees, deliver wood, sleep, cook, eat – with very little human exchange. But because of the film's dynamic and menacing opening, because we don't know its narrative parameters, we watch the entire time, responsive, appreciating that single day with the keen eyes and ears with which Alonso himself has recorded it. We are led, too, to accept the director's astute assertion that as dull or solitary as people's lives may seem from the outside, we have no idea what is going on inside their heads, of their inner life.

If the woodsman actually seems like a grounded soul, the protagonist of *Los muertos* (*The Dead*, 2004) is most unsettling. Alonso stacks our mood against him, anyway, with another striking prologue: this time a man walking, machete in hand, across a murder scene. The director then moves forward in time, to an open prison, where Argentino, the killer in question, is coming to the end of his term, a middle-aged man who wants nothing more than to return to his sister in their remote jungle home. Because of that opening, and the man's strange, faraway persona, we have no idea what he's going to do when he gets there.

While the threat of danger lends an unease to the tone of the film, its emphasis is not on melodrama but, like *La libertad*, on the observation of a man in total synchronicity with his environment: with Misael it was the forest, with Argentino the jungle riverways, through which he wends his way on an open canoe with the grace and concentration of a predator. When Argentino sees a goat on the shore, he changes direction in the boat, grabs the animal, cuts its throat, hauls it onto the vessel, where it bleeds to death, and continues on his way – in a matter of seconds, the nonchalant deed captured with equal nonchalance by the camera; when he sees a bees' nest, he dives in to help himself to honey, without a second's pause, while those watching can only think of the stings.

What is Alonso suggesting about these people so attuned to nature? With Misael, the impression is of a man, almost a technician, leading the life society has, for the moment, ascribed him; given another environment, he may well adapt. But for Argentino, and the sailor on shore leave in *Liverpool* (2008), there is something more disturbing beneath the self-contained exterior: an inability to interact, verging on sociopathic. 'Life has its pitfalls, eh?' suggests a fellow inmate to Argentino, to which he merely replies, 'That's the life of a man.'

Even though he uses non-actors, and ones with a close connection to the natural environments in which they are filmed (the lumberjack, Misael, was in fact working as exactly that, on the Alonso farm), Alonso's work could never be regarded as documentary. His admittedly scant dramatic interventions are, nonetheless, profound enough to destroy that view, while his camera also has too much of a life of its own – whether abandoning the protagonists to investigate another character, or a dog, or in *La libertad* leaving the sleeping Misael for its own creepy journey through the forest.

Alonso produces his own films, via his production company 4L, but has struck up numerous useful alliances, with the Dutch film producer Ilse Hughan among them. Though his brand of filmmaking is never going to bust out of the arthouse or the filmfestival circuit, it is one that desperately deserves to be seen.

Getting an interview with Alonso was as unusual an experience as, I imagine, meeting any one of his protagonists. After more than a year of unacknowledged emails, I arrived in Buenos Aires and hit the telephones, with a similar lack of success. Then I was tipped off that he would be attending a dinner party held by BAFICI. I went along, using a cigarette break outside the restaurant to finally say hello. He immediately recognised my name, put his hands in the air, and declared, 'I hate emails.' Later that evening he gave me an address way out in the suburbs of Buenos Aires. Two days later we sat in his office, smoking, until late into the evening. At the end of the interview I realised that he had not turned on the light. We had been talking in darkness.


*Buenos Aires, April 2007*

*Where are you from?*

From Buenos Aires, I was born here and studied here. But my father is from outside, La Pampa, in the centre of the country. He has a farm there, and also a little farm one hour from Buenos Aires. Since I was seven years old I used to go to that closer farm, every weekend. I grew up watching pigs and cows and horses and green all over the place. So I think my curiosity about these places was stronger than my curiosity about Buenos Aires. It's more interesting for me to try to discover what people outside Buenos Aires think about how they live and what they need.

After finishing high school I didn't know what to study, but I thought, 'OK, cinema, why not?' I didn't know anything about cinema. I don't know if I know anything about cinema now. At that moment my favourite film was *Dirty Harry* [Don Siegel, 1971]. Nowadays I have at least changed my taste a little. University was an interesting experience for me, because I learned about the history of films, from the Lumière brothers to Kurosawa, Welles, Fellini, Italian neo-realism, many things.


*Have any directors particularly influenced you?*

I really like some things from neo-realism. And I like Herzog a lot. Kurosawa. Nowadays Hou Hsiao-hsien from Taiwan, the first films from Bruno Dumont, *La Vie de Jésus* [1997] and *L'Humanité* [1999], Apichatpong Weerasethakul from Thailand.

*I would say there are similarities between you and Dumont.*

He has a way of taking ordinary people and putting them on screen. I can imagine he gives them the same directions.

*You studied at FUC. It seems to be the film school that everyone refers to around here.*

I think it is the best one. I was there from 1993 to 1996. At that moment it was the only university where you could study cinema with cameras, 35 mm cameras. They give you the opportunity to direct a short film, or to participate by doing the sound, or be in the camera team, whatever you wanted to do. I didn't direct a short myself, because they didn't like my script. I thank them for that, because soon after finishing the course I went back to the farm. And that's where I had the idea for *La libertad*.

*Did you not spend any time in the film industry after university?*

After finishing in the FUC, I did work a little bit in feature films for some of my friends. Many people were starting to make films – but just during weekends, for no pay, only sandwiches. I worked on *Mundo grúa* for Pablo Trapero, just for a couple of weeks as a sound assistant. I worked as a sound assistant on many, many short films, and some features. I also worked on Pablo's *El bonaerense*, for a week.

But it wasn't easy for me to get involved in the industry, so I went to La Pampa and started to work with my father – driving tractors, organising, anything. I worked there for two years. And there I met Misael, who is the lumberjack in *La libertad*. We made the movie on my father's farm.

*And is Misael actually a lumberjack?*

Yes. But now, because he has become a friend of the family and we changed, in some way, his economy, he's not cutting trees any more. Now he's with his family in another state. And he's from Chile; he is not Argentine.

Finding mystery in the mundane: *Freedom* (2001)

So I met him, and was talking with him – not about cinema, of course, just being friends. After eight months sitting there with him, talking, watching birds or whatever, I said, 'Would you like to make a movie with me?' He said, 'I don't know, what does that mean?' I said, 'OK, there will be eight people around you. You don't have to watch the camera. And don't express anything. It's that easy.'

*If you weren't working in the industry, and didn't have a daily contact with it, how did you get the funding and the equipment for a film in the countryside?*

I produced the film by myself. As you can imagine, the script was just five pages, so I didn't ask the INCAA for money. I couldn't go with five pages and say, 'Believe me, I'm going to be a film-maker, please trust me, give me some money.' So I asked my family to give me $30,000 to make the film. My father said, 'Well, OK, if you're happy. That's what you studied, so why not?'

So I got the money from my family and started to organise the production. It was ten people shooting for ten days. We shot just three and a half hours, not that much. But we did it in 35 mm, because I really like to do the best I can for the image and the sound; especially for this kind of film, where there isn't a lot of dialogue.

*And you could do that on $30,000?*

I did it. For that money I bought the film and rented the camera and some microphones. I didn't pay people. They were all friends from film school. But now they are professionals, and we continue making films together.

*You make the decision to direct* La libertad *sound incredibly casual. You met the guy, you said, 'Why don't we do this?' You didn't have a script to speak of. Yet at the same time it's a coherent, very structured piece of work.*

It's strange. I was working with my father, and I really didn't like the job that I was doing. I studied to make films, not to work on the farm; I was only there because I needed to make a living. In a way I saw in Misael how I felt in that moment of my life, with a job I didn't like, a little bit alone, you're young and you don't know what you are going to do in the future.

At that moment every film was made in Buenos Aires. And I was fed up with that. So I said, 'OK, let's go and see what happens with young people outside the capital.' I would observe Misael and let people see how he lives. Also, I thought that it was a simple film to begin with, a film that I could produce myself, a nice first step in trying to make the cinema that I wanted to make.

*Of course the title provokes a response. Why that, as opposed to 'A day in the life of a lumberjack'? Presumably you wanted to raise the question, What is freedom?*

I don't know what freedom is. I think it's about options. But I didn't see any options in Misael's life at that moment. So I was asking, 'What is freedom for you?' In a way, if you get involved with the film you will ask what freedom is for yourself. But you know, if I shot a film about myself, in the city, I could make a similar film. If you follow someone between the office, car, house, restaurant, I don't know how different that would be to Misael's experience.

*The film also evokes the age-old discussion about town and country – the cultured but pressured nature of city life, against the seeming liberation of rural life. I read Misael's life as a refreshingly free one.*

As you say, it's like that. At the same time, nature is rude. When you don't have gas, electricity, water, it's not easy. In *Los muertos*, that man, Argentino Vargas, has twenty-four kids. They drink dark water from the river. Nature is not that nice a place. I can read it in your way: as people from the cities we have an idealised view of nature, we don't think about the work and conditions. But nature is totally different from what many people think it is – 'freedom', green spaces and birds, where everything is fine. It's not that nice.

*You seem to invest your camera with a life, a curiosity of its own. There are scenes in all your films where you start on the protagonist, but then either the character moves out of the shot or the camera leaves him.*

Yeah, I like that. If you want, that's a way of us saying, 'This is cinematography,' there is an intention here, of the film-maker, or the cameraman. We are watching this person, but he is not the main subject; the environment, the forest, the river are also characters. The camera is independent from the main character. This also means that when I am showing him for four minutes, it's because I want to, because this is something I want you to see.

*By using a non-actor, essentially enacting a way of life that approximates to his day-to-day life, you are moving in that area between documentary and fiction. Are you interested in trying to blur that boundary?*

I never think about whether we are making a documentary or a fiction film. The bottom line for me, between fiction and documentary, is that if you showed this ashtray for three seconds, it's just an ashtray; but if you show it for thirty seconds, it's more than an ashtray – maybe I'm making you think 'OK, what is he trying to say?' It's in the editing. I always shoot long, three or four minutes, then I say, 'OK, do I cut it in the first minute, or the second?' Time dictates how you see the moment.

*You made* La libertad *pretty much on your own terms. How was it received?*

Once I showed the film no one cared about it, especially my family. They said, 'This is the worst film we've ever seen.' We finished the film in January 2000, I kept it on VHS and did nothing for almost a year. Then a delegate from the Cannes Film Festival came to Buenos Aires. So I went to INCAA and said, 'Maybe he will like the film.' INCAA said, 'Who are you?' I didn't have any recommendations. I just went with a VHS. For sure my film was the last one they wanted to show him. But they did, and he liked the film. In fact, it was the only film he liked.

After *La libertad* went to Cannes, in 'Un certain regard', INCAA were more friendly with me. They knew I had no money to finish the film, so they gave me the money to take the film to the lab, mix the sound, pay people. The final budget was $100,000. You know, without Cannes I definitely would not exist. If that man had not arrived in Buenos Aires, I would not be talking with you now, because INCAA doesn't like my films.

*How did you move onto your second film,* Los muertos?

The first thing was to try to find a place where I wanted to shoot. That's how it happened with *Los muertos* and then with *Fantasma* [2006] and now with *Liverpool.* I travel around. I see a place and I say, 'OK, why not here?'

I decided to shoot a film near to a jungle. First I went to Misiones, more to the north, but could not find what I was looking for. Then I found this place in Corrientes state, which has these little rivers going through the jungle. I started going there, observing people's lives, speaking a little with them, trying to get to people who are not easy to find, not easy to see. In Latin America everybody knows there are many people like this, living in very bad conditions, away from education, health, money, banks.

*Once you had settled on your location, you were looking for local people to inhabit the film?*

Yes, I was trying to find a character. I was in a boat one day and I saw some people on the shore and asked the boatman if I could meet them. He knew them, so he said sure, why not. Argentino and his family live on this little island, forty-five minutes up-river. I kept going back to this place, and Argentino was always there. I trusted him. We didn't speak much. If I'd asked him what he thought about the economic crisis and the banks, he would have said, 'I don't know. What is a bank? What crisis are you talking about?'

*Did you know what story you wanted to tell?*

A little bit. I just wrote fifteen, twenty pages. With *Los muertos* I wanted to ask, 'What is the difference for this kind of charac-

'The fact that you are still breathing doesn't mean anything.'
*The Dead* (2004)

ter, who lives in isolation anyway, between being in jail and out of jail? When a man who is in jail for thirty years for killing his brothers comes out, what will happen?'

I don't know how easy it is for these people who live isolated lives in this region to find a bed, health, food. So if they find it in prison, perhaps they don't need, especially, to be outside prison. That's my feeling, perhaps I'm wrong. I'm not talking about all of them, but the people I spoke with, especially people in their fifties, sixties. When we were shooting in the prison – it's a rural prison, as you can see, and not a very aggressive one – many people said that the only difference that exists between being inside and outside is how much alcohol you can drink.

These people are not dead – but, in a way, the fact that you are still breathing doesn't mean anything. It's the way that people and politics treat them. They are alive, but what is being alive? What is the meaning of freedom for them? Being alive means having education, food, a good hospital, that's being alive. I don't know if you read the title, as I do. Maybe you think *Los muertos* is about Argentino's brothers in the first scene. Maybe it's a little bit of that, but also I was trying to say that everybody in the film is a little bit dead.

*It's very striking that he doesn't seem to change at all, in his manner. There are two occasions when people ask him questions, and he just waves them away. There is no introspection.*

'Did you kill your brothers?' 'Well . . .'

*Yes. It's quite scary.*

That silence is scary. But how is he supposed to be? He has nothing to do outside prison. He wants to see his daughter. But once he arrives, she is not there. I don't know what is going to happen. Is he going to kill again? I don't know. It's another question. But the thing is, he has been locked up for thirty years and once he's back in his place, nothing has changed. The environment is the same. He is the same, he could kill, or not. The kids in the last scene are similar to the dead kids in the first scene.

*Do many people live in deprived conditions like this?*

The population of Argentina is thirty-eight million, and I think twenty million are poor people and do not have the choices of life.

*In both these films two things come across very strongly about the characters: they are very self-contained, able to spend days with their own company; and they are incredibly attuned to nature. Misael kills and prepares an armadillo for supper; Argentino knows how to steal honey from a bees' nest without getting stung, he kills the goat like it's second nature, he is comfortable on the water and in the jungle.*

296

I like to find people whose lives are different to the one I was born into. As you say, they know how to move in water, how to kill, how to find honey. They are isolated people, a little bit marginal, you don't know if they have decided or just want to be there, but they know how to live there. I really admire people who can live like that.

*Did you know how capable they were? For example, did you know Argentino would be able to kill the goat, or did that just happen by chance?*

Once I had spent some time with him, I knew what he was able to do. I did not see him kill an animal, but I was sure he knew how to do it. That scene was in the script. If he is going to see his daughter he does not want to go without food, because he knows what he will find there – a little house made of plastic, with no food. So when he saw an animal, he was to kill it.

Actually, did you notice that when he kills the goat he lifts it straight onto the boat, so that the boat is covered in blood? I asked him why he did that. And he said that otherwise people could see the blood in the water – and if they see blood, and they see you on the river, they will ask you if you killed their animal. He told me it's better just to put the animal and the blood in the boat, because otherwise you will have a problem.

I would ask him often what he thought about a scene: was it logical to do this, or that, where should we put the camera. Especially for the bee scene – because we were pretty nervous – and when we were shooting in the water, because it was difficult to organise the movement. It was interesting: when I'm there, I just see a tree, but he sees a tree that is good for fire; once he's in a boat it's like me walking in the street. But you know, when I brought him to Buenos Aires for the release of *Los muertos*, and then again to shoot *Fantasma*, he did not know how to move, how to walk in the city. You can see that in *Fantasma*. He never goes on a stair even.

*But in the jungle he moves a bit like an animal. In the last scene, when he follows the boy into the tent, he moves with the same speed and focus as when he saw the goat.*

You are not very optimistic.

*That moment creates such dread.*

My intention was to ask what was going to happen with that man and that boy and that house? What is their future? He has a machete, but I don't know why he killed his brothers. Of course, he doesn't know how to read and write. And in those places, if you have had nutrition problems when you're young, afterwards you cannot think so well. Then if you add alcohol . . . If there is a problem, people like this cannot talk as we can, or argue as we can. They don't say, 'Oh, what do you think about this?' Once they are totally drunk they will reach for their knives.

*Did you have any problems with him?*

No. He's a very noble person.

*When you began, did you have an idea of how you would work with him?*

As with Misael, I just explained to him: 'This is a video camera. Never look at this. And don't express anything.' I didn't say don't try to act, because they don't know how to act anyway. The thing is, I feel more comfortable working with these people, who don't even have a TV. So they don't know, are not aware, as we are. If I make a movie with you, you know what kind of people can go and see the movie, and what they might think about you and about your life, what people from cities will think about you. But they don't care, because they have never been to a cinema. The first time they go to a cinema is to watch themselves in a movie. So they don't have that problem of self-consciousness –

how shall I look, how shall I walk? If I go again to Corrientes and ask him if he wants to work now as a fisherman, he will say, 'OK, how much?' They are just working. It's just for money.

*What do you mean exactly by not expressing anything?*

I said that to myself, really: don't let them express anything. The thing is, if you put Misael in front of the camera and say, 'Eat something,' he is going to eat. He is not interpreting anything; he's just eating. That's the main problem with professional actors – they are thinking, 'Oh, I'm eating, but I'm *thinking*.' No, you're eating! TV is the same. There is a lot of over-expression. Life is not like that.

*For you, what is the chief benefit of using non-actors?*

The thing is, I'm not interested in conventional history. I'm interested in finding these people, who are almost outside history. I don't care about meeting actors. When I studied, the thing that excited me was the thought that if I had the power to find a camera and some money to make a movie, I could give that power to some people who nobody wants to see. So I think making films is my excuse for discovering these people.

I could make a film with an actor, but an actor is not what I'm looking for. And think how much time I would waste getting them to learn how to cut a tree, how to kill a goat.

*With such a foreign environment, how much did you plan your days?*

I only planned the first two scenes. Then we went wherever it took us.

*How many crew?*

With *Los muertos*, no more than fifteen. With these kinds of actors you can't put them in the middle of fifty people – make-up, costume people, the lighting – it's too much for them. Anyway, in this way I think it's a good adventure – you come down as fifteen from Buenos Aires and you connect and communicate with these local people. And that's why I prefer to go out of the capital. It's a film, but I get to learn a little bit more about my country.

*You mentioned bringing Argentino to Buenos Aires to make* Fantasma.

It was going to be a short film about this guy coming to Buenos Aires to see the release of *Los muertos* in a particular building – the Teatro San Martín. And the building is empty.

*So it's not a cinema?*

It's primarily a theatre, but it has a cinematheque. It's a strange place. For me the film was a way to speak about how hard it is to find films that I like a lot, especially because the solution to distribution is too commercial. Films from Dumont, Apichatpong are particular films, yes, but they never get a chance to connect with the audience because of poor distribution. It's very dangerous. When I have sons, they will not know anything about Rossellini. As an audience we must defend cinema. Cinema for me is not Hollywood movies all the time. You can feel something different with cinema; you can ask questions, perceive questions. So, for me, it's something other than Hollywood.

*How do you express that in* Fantasma?

By taking people from outside Buenos Aires and trying to connect them with a cultural building. But it doesn't happen, they don't connect. And in the film the kind of cinema I'm talking about doesn't exist, only as a phantom. In a way *Fantasma* is my kind of comedy. And for me it was like making a first film, a chance to experiment with sound and image.

*Was it released in Argentina?*

Yes, in the same cinema. But only about two thousand people saw it, no more than that. There is no distribution in Argentina for this kind of film. So if I am the producer, which I am, I don't want to spend the money on ten prints, because I will not receive it back from the box office. They are cheap films – once I finish them I don't have any more money for a big release, to do press, to let people know about them.

I think there exists an audience for this kind of film. The problem is that we don't know how to find them. The multiplexes don't want art-house films. And the people who go to multiplexes don't want to see them. That's why I decided not to release *Fantasma* in a multiplex. I prefer to release it in this theatre, which has a more open-minded audience. I prefer five very strong fans of my film than a million who forget the film tomorrow.

# Latin American iconoclast: Lucrecia Martel

With *La ciénaga* (*The Swamp*, 2001) and *La niña santa* (*The Holy Girl*, 2004), Lucrecia Martel established herself as the most distinctive director of the New Argentine Cinema of the late nineties and early 2000s. Indeed, if one were to piece together an informal vox pop, she might well come out as the director's director of the continent as a whole, the one most cited by peers: and the reason for that could well be that she produces work quite unlike any of them.

The strong neo-realist streak in South American cinema doesn't feature in Martel's films, not the ubiquitous use of non-actors or the conspicuous mining for material from this volatile continent's everyday life. Martel's is a deliciously unique form of film-making: sensuous and seductive, with richly textured soundtracks that add to her languid, ominous atmospheres, and narratives that are elusive, playful and mysterious. Moreover, the *mise en scène* is not the work of a fluffy stylist, but an iconoclast, whose observations on family, sexuality, religion and, particularly, Argentina's provincial bourgeoisie are both subversive and savage.

She was born in Salta, in 1966, one of seven brothers and sisters. Martel came to cinema slowly, driven – if her matter-of-fact account is to be believed – less by vocation than incremental urges: childhood home movies, a degree in communications, an animation course, some underperforming film studies; until the breakthrough came, as for a number of other key directors of the period, with the *Historias breves* script competition. Her subsequent short, *Rey muerto* (*Dead King*, 1995), is a terrific antidote to anyone opposed to the machismo of much Latin American culture. A modern-day western with a twist, its key figure is not a lone man entering town, but a woman leaving with her children – she turning the tables on the local heavy before they go. Martel's enthusiasm for the genre, the muscular, even Tarantino/ Rodriguez style direction, gave no clues as to what was to come.

The success of *Rey muerto* attracted attention, not least from that champion of New Argentine Cinema, Lita Stantic. Martel directed two television documentaries for the producer, and some children's TV, before her script for *La ciénaga* won a Sundance/ NHK Film-makers Award, and her feature career began.

As Martel explains in the interview below, her home town is profoundly conservative, a fact of which she deeply disapproves. One might deduce that her shooting all three of her features in Salta and its environs, including her latest, *La mujer sin cabeza* (*The Headless Woman*, 2008), represents admonishment, even some sort of revenge. Stantic, who produced both *La ciénaga* and *La niña santa*, observes:

What I find very interesting about Lucrecia is that she hates the middle classes that surrounded her during her teens. When she was a kid, she went to an extremely Catholic school, so was a bit isolated from the most sinister happenings of the dictatorship. She felt cheated by her parents, and by her social class, because she never really knew what was going on. That may be the engine that makes her create those characters, who are all quite sinister, especially in *La ciénaga*, which has more to do with her personal story, with the images of her adolescence.

Though some have suggested a Chekhovian character to *La ciénaga*, it's a narrow allusion, not least because Martel's dissec tion of dissolute provincials is harsher than Chekhov's, denying many of her characters even the dim self-awareness to have dreams. The opening scene is devastating: old, decrepit bodies dragging their chairs around a stagnant pool (the grating alone sending shivers down one's spine), before sinking under the weight of booze and humidity, oblivious when one of their number falls and cuts herself on wine glasses, leaving her to bleed into the concrete.

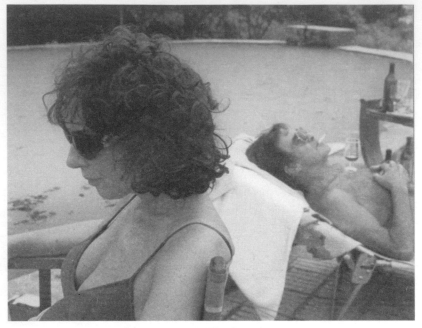

'Creepy inertia': *The Swamp* (2001)

From this moment of creepy inertia, the director builds a portrait of two families, linked by blood, but not class, during a sultry and ultimately tragic summer in the countryside of Salta province. With this film Martel introduces many of her traits and themes: the sense of unease elicited from the most mundane objects and sounds; the ability to direct children, her own family background no doubt influencing the recreation of the constant chaos of large clans; the off-putting regularity with which grown siblings (and in this film, a mother and her adult son) share beds, never quite confirming the suggestion of incest; the mockery of religion (a running TV news item involves the sighting of the Virgin on top of a water tank); and, of course, the condemnation of a class, with its emotional malaise and offensive distaste for its indigenous servants.

More than anything, what lingers are sense-memories – of overbearing nature, lassitude, the feeling that you could smell the booze in people's sweat, of unease.

Martel has said of *La ciénaga*, 'Rather than building up to a dramatic crescendo, the film proceeds through an accumulation of innocuous situations, which often lead to nothing but sometimes end fatally.' Arguably *La niña santa* has the reverse dynamic: of a series of potentially life-changing moments that could, if the characters are lucky, end without too much harm done.

The film, which was screened in competition at the Cannes Film Festival, is a sly, sensual and very mischievous account of a sixteen-year-old girl stumbling between the indoctrinations of her Catholic education and her burgeoning sexuality. Amalia (the enigmatically sullen-faced María Alche) lives with her mother Helena (Mercedes Morán) in a sprawling hotel-cum-health spa which is being overrun by a medical convention. While the girl is listening to a theremin player in the street, a man moves close behind and touches her. This is Dr Jano, one of the doctor delegates staying at the hotel. It's unclear to what extent the girl's subsequent pursuit of the middle-aged man is shaped by spiritual vocation – she says she wants to 'save' his soul – or teenage crush; the likelihood is that the girl herself doesn't know. Meanwhile, having sparked Amalia to life, the married medic is now flirting outrageously with her mother, the hotel and its popular thermal pool becoming the setting in which these ambiguous emotions heat up.

The atmosphere is again moist with family dysfunction and emotional lethargy. This time, though, there is more light to the tale. As a director, Martel's use of close-up (the girls' faces, often side by side in co-conspiracy, are extraordinary), editing and sound (the mix resonates with lapping water, catechism and the bizarre tunes played on the theremin) combine to create a mood of mystery and mischief. When Amalia whispers something in Dr Jano's ear, his response – hardly romantic – is to accidentally hit her in the eye. As a writer, Martel (who claims to get all her best lines from her mother) sprinkles the scenario with wonderfully pithy dialogue. When someone is crying, they are told, 'You're filling your eyes with microbes.' An old woman declares, 'We must have Turkish blood in the family – we all like smoking.'

*La mujer sin cabeza* also premiered in competition at Cannes. The film represents an interesting development for Martel, her first venture (other than *Dead King*) into anything remotely pertaining to genre. But while one can loosely call this a hit-and-run drama (has Veronica, a middle-class dentist, run down a boy or a dog? If a boy, is she going to be found out?), it is in fact the most overtly political film the director has made.

It features her customary concerns: the edgy co-existence between people of different classes and races, the moral weakness of the wealthy, the lack of conviction in family structures ('Has anyone in our family,' asks one character, 'ever died sane?'). But there is, too, a new theme in play. The disappearance of an Indian boy, and the closing of ranks around Verónica, represent a chilling indictment of the evasions of the dictatorship years of Martel's youth.

The craft remains extraordinary, from the composition of multiple planes of action to the blink and you'll miss it power of a child's handprint on a windscreen, from a richly textured and menacing soundtrack to the recollection of language that we all speak, but rarely note down. 'Float,' a woman tells a child as they enter a pool, 'and don't get wet.'

Yet the film did not fare well in Cannes, where pre-festival hopes that Martel would win the Palme d'Or were replaced by the sort of hostile reception only Cannes can afford. Perhaps the hothouse of a festival – with its demands for instant appraisal and gratification – was not the place for a film that evolves, gradually, in one's mind. For if Martel offers too little time to settle into the characters (the usual screenful of teeming relatives), before throwing us into the collision and Verónica's consequent mental disjunction, it's because she intends her heroine's state of mind to be shared. The result is a film that crawls under your skin and stays there, elusive and troubling.

When we met in the garden of her Cannes hotel, I found Martel chomping on a massive cigar and surprisingly upbeat. She also proved to be every bit the smart and engagingly uncommon individual one detects in the films, one who combines a deep moral sensibility with unabashed non-conformity.

*Cannes, 2008*

*You've had some extreme reactions.*

Have you seen *Le film français*? I'm the worst movie in Cannes. If this happened to me with my first film, *La niña santa*, I would be – not disappointed, but very sad. But now I think it's good, because it's a kind of Cannes tradition, to boo a film. Now I'm in the club.

*I thought the film was very strong, actually. And I found it incredibly troubling.*

I have many bad reactions, but when I hear the good ones, I have the feeling the film is perfect, because they are expressing precisely what I wanted to share with the audience.

*Which is what?*

A feeling like being in a dream, or a nightmare. It's a kind of mood during the screening of the film. They felt like they were floating; not very clear about what is happening, but at the same time enjoying this confusion.

*In your written statement on the film, you present the scenario as having arisen from conversations you have conducted, in which people speak of very violent dreams. In one, the person kills a man with a stick and hides his head on a kitchen shelf; in another, they find a black hand in their purse, which they presume belongs to the maid. Are you just being mischievous with us?*

The game is that I said it was the dreams of another person but, in fact, they are my own dreams. Nightmares, really. This is the only time – it doesn't happen very often, fortunately – that I

Lucrecia Martel

wake up crying. It's vicious. Many people have these dreams where they are chased by someone who wants to kill them, it's very common. But in my case, I am the chaser. And the killer.

*I know psychoanalysis is very common in Argentina. Do you go to a shrink?*

No, never.

*So how do you yourself interpret the dreams? Are you the pursuer because you feel guilt?*

I don't make a big effort to interpret them. But it's not guilt. It's suffering, it's pain. I always feel that I have a lucky life, which I do nothing to deserve. And I can see that there are many in my country born far less lucky, and they don't deserve that either. Of course, whether you are fortunate or not means nothing in terms of happiness. But it's easier to be happy if you can work, if you can eat, if you have a roof over your head. We should not accept this inequality. We have to do something about it. The problem is that we are educated not to have emotions on the subject. We are educated to recognise, but not feel.

*It's this complacence in society that is disturbing you so much?*

Exactly. There is no emotion. 'That's life.' I think it's the worst thing that can happen, this acceptance of this situation as natural. 'Poverty is a structure of the system.' These kinds of thoughts – to accept that the world is like this, reality is this, it's impossible to change – this is hell for me.

*In the film you use a well-worn device – of the hit-and-run, will she/won't she get away with it? – to examine this issue of a social divide and the middle-class lack of interest in it.*

It is in stages: the accident, the moment where her perception is broken, and the strange way she feels the following days; then a moment of confession; then how the family and the relatives move toward 'nothing happened'. It's like something makes you open your eyes and your reality becomes confused, then nothing happened, it falls back into place. For me it was very important to do this with very common, everyday moments. I'm not talking about criminals digging graves to hide the body. That's not necessary.

*At the beginning of the film she's lost her grounding to such an extent that she seems almost in a trance. One way you achieve this is by surrounding her with activity, hordes of family and servants, with whom she is unable to connect. And that confusion you spoke of: we too have very little idea who is who and what's going on.*

For me the idea was for the audience to be in her mind. I think she is seeing things anew. All this household is new.

*Almost like being reborn.*

Something like that.

*Can you say something about filling the frame with all these people.*

There are two elements. One is her social class moving around her, pushing her, very tenderly, with a lot of love, saying, 'It's OK, it's OK.' The other is the servants, all these people doing things for her: cooking, calling taxis, helping with everything. And through Verónica's state of mind we see that it's not natural for these tender, good people to have all these servants. I felt the best way to show this was to have them all surrounding her, like insects. It's not a comment on society, in the sense that I don't show a clear conflict. My purpose is to share with the audience a perception of reality, my point of view.

*And you do this by throwing Veró's point of view out of kilter.*

This accident, the possibility that there is a dead body out there, allowed me to shock her perception.

*As always, you've spent a lot of time on the soundtrack; by which I mean ambient sound – strange electrical noises, noises in nature, and also a cacophony of voices.*

The film is made up of different strata, all with the aim of reflecting the physical experience and the emotion of this person who seems to be floating through her life. I equate the experience of sound with being immersed in a swimming pool. When you are in a swimming pool you are surrounded by water and you can feel it because its presence has an impact on your breathing. You cannot ignore that you are under water. Sound makes you feel this sensation, in a way, of being immersed in air. And you know, it's exactly the same thing, because air is an elastic thing, and water is an elastic thing; water touches all your body, and sound touches all your body. Sound is the vibration of air. The only thing that physically touches you in the cinema is sound. You close your eyes and you will not see the movie, but sound still touches you, your body, all around.

*With Veró's sense of dislocation, or alienation, every sound seems to impact on her very strongly.*

Yes, the crash and this horrible situation she is in, this shock has opened her to all these things. In the beginning the soundtrack is more full of sounds, and then it's less and less, as she steps back into reality.

I never use incidental music. And it's double or triple the amount of work if you don't want to use music. That's why I'm exhausted. I finished the soundtrack two weeks ago. Music, like the plot and like language, always allows the viewer to anticipate and even prejudge what's next. Sound only allows the simultaneity of the experience. That's very important when you're trying to share emotions. Also sound – that is, a soundtrack with no music – allows much more uncertainty. I find that fascinating.

*Though you do have that wonderful instrument, the theremin, in* La niña santa.

It will always be something that's playing in the context of the scene, like a radio, a TV. In that case, someone is playing. What I like about the theremin is that its sound is very humorous and, for my generation, is closely associated with B-movies.

*Of course, a lot of these voices in the background are of the servants.*

Society is always divided into class and, besides that, there is a coincidence of races in different social classes. So most servants are indigenous. Still. And most of the middle class in Argentina are European, the descendants of immigrants.

*This point is also unavoidable, visually, in that everyone who helps Vero outside of her family, this whole support structure, is physically so different – darker, smaller. It's the same in* La ciénaga.

But you know what, this is the power of cinema. Because if you go to Salta, my city, you immediately get used to this situation. So cinema reminds you that it should not be 'normal': when you see something again on screen which is very familiar, you question it. I'm completely sure this is the strongest movie I've made about my city. By the way, this hit and run, of the local Indians, is common in Salta. There is a deep sense of 'Who cares?' To the whites, the life of the poor doesn't matter.

Salta is an extremely conservative city. In fact, the north of Argentina has all the more conservative cities. We have less European immigration from the nineteenth century, so the culture is very strongly linked with Spanish colonialism and this idea of society. There are more Indians in the south, there was not so much killing. In the north we have this clear idea that they are the servants, we are the owners of the land, the owners of rights, the owners of everything.

*So you don't much like the place.*

No, I love it. That's why I'm very concerned about it.

*What do you love about it?*

The food! My family is there. I very much like the way we speak, I love the singing in our language.

*Your films are powerful indictments of the bourgeoisie in this place.*

This is the class I belong to. And I think this is what bothers me most. I'm not saying that on the other side all the people are good. I think there is a danger of romanticising: poor–good, rich–bad. But I prefer to be among and to observe the middle class. Because it's my life. It's me.

*So it's complicated, for you?*

People that I love are like this. But we have to look again at the reality around us, because things are not good. I'm not trying to attack them. Just wake them up.

*What would you say is the relationship between the three films: this,* La ciénaga *and* La niña santa?

For me the deep emotional link between them is this idea that the 'reality' we live in is not natural – the meaning of relationships, the emotions, the desire, the economics, everything. We made it, we can change it.

*You say that, but Verónica has an opportunity to change things, yet doesn't take it.*

But you know, this sadness at the end of the film, because she doesn't, this disappointment in her, might make you as an audience change; at least, change your point of view.

*It's quite scary the way the family fixes things, draws ranks around her.*

They are trying to protect one of their own. But I'm completely against family. And you know, I am very happy with my family. I had the happiest childhood you can imagine. But I think the family is the beginning of corruption, because there is this idea in the family that happiness, goodness, is 'for us' only. There is a sense of exclusion. You are family, within these little walls, you are linked by possessions, inheritance, law and blood. We are together, the others are the enemy.

I don't find it a very positive institution, although I know it is very extreme what I'm saying. People say that the reason we have a moral crisis is that the family doesn't work any more. All my hope is in the dysfunctional family.

*Are you religious?*

I think I am. Without God.

*Catholic without God.*

Exactly. I had a fairly traditional Catholic education, from which I later distanced myself. From the age of eighteen until now, I've been developing my own theory of perception of the world.

*In society, family and religion are the two most important structural devices – the things that supposedly prop us all up. Families get short shrift in all three of your films; Catholicism is satirised, to a degree, in* La niña santa. *Do you anywhere propose an alternative?*

No. It's a worry. I really would like to, I do think we must be connected in some way, in some kind of community. But I don't have an alternative yet. Actually, maybe there is a proposal, in some of the relationships. In *La ciénaga*, between the two girls, which is a forbidden relationship in many ways, because they are girls, because they are from different classes, because one is a servant, the other the employer; also the relationship between the brothers in that film. For me, in a way, the softness, the ambiguity of these relationships could represent a little hope that things could be whatever we want them to be.

*The fact of young people not caring about conformity, doing what they wish to do.*

Yes. And because there are strong links between people who are divided by law, by prejudice. Also in *La niña santa*, the connection between the man and the girl, Dr Jano and Amalia, is a positive one, despite the situation. When she says, 'You are a good man,' I think this is the beginning of something.

*You've hinted at an intriguing aspect of, if you like, your alternative family, which is slightly incestuous.*

I think that desire is the only thing that cannot wait for the law, cannot accept the law, cannot accept family relations. Desire is something that moves as it must. I'm not talking about abuse. But this idea of consensual desire is something that overwhelms everything. This is something beautiful that we should pay attention to.

*In* The Headless Woman, *Veró's cousin's daughter expresses an attraction to her. She has that great line, 'Love letters are supposed to be answered, or returned.' So you're doing it again.*

Yes. And I like this very much. Also, when I write the characters, I never think of the psychology, because I know nothing about psychology. I prefer to think of the characters as children who are pretending to be adults. Whenever I see an adult, all I see is a child trying to be an adult. Here in Cannes, it's incredible.

*So much action, in all three films, takes place in or on beds; I don't mean sex, but just lying around, conversations. This adds to the mood of languor, but in some cases, also, of unspoken incestuous desire.*

I don't know how it is in other countries, but in Argentina the bed is a perfect place to have a conversation. It's comfortable. For example, in my family it's very common to say, 'Come to my bedroom, I want to talk to you.' Maybe in the siesta, maybe not. And you lie there with your relatives and you talk, and it's a comfortable talk.

*You've suggested elsewhere that you would have liked to be a doctor.*

I'm very attracted by medicine. I like very much medical instruments. Many people link this with some torture thing, some horrible fixation for blood. For me it's about a completely different thing, which is this idea of fixing things, and particularly the presumptuous, omnipotent desire of human beings to fix something as mysterious as the body. I'm fascinated by this. I have in my house a dentist's chair. And the thing that looks like a tree, which holds all the instruments. It's in my living room. And I think it's the most beautiful thing.

*Where did you find it?*

It's very weird. When I was studying in Buenos Aires, I had a small, single bed. Like all students. And I decided it was time to have a big bed. So I went to a second-hand furniture store to find my first big bed. That was a little like wanting to be an adult, actually. So I asked the man where the matrimonial beds were. And I was walking in this direction and I saw this beautiful thing, this tree full of instruments and the chair. And I asked how much it cost. It was the same price as I was going to spend on the bed. So I had to choose.

*So you continued to sleep in a single bed?*

Yes, for some months.

*But you've never fixed your friends' teeth?*

No, no. But I like to have it around.

*I think of David Cronenberg when you tell that story.* Dead Ringers, *for example.*

My sister once said to me, 'Think how many people have suffered in this chair, and you have it in your home!' But I have never suffered at the dentist's, so I have never linked it to pain.

*You never studied to be a doctor?*

No. I read a lot. I always buy books about medicine, neurology. But for me, all these technical aspects of cinema – the camera, the lighting, all the electrical equipment – it's like a way of playing doctor. The camera is like a microscope. Behind it I feel as though I am examining my characters. Except that I have the very strong feeling that the closer I get, the less I know them, the faces become more and more mysterious. It's because you are getting closer to the actor, and you don't know them.

*So the further the camera is, the more you see the performance, and the closer you get . . .*

. . . the more you see the human being. Yes. And I really like that mystery.

Filling the frame: Lucrecia Martel's *The Headless Woman* (2008)

*Is your use of Cinemascope, which affords marvellous close-ups, in some way related to this?*

Yes. I decided to adopt this format because it's ideal for getting close to the body, and to the face. Also, of course, it gives you a lot of space around the interwork with. You can put in many layers of activity.

*In* La niña santa, *of course, religion and medicine come under the same roof, in this strange hybrid of hotel and health spa that hosts the doctors' convention.*

It's true. For me, religion and religious aspects are closely linked to things medical. In religious literature there are many allusions

317

to the priest – or whoever administers religion – as a kind of doctor. The realm of the body and illness as a medical concern, and moral defects as a religious concern, are subjects that are, as a group of words, closely linked.

*One wonders if Amalia is in any way autobiographical.*

The character is based on my own experiences as a teenager. What interested me most was that power you can have being an adolescent, and also the vast mystery – life is full of secret plans. This is especially true of those girls who relate so personally to the divine. They're very powerful girls. Those were the reasons behind the creation of the character.

The 'vast mystery' of adolescence in *The Holy Girl* (2004)

*Did you always want to be a film-maker?*

No. And I'm not in love with cinema. I have this fascination with technical things because of my strange medical frustration. But, in a way, I think that cinema chose me. Maybe the first step was when I was a teenager, I used to make home videos. And in these home videos I learned about dialogue, especially the 'off-dialogue', away from the action. Many times I was just filming one of my brothers, with all my family talking in the background, and I loved this. I discovered this using the camera, I had never realised this before: as I put the camera on I understood that all around him was sound.

*Is that where you also developed an ear for dialogue? Your scripts are full of wonderful bons mots.*

It's very simple for me. My mother likes to talk. A lot. Sometimes I only have to spend two minutes with her. I would say ninety-five per cent of my dialogue comes from my mother. I have been getting this kind of shared dialogue from her for forty years.

*You first studied communications. Which means nothing, usually.*

Exactly. Semiotics, sociology, a real mix. In Argentina after the dictatorship, communications was a new career – young people who didn't know what they wanted to do went to communications. And I was one of those. So to my family it wasn't clear what I was studying. But then I took an animation workshop. This was the second step. For me it was a moment when I discovered many things, like movement, rhythm, because you have to work frame by frame.

After the animation course I went to a film school, which wasn't really working so well because of the economic crisis. But I met some guys and we worked on each other's shorts. Then I sent a script to a short-film contest, *Historias breves*. It was a way to try to find a place for myself in the world. So I made this short film in Salta, *Rey muerto*. And then what happened is that many people began to trust me in terms of cinema. So I thought, 'OK . . .'

*I think it's a fantastic short. If you see it, as I did, after your features, it's a real shock. It's like a young man's film.*

Yeah, I agree, because it's a genre film and genre is a male thing. But I love genre, and when I was a kid I loved westerns. I still do. For me *Rey muerto* is like a western, with a woman as a protagonist. So I created this inner conflict, if you like.

*You have what seems to be a rewarding relationship with the Almodóvars, who have produced your last two films. Could you make your films without European money?*

No. It's impossible. My budget for *Mujer sin cabeza* was €1.71 million. My movies are very expensive, for Argentina at least, and yet they are not commercial films. But until now I've been able to find the money, so I'm very happy.

*Always European money?*

Fonds Sud, from France. From Spain. Also from INCAA. For *La ciénaga* I had Japanese money, because I won this NHK award at Sundance.

*You've said in the past that you don't like relating your films directly to politics, and particularly the dictatorship.*

I don't want to say that publicly, for marketing reasons. No one wants to see a political film linked to the dictatorship. But they are deliberately linked. *Mujer* is like the other films: there is no precise period, it's confused, but I wanted to include some details to make you maybe connect with that time. You can see it in the clothes, the men's sideburns, the music on the radio – 'Oh Soley Soley', 'Oh Mummy Blu' – all from the seventies. And, at the same time, there is a relationship between the dead body that you never see and the *desaparecidos*.

*You would have been around sixteen when the* junta *gave up power. What are your memories of the dictatorship?*

I remember perceptions. The way various things were hidden

from you. It was very subtle. When I was nine, ten years old, sometimes I felt I was in a nightmare, but I didn't know exactly what was happening. There would be some strange news. For example, once we had a neighbour who was killed, and when the body was found he was wearing three or four shirts. Because he was changing his shirt to try to evade those who were trying to kill him – every time he moved from his house to another place, he changed his shirt.

I didn't know if this guy was a terrorist, or subversive, or belonged to the military, you only remember that he had all these shirts. This is the way you perceive the dictatorship if you are a child; and if you are not in a family that has to run away. You are at home, you are apparently safe, everything is normal, but suddenly someone is killed with four shirts on and you think, 'What is happening?' Or maybe a car appears parked in the street, with the radio on, for one day, two days, until the battery runs down. And you wonder why this car is parked with the radio running. And then a body is found in the boot. This is something that you cannot forget. This is something that you don't understand, if you are a kid, but at the same time you never forget it.

*And relating to what we said earlier, the way Veró's family pretends that nothing has happened has clear echoes of that period. Turning a blind eye was a way of surviving.*

Yes, of course. In *La ciénaga* there is also something like this. People in my films always act as though nothing bad is happening, there is a fakeness all the time. My films are completely political, but in this sense: to make a film, for me, is the desire to share this doubt about our reality.

For my generation, to participate in the history and the life of your city, as a citizen, is not that easy. In Argentina and everywhere, I think it's easier to be a consumer, who has only to try to live happily, in a comfortable house with a home theatre system. But many young people in the seventies felt they belonged to history, that they could at least try to change the world. That's something that we cannot understand. The ideology of the market has won.

So for me, to do cinema is a way to be a citizen. Because I'm speaking in public, I'm sharing with my contemporaries my concern about our lives – in my city, in my country, in the world. But first, in my city, in Salta. There is a phrase by Ovid: *Gutta cavat lapidem, non vi, sed saepe cadendo*. 'A drop hollows out the stone, not by force, but with frequent falling.' With films you can, you know . . . knock-knock.

# Quién soy?

In his short story 'The Life of Tadeo Isidoro Cruz', Borges made this characteristically elegant observation: 'Any life, no matter how long and complex it may be, is made up of a single moment, the moment in which a man finds out, once and for all, who he is.'

This instant, inevitable perhaps, but also elusive, is one of the principal themes of Argentine cinema, as it has always been of the country's literature. *Who am I?* Questions of identity posed by colonialism and immigration (as Lita Stantic bluntly puts it, 'We Porteños descended from the ships') have only been deepened or twisted by the dictatorship years – a time when families were destroyed, friendships and allegiances betrayed, and when a generation of children were orphaned, some even appropriated from the disappeared and passed on to other parents. To escape those years of repression, only to enter several more of economic hardship, maintained Argentines' sense of personal precariousness.

The directors that have emerged since the late nineties have addressed the subject of identity from a multitude of angles – personal, cultural, sociological, existential and medical. Sometimes their characters experience Borges' revelatory moment, sometimes not. The questioning, though, has been most intriguing.

Albertina Carri's *Los rubios* (*The Blondes*, 2003) is not only the best documentary I've seen on the disappeared, but one of the best documentaries I've ever seen, period. The primary reason for this is simple: unlike other pieces on the same subject, in which the existence of the film is merely incidental (at most, bearing witness) to an individual's desperate need for closure, or censure, Carri's film and the investigation of her parents' fate are one and the same thing. As her voice-over tells us: 'I have to think of something, something that will be a movie. All I have are vague memories, contaminated by so many versions. Whatever I do to get to the truth will probably take me further away.'

Ana María Caruso and Roberto Carri, political activists, were kidnapped and murdered in 1977. Albertina was one of three daughters (the blondes in question) who were left behind. Although she and her colleagues interview neighbours who witnessed the abduction, and return to the detention centre where her parents were held (now, sickeningly, a police station), the aim is not to apportion blame or even to ascertain the particulars of what happened. It is less an investigation, in fact, than a two-part reflection: on the way that the significance of such momentous acts, almost the acts themselves, can be eradicated by selective memory; and on the difficulties of being orphaned in such circumstances. 'Establishing your identity without those who gave you life can be disheartening,' she tells us. It can't help when mention of your name – usually the helpful self-identification tool in societal exchanges – signals first danger and rejection, and later confusion and pity.

Carri represents her sense of dislocation in the way she makes the film: notably by using toys (the popular 'Clicks de Famobil') to reproduce both the 'happy family' scenarios she never got to experience, and a chilling 'alien abduction' scene; and by casting an actress to play 'Albertina Carri' for the cameras. As part of her role, this alter ego (Analía Couceyro) conducts the on-screen interviews, the interviewees quite unaware that the real Carri is actually behind one of the cameras. The director herself is also filmed, by a second camera, so that the audience views Carri filming 'Carri', politely listening to the people who did nothing while her parents were taken. Loaded with pathos, this is a dazzling construct with which Borges, I'm sure, would have been very impressed.

Director Albertina Carri

*The Blondes* is a surprisingly playful film, in fact, which moves away from the earnestness with which the disappeared are usually presented. The emotional resonances of such a work are difficult to fathom if one is not from the same community. 'There were many responses, and most of them were empathetic towards the film,' reports the director, who has also made a number of increasingly accomplished features.

The strange thing about *Los rubios* is its irreverent tone. But rather than being condemned, this is what the audience in Argentina liked the most, not only those who have missing relatives but also those who don't.

I have a group of friends with whom I play a game, by which we rate our family histories based on the grade of tragedy in them. For example, if you've lost a father, your rating is much lower than if you lost a mother. My story's rating is quite high because both my father and mother are missing. But some people have lost not only their parents, but also their brothers and sisters and their uncles and aunts, etc. . . . It sounds harsh. But humour is therapeutic, it strips away the solemnity of death, the pain of living in a society without justice.

A very different kind of dilemma is expressed by the polished, comically neurosis-fuelled comedies of writer/director Daniel Burman. 'Your ancestors are Spaniards and mine are Polish. We're the typical Argentine Judeo-Christian married couple,' declares one of Burman's characters to his wife. With lines like this, spoken with the glumly sardonic delivery that is the speciality of the director's screen alter ego Daniel Hendler, it's no wonder that Burman has often been compared to Woody Allen; though, as he has said in relation to a limited allusion, Allen's characters 'live in apartments that cost at least $2 million and their fridges are always full'.

Even with a paltry parlour, his approach has proved successful. Burman is one of Argentina's most important directors, someone who enjoys both critical approval and solid box-office appeal. At the heart of a prolific output (six features, while still in his thirties) is a loose trilogy of films dealing with the search for identity, explored, as Burman elaborates, 'through the particular case of Argentine Jews, who have a very old culture surviving within an adolescent society that is still in formation', and allied to the complexities of the father–son relationship.

*Esperando al mesías* (*Waiting for the Messiah*, 2000) charts a young man's drift away from his Jewish community, including father and girlfriend, as he tries to recreate himself with a new, hip, bourgeois and Christian lover; *El abrazo partido* (*Lost Embrace*, 2004) features a full-blooded attempt to abandon community and country, before an absent father's return from Israel complicates matters; *Derecho de familia* (*Family Law*, 2006) features father and son lawyers, Perelman and Perelman, the senior a pillar of the community, the junior unable to establish his own sense of self in his father's shadow.

Of all these films, *Lost Embrace* (which won the Silver Bear and best actor prizes in Berlin) is perhaps the most incisive statement of a young man's frustration with his environment. Ariel helps his mother in a lingerie store in a multicultural shopping mall in Once (one of Buenos Aires' more bustling districts, and the biggest Jewish community in Latin America). This is not a mall in the American sense, but a small, down-at-heel emporium whose shopkeepers are feeling the pinch of recession. A malcontent feeling like a 'tourist' among people he has known all his life, Ariel is keenly plotting his escape, to Europe; moreover, he wants to leave with a European passport.

Father–son relationship: Daniel Burman's *Lost Embrace*

Ironically, while Ariel seeks his Polish grandmother's documents, so that he can apply for Polish citizenship, the old woman, a Holocaust survivor, wants to destroy them: a feckless young man coveting an identity that the older woman feels, with bitter experience, has been sullied. At the same time, throughout the film Ariel wallows in the image he has developed of his father, as an errant parent who deserted his family for ideology (to fight in the Yom Kippur war). When a very different man returns to Once, Ariel realises that his sense of alienation from his community was due merely to a missing piece of the puzzle. Up to this point, Burman's edgy, handheld camera has been constantly on the move, just like his hero, pacing the streets of Buenos Aires or the empty corridors of the mall, in search of no one or nothing in particular, other than himself.

Rediscovering a lost sense of self: Celina Murga's *Ana and the Others*

Incidentally, though Burman is a contrary fellow who rejects all connection between his work and Argentina's economic crisis, in *Waiting for the Messiah* he has provided one of the most potent symbols of the effect of the recession on personal identity. The character Santamaría is a banker who loses everything and ends up a tramp on the streets, where he makes a living by searching bins for the identity cards discarded after thefts and returning them to their owners for a fee. Ironically, if Santamaría were to discover the ID of Sylvia Prieto, the eponymous heroine of Martín Rejtman's film, she would pay him to keep it.

There are more baroque explorations of identity in Argentine cinema, two in particular from 2007: *El otro*, Ariel Rotter's existential drama in which a man in midlife crisis spends a lost weekend in a strange town, where he adopts the names of dead men in a half-hearted holiday from himself (the film won the same Berlin brace as *Lost Embrace*); and Lucía Puenzo's *XXY* (2007), a refreshingly atypical affair concerning a teenage hermaphrodite's growing pains as s/he combats pressure from her parents to decide on a gender. Puenzo is the daughter of Luis

Puenzo, director of *The Official Story*: her very modern thesis on self-determination makes a fascinating companion piece to his film about the stolen children of the disappeared, completely unaware of who they really are.

The cross-generational aspect of this predicament is underlined by Celina Murga's films. As the eponymous, twenty-something heroine of *Ana y los otros* (*Ana and the Others*, 2003) wanders her old haunts in search of a former flame, with an inscrutability not unlike the figure in *El otro*, she seems to be trying, also, to rediscover her lost sense of self. The children of Murga's second film, *Una semana solos* (*A Week Alone*, 2008), taking charge of their own lives in the comfortable confines of a gated community while their parents are away, do more than gamely run amok: they are inventing their own code of ethics, to the extent that they barely seem to be children at all.

One of the most popular Argentine films abroad of recent years features a search for personal identity by a man who, perhaps, doesn't even know he's looking, and a discovery that reverberates with the very essence of New Argentine Cinema. Carlos Sorín's *El perro* (*Bombón: El perro*, 2004) concerns Juan 'Coco' Villegas, an amiable, slightly vacant middle-aged chap who has spent his entire life working in a Patagonian service station. When it closes, he finds himself out of work, unemployable and in a fix. He drives around the countryside, trying to sell ornate knives, doing odd jobs, struggling, until someone gives him a mastiff, a beautiful brute of a dog, informing him that Bombón has the potential to be a successful show dog. The clueless Coco joins forces with an exuberant trainer, Walter Donado, and the unlikely trio – a Latin Laurel and Hardy with a sphinx-like hound on the back seat – hit the road for the dog-show circuit.

This odd, whimsical film is the sort that creates swathes of emotional resonance with the gentlest flick of the wrist. Sorín, who invariably casts non-actors, has found a couple of gems in Villegas and Donado (the pair not being troubled with having to remember different character names). He need do little more

It's a dog's life: Carlos Sorín's *El perro*

than point his camera at them to elicit humour, absurdity or, in the case of Villegas, the pathos of a man who has never had a direction in life, and is now forced to find one. In some respects 'Villegas' is a relation of Rulo, in Pablo Trapero's *Mundo grúa*, struggling with quiet dignity for a second chance in middle age. 'I haven't been doing well economically,' is the closest he will come to a complaint.

Sorín likes dogs. One plays a crucial role in his earlier film, *Historias mínimas*, its fate synonymous with an elderly character's loss of self-respect and eventual redemption. And here, within the context of the soul-destroying effect of unemployment, the suggestion is that Coco gradually wins back his self-esteem and purpose through Bombón. The director laughs:

In this relationship, the master is the dog. At the same time, I wanted a dog that didn't behave like a dog, but was mysterious. That's where the humour lies, that here is this unemployed guy of fifty years old, in our country that doesn't give second chances. And when he gets one, he is in the hands of a dog. And he doesn't have a clue what the dog is thinking.

Sorín calls his filming process 'chaotic', a condition created to some degree by the fact that he doesn't give his actors scripts, merely creating situations in which they must perform. With his large, brown, glazed-over eyes and almost dainty delivery, Villegas genuinely looks as though he is suffering with his character. But Sorín reveals at least one moment when Coco's visible, triumphal joy is shared by the actor: when Juan Villegas receives his first dog-show trophy.

In that moment I wanted the character to be truly happy. The person Juan Villegas had been working in the solitude of a parking lot, parking cars, for thirty years. And never in his life had he had a crowd of people cheering him. So I put four hundred extras around him, clapping enthusiastically, cheering. And then his emotion became real.

Could it be that as Coco discovers his true *métier*, something that makes him almost inexplicably happy, the real-life Juan Villegas also discovered himself, in front of the camera? Actor, character, man, merged in their own Borgesian moment of self-discovery.

# *Whisky* and wattage in Uruguay

'There is not much of a film industry in my country,' admits Uruguayan Manuel Nieto Zas, while counting the working directors in his head. 'There are ten. And between us we make one and a half films a year.'

It's always been like that in Uruguay. There have been whole decades in Argentina's diminutive neighbour when no films have been made at all. And although in the past the country has had a strong film-*going* tradition (apparently in 1959, when the country had less than its current three million population, nineteen million tickets were sold), a faltering economy has led to fewer people going to the cinema. Add to that the tiny size of the population, and the fact that there is just one city, and it is inevitable that the market for the few home-grown films that are made is small.

Yet, in keeping with the currently passionate, continent-wide desire to make films, this small community of Uruguayan filmmakers is making itself felt, both in the quality of the films they are making – including, in Juan Pablo Rebella and Pablo Stoll's *Whisky* (2004), one of the very best South American films of the past decade – and in the way individuals are connecting with fellow Latin film-makers.

In 1985 the country emerged from twelve years of military dictatorship, which earned it the unwholesome moniker of 'the torture chamber of Latin America'. During this time the primary activity of film production was in documentaries, with virtually no features made at all. Then in the nineties the government in Montevideo started to develop cultural programmes and, since 1995, there has been a national film fund, FONA. Grants are still absurdly small, but the period has also seen the founding of a national film school and the emergence of a predominantly young generation that has started to make feature films.

The comparatively seasoned César Charlone, the Uruguayan who made his name as a cinematographer in Brazil on *City of God* but recently returned to his country to direct his first film, makes an astute distinction.

In Uruguay this is not a *retomada*, a rebirth, as it was in Brazil. It's a birth. As it is a birth in Paraguay, as it is a birth in Ecuador.

I think it's part of a social movement, like the reverse mood after dictatorship. We had the very dark period of the dictatorship, when people were making short, political documentaries, but nobody thought of a feature film. Now film schools and film culture are more popular.

It's a birth that has been accompanied by a tragic loss. In July 2006 Juan Pablo Rebella committed suicide, aged just thirty-two. The film community in Montevideo being so small, his death affected everyone in it, personally and deeply (a year later Stoll, who felt he could not speak to me for this book, was still not thinking about directing movies). Until Rebella's death, however, the pair had been the leading lights of the country's film industry – the ones, arguably, who had put it on the map.

Both born in 1974, Rebella and Stoll met while studying social communications at the Universidad Católica in Montevideo. While there, and beginning to direct work on video, they saw a film by the Argentine director Raúl Perrone, *Labios de churrasco* (1994). 'We loved it,' recalled Rebella later. 'And we just said, "Wow, that's a movie about nothing."' They decided to start writing.

They made *25 Watts* (2001) for a mere $26,000, acquired partly from a local film fund, partly from private sponsors, with a rented 16 mm camera and a crew working for free: the electricians were the only ones, not excluding Rebella and Stoll, who were not, in the directors' own words, 'amateurs'. Still lacking money to finish the film, the Uruguayans discovered a benefactor that has been crucial for many Argentines – the Hubert Bals

Fund in Rotterdam, which helped finance the transfer to 35 mm. They borrowed a further $20,000 themselves – another bold move, considering Uruguay was embroiled in an economic crisis with a worrying resemblance to the one in Argentina – and completed their debut.

25 Watts is regarded as the first Uruguayan film to be made by, about and for the country's youth. Shot in black and white on the disconcertingly empty streets of Montevideo, it is akin to their inspiration, 'a movie about nothing'. The film follows a day in the listless lives of three slackers, unmotivated and aimless, undecided between study or work, obsessed by but not able to do anything particularly constructive with girls. These guys may be the closest to genuine losers that the slacker genre has ever offered. But while the title refers to the very low wattage of their ideas, the film itself buzzes with wit and invention, in both the script and the camera. And Daniel Hendler, a local boy who was soon to become a familiar face in Argentine cinema, makes his mark as the most charismatic of the anti-heroes, one with no compunction about using his elderly, barely cognisant grandmother as an aerial stand when his TV isn't working.

The directors also make a joke of the country's relative obscurity, as the characters mull over the only Uruguayan in the Guinness Book of Records – a man who clapped his hands for five days straight. 'What', they ask, 'was he applauding?'

Suddenly Rebella and Stoll were being applauded themselves. The film won a Tiger Award for best film in Rotterdam, as well as the best first feature-film prize at the New Latin American Film Festival in Havana. Then their script for Whisky won the coveted Sundance/NHK International Film-makers' Award (a cash prize, plus guaranteed purchase of the Japanese television rights), setting them on their way for their second film, which was co-produced by companies from Argentina, Germany and Spain.

While 25 Watts portrayed the wanton aimlessness of youth, Whisky (2004) looks at three people at the other end of the line. Jacobo is a sixty-something owner of a clunky and outdated

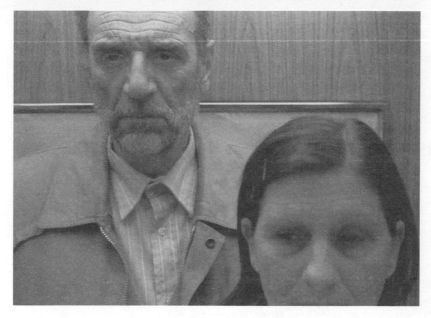

Say cheese: Rebella and Stoll's *Whisky* (2004)

sock factory, who with his loyal assistant Marta goes through each and every day with exactly the same monotonous, miserable routine; it's difficult to say who is the most taciturn in their daily exchanges. When his estranged, much more successful brother Herman visits from Brazil, Jacobo enlists Marta to move into his apartment and pose as his wife, so that his life doesn't look quite the failure that it is.

Their efforts to sustain the pretence, while Marta is drawn to the gregarious Herman, are shot through with the sort of absurdity and melancholy (and hilarity) that have already earned the directors comparison with that doyen of deadpan, Aki Kaurismäki. (It's not surprising, incidentally, that their Argentine co-producer is Hernán Musaluppi, of Rizoma Films, who also produced Martín Rejtman's *The Magic Gloves*. There is clearly a shared sensibility between the Buenos Aires-based producer and these directors either side of the border.)

With *Whisky* Rebella and Stoll, still not in their thirties at the time, showed a remarkable maturity in their storytelling, achieving with a frame or two an insight for which others would require pages of dialogue: the presence of an air compressor tells us all we need to know about Jacobo's limited life caring for his mother; the presentation of socks as greeting gifts (and holiday-resort T-shirts at parting) reveals the extent of the rapport between the brothers; close-ups of their faces – all pores, crows' feet and glumness – betray everything about their loneliness. (Interestingly, there were virtually no close-ups in 25 *Watts*, suggesting that there was, as yet, nothing of note written into those young faces.)

The directors are served admirably by their actors, Andrés Pazos, Jorge Bolani and, in particular, Mirella Pascual, whose expression barely changes throughout the film. The title, by the way, is both particular and ironic – 'whisky' being the Uruguayan equivalent of saying 'cheese' for the camera.

The pair shot the film in a brisk eight weeks, using many technicians with whom they had been friends for a decade. The hand-to-mouth experience of the production is summed up by the fate of their chief prop: one day during shooting in Montevideo, their assistant director (one Manuel Nieto Zas) sheepishly announced that Jacobo's car had been inadvertently sold to a junk yard.

At the time, Stoll raised and answered an obvious question about their choice of subject:

Why, after a youthful and autobiographical film like 25 *Watts*, did we produce a film about two sixty-year-old Jewish brothers, a woman and a stocking factory? Well, as we wrote the script, we started to realise that perhaps these characters were not so different from ourselves; that we were not so far away from these kinds of loneliness. They could be a projection of ourselves in twenty or thirty years' time.

There's an unavoidable and unfortunate resonance in this comment. Yet it also displays, as does the film, the remarkable thoughtfulness and empathy of these directors. It's to be hoped that Stoll will return behind the film camera. In the meantime, the company he founded with his co-director and their stalwart editor and producer Fernando Epstein, Control Z, is becoming the most dynamic production company in this small industry, building on its relationship with Argentine and European companies, handling its own distribution, nurturing new talent.

One of the films Control Z has produced, and another Tiger Award-winner at Rotterdam (that festival having the same liking for Uruguayan films as it does Argentine), is by Rebella and Stoll's former university classmate and assistant director, Manuel Zas.

Like 25 *Watts* and *Whisky*, *La perrera* (*The Dog Pound*, 2006) features both characters who have been beaten down by life and those trying to sidestep it altogether. Zas's chief protagonist, David, is a university drop-out who is spending the summer at his father's country home, ostensibly to oversee the building of another house. Too doped up and indolent to make any progress, he is the laughing stock of the locals – until he promises to bring a bus full of girls from the city to repay them for their labours.

It's a wry, tough film, with a good eye for the idiosyncrasies of human behaviour. Yet it's also a frustrating experience to watch this handsome young man letting life slip through his fingers. 'I like depressing environments. I like the bad side of life,' sighs Zas. 'I don't like happy things and beautiful things. They don't interest me. But I think this is a Uruguayan artistic sensibility, because in writing there are similar examples.' But do these artists reflect a national sensibility? 'In some way. Not the whole country is depressed. But the melancholy, yes the melancholy is all over Uruguay.'

He's a droll fellow, Zas, but passionate too. And he is one of the primary representatives of the cross-border liaisons with which Uruguayan film is involved. Zas has acted as assistant director on Lisandro Alonso's *Los muertos* and *Liverpool*, and on the first film to be made in Paraguay, Paz Encina's *Hamaca paraguaya* (*Paraguayan Hammock,* 2006); Fernando Epstein edited *Liverpool*; Daniel Hendler is a regular in Daniel Burman's films. Moving in the other direction, Hernán Musaluppi's Rizoma has just co-produced another Uruguayan film with Control Z, *Acné* (2007).

'Uruguayans are very much *South American*,' says César Charlone, 'because we're so small that we need to be South American. And because we're so small, we have a space in our mind to absorb other cultures. Uruguayans are very conscious of what's going on outside the country: they see lots of Argentine films in Uruguay, lots of Brazilian films.'

Born in 1958 in Montevideo, Charlone left Uruguay in the seventies to attend film school in São Paulo and, with news of the violent coup behind him, decided to stay. He remembers, though, being a member of a film club in Uruguay as a youth, imbued with the left-wing militancy of the time, watching Solanas films, eager to change the world. 'I still keep with me the accreditation of this cinematheque, which used the same high contrast as the famous Che Guevara portrait – a guy with a camera, which has a handle that looks like a machine gun. I keep it with me to remind me.'

While developing his career as a director of photography in Brazil, Charlone also directed documentaries with Uruguayan – and always political – subject matter.

I think I became a DoP more because I was a foreigner in Brazil than because I had a vocation for it. I didn't think I could direct films in a country that wasn't mine, because I [wasn't close to] subjects, or to money and production. I don't think I would have got grants to produce a film of my own, being a shy foreigner. [Hector] Babenco was a foreigner, of course, but he's not shy!

It was inevitable, he says, that when he came to direct a feature, it would be back home. And *El baño del Papa* (*The Pope's Toilet*, 2007), co-directed with Enrique Fernández, has a tough social subject befitting his origins and inclinations. A film of

*The Pope's Toilet* (2007)

great pathos and humanity, it relates the true story of the visit by John Paul II (the 'travelling Pope') to an impoverished border town in 1988. With the media promising thousands of visitors from Brazil, the eager locals go into hock for the food stalls that will make their fortunes. The film's flawed hero, the smuggler Beto, has his own shrewd idea: he will build them a top-quality loo. But, as anyone who saw *Elite Squad* will know, the Pope's visits to South America usually ended in tears.

Not surprisingly, the film is quite unlike other recent Uruguayan films, being made with a social-realist approach more familiar in Brazilian cinema. Cinematically and emotionally, one sees Salles rather than Meirelles in the mix: the pursuit of the smugglers over the Brazilian border by customs officers has some of the wind in the sails of Salles' road movies; the array of townsfolk talking directly to the camera, describing the wares they've bought and intend to sell, brings to mind the initial letter-writing sequence in *Central Station*.

Charlone himself declares:

It is a Uruguayan film, with Brazilian help. And the Brazilian help is what I have learned from the Brazilian sense of humour. The original, Uruguayan ending of the film is kind of melancholic. But I think it's a reality, a truth – this I learned on *City of God* – that people in that kind of adversity are in a way happier and gayer than we middle-class people. They have to find a way to be happy, even in the worst situations. So the optimistic and jokey part of the film comes from Brazil, from me.

Charlone recently brought production work to the country in a different way, by persuading Meirelles that the controllable, empty streets on which he wanted to shoot parts of *Blindness* could be found in Uruguay. 'I convinced Fernando that we should take a week of the film to Montevideo. And we had there all the Uruguayan crew who in one way or another had worked with Rebella and Stoll. Because it's a very small film community, it's one family that makes all the films.'

It's a powerful sentiment, echoed by Zas. 'I would not say there is a movement in Uruguay, or even a generation. However, I feel close to Pablo Stoll, because we are friends. And when I think of making a movie I think of friendship. It's crazy, but maybe this is our connection.'

# After Pinochet: Andrés Wood's *Machuca*

In 1973 the Chilean president Salvador Allende, the first avowed Marxist to win a free election, was overthrown in a violent coup by the CIA-backed General Augusto Pinochet. Pinochet oversaw one of the most murderous and repressive of the Latin American dictatorships, a seventeen-year period of darkness during which opposition parties were outlawed and it is estimated that more than three thousand people were killed for political reasons, and thirty thousand tortured. During this time, also, film production rapidly ground to a standstill. It was a difficult time to be an artist, or indeed anyone with a left-leaning point of view, and a number of Chilean directors numbered among the *desaparecidos*.

This was also when a number of directors, notably Miguel Littín and Raoul Ruiz, who were at the forefront of Chilean cinema's most exciting moment in the late sixties and early seventies, joined the thousands in exile. While Ruiz is now thought of as an essential part of the French art-house cinema, his work in Europe is sprinkled with intelligent commentaries on the experience of exile. Meanwhile, back home, cinema was dying. 'The dictatorship was never concerned with art,' Ruiz recalls today of the dictators who even burned the country's film archives. 'Pinochet said that art was for old ladies, homosexuals and Jews.'

Although Chile returned to democracy in 1990, it has been a long road back for the country's film-makers. The closure of film schools and withdrawal of state support for cinema under Pinochet, aspects of his philistine monetarist misadventure, were not quickly reversed.

One film that was made soon after the return to democracy, *La frontera*, by Ricardo Larraín, was an intelligent, careful

341

indictment of the military regime which used a bucolic satire about a mathematics teacher cast into internal exile in a sea-lashed backwater to convey the absurdity and malign pettiness of totalitarianism. The film won a number of awards, including the Silver Bear in Berlin and a Goya, and did well at the Chilean box office. But that was in 1991. There was no state-funded Chilean film industry to which Larraín, who had made *La frontera* as a Spanish co-production, could return in triumph to make more films; nor was there a guaranteed local audience for Chilean film. And it would be almost a decade before any semblance of either would be apparent.

Moreover, as the 'transition' period of the nineties progressed with no attempt to censure the wrongdoers of the dictatorship, Chile fell into a sort of impasse, psychologically and, arguably, artistically. Hated by many, loved by some who felt he had rescued the country from communism, Pinochet remained commander-in-chief for several years after he lost power, and had himself appointed a 'senator for life', immune from prosecution. When that immunity was finally stripped from him, alleged ill health saved him from facing the amassed charges of human-rights abuses and fraud. His death in 2006 has denied the country a sort of closure, perhaps for ever.

In keeping with this impasse, few film-makers returned to the dictatorship as a subject. Whereas contemporary directors in Argentina have a generation of *junta*-bashing films to rebel against, there is no such legacy in Chile today. It is as if Larraín and a few others made their films despite the prevailing lack of interest among Chileans in facing their history on screen. Tellingly, the country's biggest box-office hit since democracy has been *Sexo con amor* (*Sex with Love*, 2003), an inanely risqué sex comedy whose only political message might be the decline of sex education during the years of repression.

Nevertheless, the success of *Sexo con amor*, which broke the Chilean box-office record with 1.2 million tickets, and before that another comedy, *El chacotero sentimental* (*The Sentimental*

*Teaser*, 1999), did suggest that audiences were willing to return in numbers to Chilean films – albeit those whose primary ingredients were, let's say, *sexo con comedia*. At the same time a new film law was introduced that approved subsidies for production, promotion and foreign distribution, which have been steadily increasing in the 2000s – and with them the number of films made: the average of two a year in the nineties has risen to twelve in the 2000s, with an estimated twenty in 2008.

Then, in 2004, came a commercially minded film that dealt directly with that moment when democracy was lost in the country. Andrés Wood's *Machuca* was released in Chile just after Pinochet was stripped of his immunity, and just before the publication of a major report on the torture and detentions of his regime: it was the right moment, perhaps, for such a film to engage with the Chilean public.

Prelude to a coup: Andrés Wood's *Machuca* (2004)

*Machuca* marks a double watershed: here was a well-made, serious yet accessible film dealing directly with the coup which both touched Chilean audiences (with seven hundred thousand tickets it was the third most successful Chilean film ever) and gained international distribution: UK audiences, knowing of their own country's shameful collusion with Pinochet, were among those who welcomed an honest take on the man's dire legacy.

The film also won a clutch of film-festival prizes, both around Latin America (Bogotá, Lima, Mexico City and Chile's own, famous Viña del Mar, by then reinstated) as well as in the US, while in Europe it was selected for the Directors' Fortnight in Cannes.

Wood was a child at the time of the coup, and it is through a child's eyes that he recalls the tension, confusion and personal and political conflicts of ordinary people who had little idea what was in store for them. A boy, Gonzalo Infante, lives in a wealthy Santiago neighbourhood and attends an exclusive private school which, as part of Allende's liberal social experiment, has opened its doors to poor boys from a nearby shanty town. One of these is Pedro Machuca. The pair become friends. At home Gonzalo becomes acutely aware of the divisions between his socialist father and his materialist, self-centred mother; on the streets with Pedro, he experiences the political unrest, walking among demonstrators of both left and right as Allende's hold on power becomes ever more precarious.

This is an understated film, about what might have been, which evokes the period through a steady accumulation of detail: the chic seventies clothes marking the time, the closed grocery shops and bulging black-market warehouses the country's faltering economy, the graffiti slogans on the walls providing a running commentary on the political state of play.

While *Machuca* is concerned with bitter reality, it makes a conscious attempt, like *Central Station*, to open itself to audiences, with extremely polished production values and the softening prism of a child's perspective. Not that Wood doesn't pack a punch in *Machuca*. When the coup arrives and imposes the grimmest reality check on the children's adventure – when soldiers take over the school and destroy the slum, people die, and the hitherto jaunty soundtrack suddenly sounds terribly jaundiced – the result is heartbreaking.

*Santiago, 2007*

*You started as an economist?*

Yes, I worked as an economist for one year, in 1988, for the research part of a small company that had investments in different parts of Chile. I had to study golf courses, hotels and hot springs! I enjoyed it, but I was really living after work. I was trying a lot of new things – photography, going to films and taking very funny film classes.

*Why funny?*

Because they were very bad. Anyway, I quit my job. And a friend, a film-maker whom I've known for a long time, hired me to assist him on a documentary about Chilean wine. But he wanted me to be the producer, because I was an economist, and I wanted to learn directing, so we had a sort of difference. I thought, perhaps I should learn this away from here – away from Chile. So I went to the United States, and I got a job there, and I entered university in New York.

*You make it sound easy.*

Actually, it was very difficult. I was naive. I just applied for a graduate programme at NYU – it was the only application I did, because I wanted to go to New York – but I didn't have the money to do it, and I didn't have the scholarship. So I didn't enter the programme. But I managed to get a job, doing research on human rights in Chile, for Notre Dame University in Chicago. It was very important to me, to do that work. And it also gave me a lot of freedom. I could work on the computer from my apartment in New York, and at the same time I took classes in cinema studies at NYU, for free – so I attended their film course through the back door. I never took a degree, but in three years I covered the curriculum.

*Did those NYU courses cover the gamut?*

We did a lot of theory. I wanted to be a director of photography at first, so did a lot of photography courses. And I was the DoP for a lot of shorts for my friends in class. Then one moment I thought I'd try to direct my own short film. It was based on a short story, a love story, looking at the issues this couple faces from their different points of view. It has a couple of good sequences. Making the film was a revelation for me. I found it a sort of magic process, creating a fiction under lights. I was also amazed how the film had its own spirit. That was the first time I realised that. I'm talking about movies in general. You expose yourself in a way that is incredibly significant but, at the same time, the movie is not directly related to all the energies put into it, and all the talent. It has its own life. So it's a very risky medium.

With that first short I thought, 'I don't know if I'm good or bad at this, but I want to keep trying.' I stayed in New York for another six or seven months, trying to find a film job, while doing everything to pay the bills – selling ice creams, selling jewellery, doing camerawork for TV. But there came a moment when the spirit to direct was so strong that I thought, 'I don't need New York to do films. Let's go back.' That was the end of 1992.

*And how did you find Chile on your return?*

We were living with incredible change. Democracy had just been returned, but things were not going as fast as a lot of people wanted in terms of human rights, and Pinochet still had power in the army and the senate. So it was emotionally hard, there was still a lot of depression. On the other hand, we were doing incredibly well economically. Between 1985 and 1997 Chile had a growth rate over seven per cent per annum. We had the arrogance of being the 'tiger of Latin America'.

In film it wasn't good. Between 1974 and 1989 in Chile there had been just six, seven, eight feature films. Hardly any. There were a lot of small documentaries that were really brave, because they were dealing with the situation in Chile, as it was going on. There were a lot of brave people whom they didn't kill. But a film was really something if it came out. 'A Chilean film – what's that?' And there was a lot of censorship. The most important Chilean film-makers, for the world I would say, were exiles, outside the country. Raoul Ruiz, Patricio Guzmán, a lot of people.

Ruiz is a special figure, you know. He has made incredibly good, *Chilean* films: *Tres tristes tigres* [*Three Sad Tigers*, 1968] is a very important film, for example. Then, outside the country, *Diálogos de exiliados* [Dialogues of Exiles, 1975] was incredible, because in 1974 he was laughing about exiles, while being one of them. He's the most important film-maker here, even though he isn't here.

*It's an interesting way of describing him.*

He seems very free. And he has captured Chilean culture so profoundly, in a way that maybe no one has. So, after Pinochet left the presidency, there was a lot of political impetus for films to be made. Some of the exiles returned and they regrouped. There was an experiment called Cine Chile: a state bank would lend money for a package of ten films. That was around the time I moved back to Chile. But it was very short-lived. After just a couple of films the agreement between the political world and the film-makers fell apart. There was the hope that the state would help the film industry, but the problem is that the free-market economy is not very keen to do that.

It was very hard on those film-makers. Can you imagine being twenty years away from your country – dreaming about filming in Chile – and you return and it's not your country any more, they don't appreciate what you're doing? The press is absolutely on the right, and is against you. They want to know why you are talking about the past.

*So film-makers wanted to comment on the situation and the country they saw, but no one was interested?*

It wasn't that no one was interested, but that the movies didn't have the chance to attract people. In Chile we hadn't made films for almost twenty years. We lost our film tradition. People weren't used to Chilean movies. That's something very difficult to overcome. If you haven't seen English movies for a long time and suddenly you're hearing your language and seeing your streets, you may well say, 'I don't like that, I prefer to see San Francisco.' It wasn't possible to re-enter our own world, just like that.

*So even after Pinochet left power there was not an immediate return to Chilean film-making on any significant scale?*

No. And there was no young generation of film-makers who had been to film school. There was no film school in Chile. They closed it in 1974. Instead there was this new generation of people from different areas of life – I was an economist, my friend was a lawyer – who loved film, wanted to do film. And we got together making short films. And we created a very strong movement, an independent movement, of people who felt you could do it without money. And, in a way, we were against the old school. Of course, you always have to kill your father.

*Were you showing these shorts?*

Yes. In festivals, film clubs, we tried to put them on TV. And we were putting shorts in cinemas, before features. We also showed them in the Chilean film festival, Viña del Mar. The festival had been very important in the sixties, then stopped, then in 1991–2 it returned and was important again in terms of Latin America. There was an incredible spirit. Ironically, if you go there right now, it's dead. Because there's no money.

*Viña del Mar played a key part in that almost homogenous Latin American film movement in the sixties.*

Exactly. But it lost that strong identity, because Chile lost that. We were part of the soul of Latin America and we're not any more.

*Film-wise?*

In every way. The country. You can see what is happening in Latin America, politically, right now. But even though our president is a woman [Michelle Bachelet] whose father was killed by the dictatorship, she is absolutely to the right of Chávez and everyone else. The country moved to a place that I am not criticising easily. I'm saying it's the reality. Sometimes I'm proud of that, sometimes I'm ashamed of it. I feel that sometimes the government has been very brave not to be populist. I'm ashamed because our transition was so slow in terms of justice. There is still a lot of pain.

*Having those conflicted feelings is a good place to be as a film-maker.*

You're absolutely right. And I think sometimes our crisis in films is because we are not critical enough. I really believe in that comment by Lindsay Anderson, that if you want to be an artist you have to bite the hand that feeds you.

*But if it's likely to kill you, you might not want to do it.*

Of course. But as a film-maker in this kind of country you have more than the right to do it, you have the obligation.

*How did you progress from the shorts to your first feature,*
Football Stories?

I wanted to do a TV series of twelve chapters, with different
Latin American directors making stories about football. I love
football. In England I support Arsenal. I wasn't a great football
player, OK in midfield I guess. But I like to go to the stadium. It
is a democratic place. In countries like this sometimes you need
to go to the stadium and feel part of that circus. There is something deeply social there, which I love. In *Football Stories* someone says, 'In Chile we used to belong to political parties and now
we belong to football teams.'

Anyway, I thought it would be a nice idea to do something
about football and I started talking to the TV people here in
Chile. I would be a producer, and direct one of the stories. But I
realised that they were thinking of using big-name television
directors, and I would probably not do anything. So I said, 'OK,
forget it.' And I decided to do a film, made up of three different
shorts in a sense which are related by football and the country.
There was no money. We formed a cooperative – the actors,
crew, everyone did it for nothing. And we had no expectations.
It was very difficult to finish it – we started shooting at the end
of 1995, then in March 1997 a different part, and finished it in
June 1997. But we had a great time.

We had three prints. And there was no theatre that wanted to
show it, because Chilean film had pretty much disappeared at
that point. I took one of the copies to festivals and the other two
to cinemas in Santiago. I got the worst theatres. We opened it in
a theatre called 'The Kiss of Death' – every movie goes there to
die! It's a one-week theatre, but the film stayed there.

For me, the good thing about *Football Stories* was that other
film-makers were saying, 'If this guy can do this, I can do it.'
There was a sense, a realisation that it was much easier to do a
movie than people imagined; and that maybe people could and
should tell their neighbourhood stories, rather than formulaic

stories. I think it opened people's minds. I have had this conversation with a lot of Chilean film-makers, who say, 'I didn't like *Football Stories*, you know. But it made me think I could do a movie.'

*Is it correct that your wife urged you to relate your childhood experience in* Machuca?

Exactly. I had received a script treatment from a friend, set in 1978, during the dictatorship. I really liked the idea, and we talked about writing it together. But I found we had different points of view about the material. One day I got home depressed, and my wife said, 'Well, the story you should write is about your childhood, about the kids in those days, the story you have told me thousands of times.'

I attended a very similar school to the one I have depicted in the film. It was run by priests, led by the American priest, and the original pupils came from that same socio-economic class, that is to say upper class. And in 1970 they introduced kids from the shanty towns into the school. It was a very strange experiment for Chilean society, to create that kind of social mix, and on such a large scale. In my class fifteen out of forty kids were from the shanty towns – so one third from a completely different social background. But it ended with the coup, when the shanty towns were moved to the edge of the city. The military took the school, the priests were expelled, and an officer from the military became the principal. That was all true.

*Machuca* is not autobiographical. I wasn't in a riot in my life, I didn't see a killing, I was younger than the boy in the film – I was seven when the new kids first arrived. And there were two other scriptwriters [Roberto Brodsky, Mamoun Hassan], who brought their own perspectives. Nevertheless, it is a very personal film for me. I reconstructed everything through interviews with the American priest and with my former classmates. It was very touching, to speak with them again. It was therapy for me, because when you are very young there are a lot of things you don't realise – for example, about the reality of how other people are living.

*'Therapy' suggests you had something you needed to resolve.*

I'm a very melancholy person. I went to university in Chile, university in the United States, I have had a lot of friends all my life, but those days stayed with me. Making the film was a way of saying, 'This is why it stayed with me.' Not good or bad, but very particular to this country.

*What was your awareness of the coup at the time?*

I remember the coup, but I don't remember it as a political act. I remember all these armed men coming into the school, but it was a game for us. And I didn't have the experience of those people who knew someone who had disappeared – that's something that would quickly change your point of view. I did have this strange experience of having a good time in a strange country. And I tried to put that in the movie. All the fun of being kids and discovering kisses and play and friends and films and whatever – but in a strange country.

*What did this social experiment mean to you?*

I said it ended with the coup, but not abruptly. My class was a sort of island for this experiment – and six of the shanty kids stayed until the last year of high school. So I lived with that very particular reality till I was eighteen years old. I spent all my teenage years with these children. In that sense, you start living with another reality. And you start losing the fear of different people. You see that he is the same as yourself – although he's smarter, because he has to work all summer. For me, that's the thing: no fear. For my kids, and as a country, I would love to have a more socially mixed society.

'Like the point of view of an alien': the child's perspective, in *Machuca*

I have kept in touch with some students from my class. Three of them are engineers now, and a number of the others have good jobs. And if not, they still have a sophisticated way of seeing things. I believe this experiment was a real success, even though at the end it was very painful. And as far as I am concerned, I feel very lucky to have studied with people from different social backgrounds. Maybe that's natural in England or wherever, but not in Chile. For me, it was a life experience and I think I do films because of that experience. Politically it affected me also. My family is from the right, but I have never been on the right. I had a political conscience at thirteen, fourteen. And I jumped. I said, 'I don't belong here.'

*Machuca is about a particular period, the seventies, but I gather that divide between rich and poor still exists. Is the film commenting a little about Chile today?*

Of course this is a personal movie, about these two kids who meet, at that particular time. But I think the film does touch the present. The social issues, the gap between rich and poor, the opportunities for education, or lack of opportunities, are similar. We are a much richer country right now – kids in those days had no shoes. But the gap between rich and poor has remained, and maybe even increased.

And that was a point that came across very naturally. It was not that I was saying, 'I will talk about today.' It was there in the first script reading and the audience in Chile also read it like that. People were very touched. The discussion about the film here was social, as well as political. You might think that we had to do a lot to recreate the city, but when we shot in a shanty town we just did it, because they are the same, only in different areas.

*And why centre the film on the child's perspective?*

With a kid's subjective point of view you can include whatever you want and however you want – you can make a riot as strong or soft as you want, for example. It's like the point of view of an alien: you don't have obvious judgement, but you are judging, from a distance. And I like that.

*That kind of perspective is very interesting for this particular historical moment, because of the complexity of the situation leading up to the coup, with the different factions for and against Allende.*

Yes, it was very difficult to understand at the time. And that was another decision we made: at first we opened with a big scroll saying, 'In 1973 . . .' We even had some images of the Congress electing Allende. But we scrapped it. This movie doesn't need any explanation.

*You allowed that complexity just to exist.*

Yes.

*Watching the film, one does get the feeling that, after a certain point, the coup became inevitable.*

I really don't know if it was possible to avoid. I know it wasn't good. That's the only thing I can tell you. If Allende had been supported, who knows? It was a very complex situation. I don't know if it's very well portrayed in the movie, but I'm saying that, through the eyes of the kids, we are watching this adult world acting like kids. And the ones that really suffer are the innocents.

   For me the strongest part of the film is after the riot. We had a big discussion, because I showed the movie, and some said I should finish it when the kid is riding the bicycle after the destruction of the shanty town. And I said forget it, this is not an action movie, I need to say how it will be in the years to come, when the shanty town will have moved, the rich will have become richer, everyone will be different and people will say, 'That was a dream.' Even though a lot of people say I have three or four endings – well, sorry, I wanted to talk about that.

*Did you have to go to a lot of cost and effort to recreate the period?*

It was very difficult to find what we needed. We have big earthquakes here. Also we have a neo-liberal economics that doesn't care about the past, and just destroys the old buildings. So the city has changed a lot. We had to shoot with a lot of care. And we worked with a Job that did a lot of detailed stuff.

*So you didn't build new streets or anything.*

No, it was impossible. It wasn't part of the budget. I used the corners that I needed. I shot very carefully.

*Was it an emotional experience for the crew, recreating that period? During the riot scenes, or when the shanty town is destroyed?*

It was strange: we had a great time. It was very calm, because, in a sense, we were in the rhythm of the kids. There were some very touching sequences, and of course the riot was special. We fixed on the street that we were going to use, we had been shooting for four or five days there, we dressed everyone and everyone was joking – until we did the take. Then, after that, there was a sort of silence. As the director you are crazy, you're up against time, constantly moving on to the next set-up. But I could see that a lot of people were very emotionally involved in those scenes.

*You said that when you made* Machuca *audiences didn't want films about the coup or the dictatorship. Was it a risky project in that sense?*

I felt very secure that I wanted to do the movie, and insecure, of course, about the reaction, because as Chilean film-makers we were avoiding those years. I was so insecure, in fact, that the poster says, 'Dedicated to the kids of yesterday.' Because we thought that only the people who experienced those days would like the movie, and no one else would care. So we were really afraid. I remember the owner of the film lab, who was also a partner of the movie, said to me, 'OK, it's a good movie, but I don't think a lot of people will come to see it. So when will you do a movie that's audience-oriented?'

Of course, it has been a big success and a very important film here in Chile. And to me that was an enormous surprise. Writing, finding the money, making the film was a process of three years. Six months before *Machuca* was released we had the thirtieth anniversary of the coup. On television there was a lot of material I had never seen before. On the one hand, I was crying, because I had already done my movie and I hadn't seen those images and I was saying, 'Why didn't we shoot the movie there, or there?' On the other hand, I think I was lucky that the movie arrived just at that moment. It was the anniversary, and Pinochet was in England, and something changed. In a way, the country opened up.

*I've heard you refer to the Pinochet years as 'an open wound' in Chilean society. Presumably what we're talking about is a similar problem in the national psyche as, say, Germany experienced for several decades after the Second World War, when people simply didn't want to talk about or acknowledge what had happened.*

And not just in Germany. My mother-in-law was in France in the early seventies, and told me that they were still fighting over who helped the Nazis and who didn't. There is no way that in Chile we will get together and have a common story about what happened. My generation and older has to die before the country can recover from that. But it's very important in my opinion that we have to say, 'Well, look, it really hurts but it's part of our story – our mother is a prostitute, but let's accept it, it's our family.'

*Has* Machuca *helped to close the wound?*

It would have been very ambitious to think that a movie would help, it's not something that you can aim for or plan for in advance. But I really think that it did. There was a big discussion about the film from the beginning, in the film press then jumping to the editorial pages, about the political vision of the film, about the social differences still existing today. And there was a big catharsis. On a more personal level, half of the people from my school said I was a liar, the other half said it was absolutely the truth. I got a lot of emails.

In a way, *Machuca* put a marker down in terms of how Chilean films can deal with the coup. Of course, Guzmán's *Battle of Chile* is an incredible documentary; I'm not comparing my film with that. But in terms of fiction, I think that we achieved something that no one has up to now. I'm very proud of it. I'm waiting for another movie to go there, in the sense of making a personal movie that is important for the country, as a cathartic experience. The box office in Chile was very good: with thirty copies, we had almost seven hundred thousand admissions. The third-highest Chilean movie in history. The other two movies were sex comedies. They are good movies, but I want us to move on from that, of course.

Film-makers have dealt with the transition with a lot of fear, always thinking that the audience wouldn't want it. *Football Stories* did something for film-makers – it encouraged them to say, 'Let's do movies, who cares?' And *Machuca*, I think, has helped them to say, 'Let's do personal movies – who cares?'

*There is this very striking theme relating to the film-makers throughout the continent, particularly Argentina and Brazil, of having this still recent history to draw on for material – incredible material – but not wanting to use it. Argentine film-makers say that their predecessors made political films in the seventies and eighties and they don't want to do that. However, I think you are all making political films, simply ones that are not overtly political, but dressed as personal films.*

As I said, when you are young you are trying to *kill your father*. And you say, 'No, I want to do something else.' But the best films are often political, everywhere – the best English films are political – in the sense that they have a social relevance, they show a part of our society, maybe through one person, it doesn't matter. As a spectator I like personal stories. I don't want the big speech, I don't want a talking head, I don't like polemics. I want to enter through the heart. I like to be engaged, to love the characters, to see life, very simply – but all of that, in a social context. I think that all my movies are political, absolutely. Even *Football Stories*: I am talking about social classes, some parts of our culture, I choose some and not others, I am showing the country. It's political.

*How would you define the cinema scene in Chile today? A good time, bad?*

There are at least three generations of directors making films, which is incredible for Chile. There is a strong group of young people who have studied at film schools, and they *really* want to kill their fathers – they're killing me. They're doing good things, I'm proud of them, even though I don't care a lot about their themes; I'm not that old compared to them, but in spirit I'm older, I come from another generation.

In terms of the country, the public is more interested in Chilean films. Every year there is even a Chilean film that fights with an American blockbuster. Chilean films are here to stay. And I can't tell you how important that is.

# A second wave from Chile

*Santiago, 2007 – San Sebastián, 2008*

An emerging generation of twenty- and thirty-something film-makers in Chile represents one of the most distinctive strands of development on the continent. With ambition far outstripping their finances, many of these directors have embraced the digital revolution to tell their stories. Allied to this, while Latin American cinema has traditionally looked to Europe for inspiration, a number of these young Chileans seem to have imbibed the formal inventiveness and quirky spirit of US independent cinema. The result is a tone of film quite different to elsewhere on the continent.

It's tempting to compare the Chileans with their Argentine near-contemporaries. Like the Argentines, the Chileans have a dictatorship in their recent history, which they were born into but were too young to experience directly; like the Argentines, they profess a keen desire not to make overtly political films, but to deal with the here and now of Chilean society, particularly the day-to-day experience of young people. And like the Argentines, too, directors such as Pablo Larraín, Matías Bize and Alicia Scherson are essentially self-made – born not of a film tradition and an active, professional support system, but of go-it-alone, resourceful determination.

There are, however, significant differences, not least the fact that post-*junta* Argentina quickly re-energised its film industry, something Chile has been slow to do. And the absence of Chilean film schools until very recently has meant that the directors who are following Andrés Wood are, like him, seeking training outside the country, principally in Cuba and the United

360

States, before returning to a country whose film industry is still, even in South American terms, relatively impoverished.

Perhaps this is why the cheaper digital technology has been embraced more by Chilean directors than their neighbours. Matías Bize, young enough to have attended Chile's first dedicated film school, was just twenty-three when he made his debut, *Sábado* (*Saturday*, 2003), shooting with friends and a borrowed digital camera, in a single sixty-five-minute take, for the princely sum of €40 – which was simply the price of the mobile-phone cards used by the crew. Alicia Scherson speaks of how the discovery of a particular Argentine HD camera effectively paved the way, creatively and financially, for her award-winning debut, *Play* (2005). And it's significant that a number of these film-makers cite, among their influences, the UK director Mike Figgis and American Richard Linklater, indicating the degree to which they embrace, like those two experienced directors, the experimental as well as the budgetary possibilities offered by digital technology.

Bize particularly emulates Linklater – that is, the Linklater of *Before Sunset/Sunrise* romantic mode. *Sábado*, *En la cama* (*In Bed*, 2005) and *Lo bueno de llorar* (*About Crying*, 2006) each investigates a key relationship phase: respectively, a wedding in the process of being wrecked, a one-night stand that might turn into something more substantial, and – a flipside – a couple spending what could be their last evening together. The director obviously enjoys setting himself formal parameters, whether they be temporal, spatial (the whole of *En la cama* takes place in a single fixed set, the bedroom of a Santiago sex motel) or visual – for example, the fact of our watching the action in *Sábado* through a character's own camera, as he follows the warring bride and groom. Bize's adventurous nature has led none other than Raoul Ruiz, himself incorrigibly experimental – and now sporadically returning home to make his own digital films – to cite him as among his favourite young directors in his homeland.

An important difference between the two, however, certainly at this point, is subject matter: the younger man is unconcerned with the dazzling array of concerns – politics, art, literature, philosophy – that have engaged the veteran for his entire career. Bize says:

I want to tell stories about couples, about love, about things that could be happening to me and my friends. It's funny, *En la cama* is not what people outside our country would expect a Chilean movie to be – Pinochet, poor people, people with guns. It could be from any part of the world. And I think that could be said of many of the movies made by young Chileans today.

Francisca Schweitzer, who directed the similarly relationship-themed *Paréntesis* (*Time Off*, 2005) with Pablo Solis, concurs.

We were bored with Chilean cinema – folklore, poor people in poor places, drugs, crime. I wanted to show my world, where I work, where I live, to talk about my place in the world. The generation before us was a political generation. The new cinema is about emotions. Also, people in the United States and Europe have a caricature of what South Americans are like. But we are what we see, and we look at you: I identify more with your movies than with our movies.

So much so, in fact, that her film – about a video-store clerk who begrudgingly accepts a trial separation from his girlfriend, then finds he rather enjoys it – has blatant references to Kevin Smith's *Clerks* and Vincent Gallo's *Buffalo 66*; Schweitzer agrees that the hero's best buddy is a riff on Smith's classic creation, Silent Bob. Curiously, to us, but not that surprising given the continent's dearth of good comedy, Smith's slacker humour is replaced by Latin angst.

But Schweitzer's dogmatic point of view reflects only part of the picture, for other of her contemporaries are more akin to Andrés Wood, considering social as well as personal subjects. One devastatingly effective example of micro-budget digital cinema is Oscar Cárdenas's *La rabia* (*Rage*, 2006), which follows an unemployed secretary on a humiliating round of job interviews.

'Moved by an absolute lack of commitment': self-exile in Andrés Waissbluth's
*199 Tips to Be Happy* (2008)

Cárdenas's simple technique of throwing different women together in waiting rooms and corridors, their conversations alternately
friendly and competitive ('You have to be bilingual: if you don't
speak English, you're no one.') expresses the bitter underbelly of
the so-called 'Latin American tiger' with brutal efficiency.

Andrés Waissbluth, who like Alicia Scherson studied film in
Havana, has now made two films: while the first, *Los debutantes*
(2003), was a technically accomplished, but derivative and
slightly unsavoury crime thriller, the second, *199 recetas para ser
feliz* (*199 Tips to Be Happy*, 2008), comes as a mature addition
to the genre of Latin American films about exile.

Set in Barcelona, it plays on the surface as a steamy *ménage à
trois* involving a Chilean couple, Tomás and Helena, who have
relocated unhappily to Europe, and a mysterious young woman
claiming to be the girlfriend of Helena's dead brother. Yet bub-
bling beneath Tomás's sexual obsession and the drama it creates
is the couple's crippling ennui, a sense of uprootedness, of unfin-
ished business, of deep psychological trauma. It makes one think

of the lonely characters in the Santiago of *Paréntesis*, who talk wistfully of Europe but would probably be just as clueless if they moved there.

Waissbluth, who was raised in exile in Mexico, suggests:

The film explores the deep sensation of loss that is characteristic of my generation. Behind the characters' conflicts are subjects like the loss of identity, and a disorientation so intense that it drives one to perplexity. These are essential to understanding the way our generation lives.

I think the film renews the notion of exile, which for the generation of our parents was linked to political commitment and conflict, and which for my generation is reinterpreted as a form of self-exile, moved by an absolute lack of commitment of any kind. In that way, the life of thousands of young Chilean people in Barcelona offers a unique mirror of the unrest of this generation. What makes them choose to go somewhere else? As if happiness is, necessarily, somewhere else.

Four years after *Machuca*, Pablo Larraín has returned to that period of enforced exile under the dictatorship. Larraín's second film, *Tony Manero* (2008), is founded on an extraordinary conceit. Set in 1979, it follows an illiterate, brutal sociopath who dreams of emulating his American hero, the eponymous disco dancer played by John Travolta in *Saturday Night Fever* (which played in Santiago for eight months in 1978–9, to six hundred thousand people). The weasel-like Raúl operates his own little dance troupe on the outskirts of the city: while he obsesses about finding glass blocks for his dance floor and winning a TV impersonation contest, his dancers are risking their lives covertly campaigning against the regime.

It's a savage, darkly comic film which Larraín says was made to reflect the moment when 'the new Chile began': in thrall to First World culture, 'driven by a massive communication tool, which is cinema', and imposed largely by the US.

In 1976 Pinochet hired a few young people who were studying at Chicago University, with all these new capitalist systems that they were learning over there with Milton Friedman, and he put these Chicago Boys into the government. So Chile became an open-market economy

© Tomas Dittborn

Dancing around the dictatorship: the Travolta wannabe of
*Tony Manero* (2008)

and, when he did that, a lot of things changed socially. We began to import a lot of stuff, cultural and economic. And that's what the film is about. The Pinochet regime did enormous damage to our folk traditions. Pinochet was very ignorant. He probably never watched cinema in his life. He certainly didn't care about it.

This observation seems entirely accurate, not least when viewed alongside Francisca Schweitzer's earlier comment about looking at films other than those of her own culture, and considering the influence of American directors on many of Larraín's fellow film-makers.

*Tony Manero* is a step on a faltering path, from *La frontera* in the nineties, via *Machuca*, to Chile finally laying to rest the dictatorship nightmare. 'You know, no one has done a film about Pinochet himself,' observes Larraín.

You have to remember that the Germans took fifty years to make *Downfall.*\* You have to stay away from it, for a while. But someday someone is going to make a film about Pinochet. We'll face it: we'll look at him, close-up. How long do we need to get there? I don't know.

Alicia Scherson offers an interesting amalgam of the competing inclinations among contemporary Chilean directors. On the surface, *Play* belongs in that school of intimate relationship stories, told via an inventive use of digital technology (and a narrative style and aesthetic that reflects this director's keen interest in video art); below the surface, she investigates such intrinsic themes as Chile's rural/urban divide, and the identity issues that arise from yet another South American country residing on the subjugation of its indigenous community. It's a rich brew, which the gifted writer/director pulls off with a lightness of touch and a penchant for the enigmatic that do justice to her title.

*Play* concerns two central characters who are poles apart in their experience: Cristina (Viviana Herrera), a young Mapuche woman from the south of the country, working in Santiago as a private nurse, without friends, spending her spare time in video-game arcades or walking the streets of the city; and Tristán (Andrés Ulloa), an affluent middle-class local, distraught and anchorless after a recent break-up. After Tristán is mugged, Cristina finds his abandoned briefcase: puffing on his cigarettes (she doesn't smoke) and listening to his iPod, she starts to draw vicariously on his life; then, tracking him down, she follows Tristán through Santiago, observing him just as he is trying to reinvent himself.

Though Scherson claims such disparate inspirations as a curiosity about garbage collectors and the loss of a wallet (and consequent musing as to what would be gleaned about her by

\**Der Untergang* (*Downfall*, 2004). Directed by Oliver Hirschbiegel.

the thief), she admits that the Italian proverb with which she opens *Play* – 'The times were hard, but they were modern' – signals her wider intent.

It's an acknowledgement that I would try to understand Chile. I think it's much harder for Latin Americans to understand Latin America, than it is for Europeans to understand Europe, because of the *mestizo*, the mix of blood, and what that means – which is that we don't, truly, belong to any culture. That has to be the main issue of reflection for us citizens of Latin America. For me it is an important issue, and it has to do with progress, with pain, and also with identity.

As opposed to the English colonies, in Spanish ones there was a lot of blood mix with the Indians. In my case I probably have Ukrainian Jewish, Italian, Spanish and Mapuche blood. Most people here have mixed heritage. But the Indian population itself is small now and, after all the discrimination and violence against them, they sometimes are like outsiders in their own land, like Cristina.

This is one reason, alongside a desire to follow her characters around a little-known Santiago, why she fashioned her heroine as a sort of detective. 'If you want to be a detective you have to be invisible. And, of course, the Indian people are sort of invisible to us, in the city.'

In 2005 Scherson won the best new narrative film-maker award at Robert De Niro's Tribeca Film Festival, with *Play* opening in Chile later that year and in Europe over 2006–7. Although there is a discernible strain of old-school US indie sensibility in *Play* – her interest and approach to marginal figures evoking Jim Jarmusch, her arch dialogue and unexpected physical moments (a sudden kiss, the drop of a head into a lap, the absurd mugging) early Hal Hartley – she also cites the Argentines Martín Rejtman and Lucrecia Martel as favourite directors.

I feel a very strong connection with the New Argentine Cinema, particularly their model of making movies, from the production point of view. They made movies in the middle of their financial crisis, and they made cheap movies, and they were great. They had this attitude that I

Alicia Scherson captured top prize at New York's Tribeca film festival, with *Play* (2005)

call *modest*, in a good way: they didn't want to make the big movie of the year, in commercial terms, nor even in terms of the artistic challenge; they made these little movies that were very specific and precise, like *La ciénaga*. And for me that was very inspiring.

They suggested this idea of how to face movie-making in a way that is possible for our reality, for our money, our time. I think the great gift that the New Argentine Cinema gave to us was this idea that independent film is possible from South America. We knew indie from Sundance, for example, but we thought we couldn't do it. It's interesting, they don't do it in Spain either. I have friends in Spain and I say to them, 'Why don't you just make a movie?' But they don't have that mindset, that understanding that you don't need to wait until you have €2 million to make a movie. There are other ways.

In the meantime, these Chilean film-makers daring to cover important subjects, or daring to tell their relationship stories in an experimental, cinematic way outside the mainstream, share the South American experience of struggling for local audiences. *Machuca* is a contemporary exception: compared to its audience figures of seven hundred thousand, Larraín and Bize – both of whom profess themselves happy with the results – achieved below a hundred thousand. At once forced and willing to look outward, the directors of what I regard as the 'second wave' of new Latin American cinema are, like their Argentine precursors, increasingly adept at mining the co-production potential that a festival prize or two opens up. And with co-production usually comes a guaranteed distribution in that country.

They also share that ability for marvellous improvisation. Larraín made his $700,000 movie in a slightly different fashion from that outlined above: pre-selling it to Chilean TV and borrowing cameras and a student crew from his old film school. When he decided he wanted to shoot not on the cheaper digital, but on Super 16, he shopped for film in Canada: noting that in that country it is illegal to sell film less than three months before its expiration date, Larraín snapped up the ageing product, finding the rough quality exactly what he wanted for his recreation of seventies Santiago.

'In a way we are approaching a door that the Argentines passed through in the nineties,' he says.

We're making more international films all the time. And they're very diverse, which I love, people are making genre films – comedies, horror films, social-realist films. And the more we travel with our films to festivals and see other films that we don't usually get to see in Chile, the more we learn and the more we will understand that we have to make films for the world. We have to export our films.

What that means is that we have to make films about our reality, our traditions, our customs – you must always shoot for a Chilean audience, first, otherwise you will not have a connection with them – but, at the same time, they have to be somehow universal.

Larraín refuses to complain about the dominance of Hollywood products in local cinemas.

There's something Andrés Wood told me once, which is very nice and very smart: that without those American films, without that industry that fills all these cinemas, we probably wouldn't have a space to show our films. Because we don't have an industry. Maybe we could all get together to have one or two cinemas, you know. But there are three hundred in Chile, and that is because of the Americans.

It's a contradiction, of course. Because we have to fight for space. *Tony Manero* is now in cinemas, and tomorrow they are releasing *WALL-E* and we are going to be kicked out. But this is the reality. If you want to make an artistic, experimental film, or a festival film, just do it and release your film on one print as Lisandro Alonso does in Argentina. He's happy. He doesn't care. And if you want to make popular films, you'd better make a good film, so people will go to see it. This is the competition. This is the way it is. No one's going to change it. *Harry Potter* will always be here.

# Peruvian tales

Peru does not have as powerful a film tradition as some of its neighbours, and its current industry is a small one. However, two directors, Josué Méndez and Claudia Llosa, have recently burst onto the Latin American film scene with films that not only signal precocious talents, but also offer a compelling snapshot of a troubled country.

One could argue that Méndez and Llosa provide a 'town and country' survey of Peru: his *Días de Santiago* (*Days of Santiago*, 2004) and *Dioses* (2008) giving two very different accounts of life in Lima – between working-class life on the streets, and the upper middle classes isolated in their glass apartments and beach houses; her *Madeinusa* (2006) an unsettling account of twisted religiosity in an Andean village, imagined, yet rooted in reality.

As with many of the younger directors in Chile, the Peruvians, without a dedicated film school in their own country, have found film training abroad. Gianfranco Quattrini (whose *Chicha tu madre* was discussed in the chapter 'Football stories') lived and trained in Argentina, Méndez at Yale, Llosa in Madrid. It's interesting that they should then return home to find their subjects, not least when the mechanisms for making film in Peru are so scant: at present the film body Conacine awards a total of around half a million dollars a year to no more than four films. Méndez's debut, which did not receive any Peruvian state funding, went on to win thirty-five international prizes, becoming the most lauded film in Peru's history; as ever, one wonders who exactly is operating these funds.

Yet these directors do return, employing the customary beg, borrow and co-production approach that is working for a lot of their fellow South Americans. *Chicha tu madre* was co-produced with Daniel Burman's BD Cine in Argentina (which enabled that country's funding body, INCAA, to be involved); Llosa had a Spanish producer (and the cash from a script-writing prize); Méndez, having had to borrow the money for his first, found Conacine more accommodating second time around, allied to German and Argentine co-producers.

As Méndez suggests below, an obvious reason for making their films on home soil is that an artist often follows the subject or culture he or she knows best. At the same time, these subjects are so very rich. Méndez and Llosa were both born in 1976: as they were growing up, the country moved from dictatorship to democracy, was embroiled in more than a decade of internal violence with guerilla groups – the Maoist rebels Sendero Luminoso ('The Shining Path') and the Cuban-inspired Tupac Amaru Revolutionary Movement – which accounts for an estimated seventy thousand deaths, waged war with Ecuador and experienced an increase in drug trafficking. All the while the majority of its indigenous population has continued to live in abject poverty.

Méndez's films are the more overtly political. *Days of Santiago* follows its eponymous twenty-something ex-soldier, struggling to carve out a new life for himself in a city that has no respect for its war heroes, while despairing at the brutish behaviour of his father and brother, and suffering terrible guilt over the atrocities he committed on his country's behalf. Méndez's handheld camera rarely leaves Santiago's shoulder, first as he strides attitudinally around downtown Lima, holding back the regular temptation to beat some respect into those around him, then in his taxi, earning the money for the education he desperately wants. Meanwhile, one of his old war buddies, an amputee, kills himself, while others have other ideas about how to make the city take notice.

With Santiago (a frighteningly intense but also sympathetic performance by stage actor Pietro Sibille) breathing contempt behind the wheel of his cab, one obviously thinks of Scorsese's *Taxi Driver*: the film's protagonist is, like Vietnam vet Travis

Bickle, part victim, part potential nemesis of a corrupted society. Shot in just twenty-three days, this is a powerful and troubling film.

While *Days of Santiago* often flits into black and white (usually to signal Santiago's most isolated and enraged moments), *Dioses'* photography and locations evoke Hockney's colour-saturated LA swimming pools. For this is the world of the Lima über-rich, whose money separates them from those bitter realities of downtown, the wives filling their empty heads with Bible class, gossip and plants (they know the Latin name for a house-plant, but probably not the name of their political representative), their spoilt children high on drugs, sleeping with each other indiscriminately, heedless of the consequences. So morally reprehensible are these people that an incest theme is actually unnecessary.

The underclass of *Days of Santiago* is still in evidence here, in the form of the servants without whom these pampered monsters would barely be able to get out of bed; but while the film emotionally works in their favour, Méndez's portrait is of a society compliant on both sides of the social divide. Its 'gods' are much more frightening than the earlier film's anchorless killers.

On the surface, Llosa's *Madeinusa* may seem the closest that contemporary Latin film-makers, so intent on *vérité*, get to magic realism. Yet even proximity to that hoary form is a trick of the light: nothing happens in this strange film that could not, conceivably, take place in a material world governed, in no small part, by hypocrisy; its fantastical tone is a triumphant meeting of imagination and anthropology.

The story takes place in a remote Andean village whose fervently religious inhabitants have an unusual spin on the Easter festivity: during their *tiempo santo*, Holy Time, God is deemed to be dead, allowing one and all to sin with impunity before He revives on Easter Sunday. Unhappily for local girl Madeinusa (Magaly Solier), her loathsome father – the mayor of the town – intends to use his 'get out of jail free card' to take her virginity.

Madeinusa's is a dismal, impoverished life: lusted after by Dad, hated by her jealous sister, Chale, her days taken up by such onerous domestic tasks as killing rats and plucking the lice from her sister's hair. Being chosen to portray the Immaculate Virgin in the *tiempo santo* parade is just the latest ironic trick that life is playing on her. But then Salvador, a young Lima man stranded in the town on his way to another village and immediately attracted to the girl, offers an escape.

The film plays on a number of levels: as a culture clash of old and new, as a western in which the stranger shakes up the locals, as a Buñuelian satire, as a spin on the British horror film *The Wicker Man*. It is also a piquant reversal of the traveller's idyll: finding a town where the road ends. Being all of these things, to varying degrees, *Madeinusa* can only seem wholly original – ravishingly shot, troubling, and sinister.

I met the two directors as they accompanied their films on the festival circuit: Llosa in Rio de Janeiro, Mendéz in San Sebastián.

# Claudia Llosa

*Rio de Janeiro, 2006*

*It's quite rare to see a Peruvian film in a festival.*

It's true. It's very difficult to work in cinema in Peru. There are very few directors who can work constantly. There is a long history of film-making in my country, but the communication between generations is non-existent. So everyone thinks they are the Adam or Eve of film-making in Peru. It might not be the reality, but that's the sensation – of starting over.

*You didn't study film at first.*

I studied science of communications, at the University of Lima, from 1994 till 1998. It was very general. Film is a part of it, but you don't come out with the feeling that you know anything about it. Then I worked for three years in advertising, as a creative copywriter. I was the only woman in my agency. It was a pretty big company, I could do a lot of work and had a lot of responsibility very quickly. It was fun. But something was missing. So I just told my family and my boss that I was going to Madrid to study scriptwriting.

*Specifically scriptwriting?*

Yes, I really wanted to be a scriptwriter. My experience in life was always writing, even though I'm dyslexic – I always have people who correct my writing for me.

*And you're related to Mario Vargas Llosa.*

My father is a second-generation cousin of the author. Actually, my influence comes from my mother, who is an artist. She started with painting, then, many years ago, began working with video art and installation. And she was the art director on *Madeinusa*. When I made *Madeinusa* I didn't have any experience as a director, I needed to find my own way. And I think I drew from her way of working as I had seen it, all my life, from video art, the process of narrative in film-making.

*In terms of conceptualising the work?*

Yes. Though it's hard to be specific about the influence. It's like trying to understand how being Peruvian or even being a woman influences me. It's obvious and obtuse, and has too many layers for me to peel. But it's easy to recognise that as the daughter of an artist, it is much easier to gather information and to access a certain kind of prism through which to look at life than it is as the daughter of somebody who doesn't appreciate art at all.

*Why Madrid?*

Because I wanted to learn scriptwriting in my language. I wanted to feel free to write. But also I wanted to go out of Latin America. I wanted a different culture. I wanted to go to Europe, really. I travelled a lot. And I spent a whole year rebuilding myself.

At that point I felt so far away from film-making. It was like trying to be an astronaut, you know. When I was young everything was difficult in Peru. Actually, I think my generation needed to run, to leave the past, to start over again, and to start thinking that things could happen for them.

*When did your thinking move towards directing?*

I finished the course in Madrid, and went to Barcelona, because I wanted to stay in Europe. Actually, I started doing creative copywriting once again, for a year, while I started to write *Madeinusa*. At that point only my mother was reading my stuff. When I finished, I sent the script to the Havana Film Festival. And I won the original feature script prize. The prize came with sponsorship from Canal Plus, $125,000, so a pretty big start for the film. It was amazing for me.

So I got this prize, with two years to start shooting – and with no history in cinema, no experience at all. I didn't know one person who worked in film. The manager at Canal Plus told me I needed to get a co-production. Meanwhile, I started rebuilding the script. And I applied and was accepted to the Sundance scriptwriters' lab. As well as helping you with your script, the lab helps raise the profile of the project, putting you in touch with producers.

Then a friend of mine in Peru told me about Antonio Chavarrías, the Spanish producer. I called him in Madrid and sent him the script. He was the first one to actually read it before he met me. He sat with me and said, 'I'm interested, and I will help you raise the money, but only if you direct it.' He told me that it was such a personal script, and such a personal way of seeing the world, that for him letting someone else direct it would be wrong. 'Directing is easy,' he said. 'Don't worry.' My God, I remembered that shit when I was shooting!

He also suggested that I go on a course. So I used the money I won as a scriptwriter and I went to a New York University summer course. But it was nothing – one month, fixed camera. I couldn't learn anything, really. At the end of that I moved to Peru and started working, working, working.

*How useful was the Sundance lab?*

Very. It was interesting primarily because of one thing. At Sundance they are very careful not to make their own movies: they work for you. That's quite rare. The teachers – scriptwriters, with one producer – were American, Mexican, Spanish. They didn't know Peru. And they were very smart about not questioning the content, the culture. Instead they focused their work with me on the structure. And for me that was good. I did three more drafts of the script, but did not change the content.

*What gave you the idea for* Madeinusa?

How can I start? The story is invented. Everything is fiction: the festival, all the rituals that you see are invention. But at the same time, everything is inspired by reality. I've travelled all my life all around the country, going to different villages and all kinds of festivities; not as a tourist, because these are not tourist places, but as a spectator, a viewer, as a child.

*Presumably a lot of these villages are inaccessible.*

It depends on the area. In terms of getting to them – yes, often very difficult. There are a lot of places where no car can go, and you have to walk for two days. Also, there are areas that are very friendly, and areas that are less so.

© Evelyng Marino-Reyna

Culture clash, Peruvian style: Claudia Llosa's *Madeinusa* (2006)

*When one goes up to the mountains, both in South America and Central America, you discover these indigenous communities where you feel like you're stepping back in time.*

And for me it was about understanding the difference between Lima and the other Peru, the contradictions between Spanish and Quechua, between European thinking and native South American thinking. It's a divided country. Two ways of being.

If you are a little girl in Lima and you want to visit your grandmother, you will have a shower, your mother combs your hair, and you're going to walk with her or take a cab or a car and go and visit your grandmother. That is the same all over the world. But if you're a little girl in the Andes and your mother says, 'Go and visit your grandmother,' you are going to go into the mountain range and maybe walk for two or three hours. On the way, you fall and hurt your knee. And you have to forget that you are crying and keep on walking. You could be three years old. Even in that simple experience, you can imagine how differently a child can grow up.

I'm not talking about the cultural differences, or linguistic, just the basic differences, physical and psychological. They are huge. If I asked my little niece to sing, she would sing songs about bubbles in the sky, *la-la-la*. And when you go into the mountains and you ask a child to sing for you, she's going to sing, 'Why do you leave me? I'm dying with the snakes. I'm alone and I'm sad and I'm going to kill myself.' And that's what makes it really difficult to cast somebody from the city to portray somebody from the Andes. There is no such actor that can nail it, in my opinion.

*Then there's her name, of course. Any chance that it's a coincidence is dashed when we see the Made in USA label on Salvador's T-shirt. It seems that, as for Madeinusa's mother before her, the US – through those magazines and Hollywood stars – represents escape.*

It has to do with miscegenation, and transculturation, how identities are in constant transformation, influenced by others and by their past and present. It's another way of talking about the cultural divide. To me, those with less power have much more capacity to immerse themselves in the 'other' influence, while keeping their own. And the other, the more powerful, is incapable of accepting the differences; there is always more condescension.

By the way, Madeinusa is actually a proper name in Peru. There are lots of other great examples: Usanavi, Jhonfkenedi, Marlonbrando. It's disconcerting, but fascinating.

*You were considering these themes from a distance, from Spain.*

That's right. I was in a new country, I was 'resetting' myself. But I've always had this kind of reflection: what are we, what do we really want to be, need to be? Thinking about this very difficult frontier between instinct and desire, and necessity. And I wanted to think about what would happen if there's no state, no Big

Brother looking over you, telling you how to act. It is then that surprising things happen. But I didn't want to make this a political movie, I wanted it to be more of a psychological movie, so I moved away from the idea about the government and started to focus on beliefs.

*You said it's an invention, but what about this strange mixture of Catholicism and paganism?*

Of course that does exist. Maybe there is no such a thing as a contest for a virgin, but you can find things such as the Niño Manuelito, a foetus that has been turned into a saint. People bring it toys – his altar is made of toys. The family has developed the belief that this Niño can make your miracle come true. But if you talk to the mother, my grandmother's age, she's still crying for the loss of this miscarried child that is now a saint.

Actually, we have a figure that resembles the Niño Manuelito in the film, following the virgin Madeinusa in the holy procession. We called him El Santo Sastre, the tailor saint. This icon is invented for the film. We thought it was really important to accompany the virgin, because in life she never goes alone in a ritual. But we used an ancient story about an Indian tailor who was never accepted as a saint by the church, because of his origins. We thought it would be nice to recognise his miracles and give him the chance to become a saint. Better in fiction than never.

There are also festivals, like Paucartambo, where men can dress as women. At the end of the festivity the mayor is still the mayor, no one will say anything. You can see something similar in carnivals, with these cathartic rituals that help society to experience something new, maybe repressed, for a certain period of time, and then return to normal as if nothing has happened. That same effect is what we show in *el tiempo santo*.

*Where did you shoot* Madeinusa?

In a town in Huaraz province, 3,500 metres above sea level. It's a beautiful place, not so well known. But we changed everything – the clothes, even the bridal gowns – to make the viewer feel that we were not talking about a specific area of Peru. If there was a sign giving away the location, we didn't shoot it.

I wanted to create this whole new universe. The town's name in the film is Manayaycuna, which is Quechua, and its Spanish translation means something like 'village that you should never enter'. Richcane, the village where Salvador wanted to go, means 'you will never get there'. In a way, I wanted to wink at the audience. If Salvador knew a little Quechua, maybe he would never have stopped in that little lost village.

*It's all very strange.*

There's more. When the terrorism got worse and worse in Peru, and lots of people were disappearing, the people in these rural communities invented a kind of white monster that eats you. If you talk to people from these areas, they would insist that these monsters exist. They are intelligent people, some have been to university. But somehow fiction has managed to create this tunnel with reality. And that's what I'm into. I wanted people in the audience to feel like they were in a playground where you think, 'No, this can't be true.' And then you start to believe in it.

*The* tiempo santo *is the background to the story, but the focus is this very dysfunctional family and Madeinusa's desire to escape it, to follow her absent mother. There is an incredible intensity to it, which is best summed up when her sister Chale maliciously cuts off her hair.*

Hair is a thing of life, of fertility. That's why the Indians always grow it so long. That's why it is so horrifying for Madeinusa when her sister cuts it off. The hair represents your ancestry, what you're going to be, your fertility. It's your renewal, your force. There's a comparison with Samson, but it's much stronger for a woman to cut her sister's hair like that.

*Then Salvador offers a way out, by offering to take her to Lima.*

Freedom is a thing that every human being is looking for, the perfect freedom. And that is never going to happen. For Madeinusa, Lima represents that and the mother represents that.

*So the ending is no resolution for her?*

You never know. It's a weird image at the end, that look in her eyes. She's so innocent, but she has also grown up. You don't know if she's feeling bad or perfect. But I think she's going to make it.

*I don't see it myself, but it has been suggested that the film is in the magic-realist tradition.*

I don't see it either. More than one time I have found myself explaining the difference between *Madeinusa* and magic realism. Magic realism is based on hyperbole: 'The girl cried till the room was full of tears and she drowned in her pain.' This kind of exaggeration does not exist in my film. In *Madeinusa*, for good or ill, everything that is shown could be true. You can never find babies with a pigtail, as in Macondo.* But I understand why people make this kind of association, because there is a big gap in the film between what common sense expects from reality and this reality itself. Magic realism sometimes is the nearest device to help you accept that gap.

*Conversely, would you say that you wanted there to be a sort of documentary feel to the film?*

*Macondo is the name of the town in Gabriel García Márquez's *One Hundred Years of Solitude*.

I needed to gain the viewers' trust, and so to create a truthful environment that is only afforded by documentaries. Nowadays people understand movies perhaps too much; in fact, sometimes they are watching an actor's performance, and not the character of the story. I wanted to get rid of that over-awareness. It's not always possible though.

*The choice of non-actors can help. Were yours all non-actors?*

Yes. I wanted to use non-actors, because I needed to believe in my own movie. I found them in different places, as I was looking for my locations. For *Madeinusa* we invited people in advertisements and on the radio. A lot of girls came, we looked at maybe a thousand. It's very difficult to find somebody who really has it, but Magaly Solier is amazing. She's from a little village in Huanta, which was at the epicentre of the terrorism in Peru. That's a big, big thing for a Peruvian to experience, you know. She's very talented and brought a lot of intelligence to the film. Everyone who does an interview with her falls in love. And I think that helped the movie when it opened.

*How old was she when you shot the film?*

Seventeen. She finished school at sixteen and was selling food in the street. Now she's studying opera, she's studying piano, she is studying to go to university. And she's going to work in my next movie. And she's still very down to earth.

*You shot the film on HD. Had your cinematographer, Raúl Perez Ureta, worked with digital before?*

No, this was the first time. And he was suffering a lot because of it. He was so sure that if he was working with film, the material would be much, much better. He was always saying, 'If we had 35 . . .' But we talked a lot with the laboratory during the process, and they applauded our work. They told us it was one of the most beautiful registers they had seen with HD up to then. Actually, I feel that in *Madeinusa* the cinematography is totally connected with the art direction; the content really helps the image.

*I think it looks extraordinary. What cameras did you use?*

Panasonic. Typical ones. But with Digi-prime lenses, which means you are not using the lens from the camera but very expensive film lenses. Totally different. You get what you pay for.

*Which directors have inspired you?*

I have a lot of influences, a lot of directors I love. But I didn't approach anyone whom I wanted to emulate. It's more instinctive. I start really with Buñuel. My obsession with film started with him. *Viridiana* [1961] is one of my favourite movies. I love also Arturo Ripstein. Bergman. And then I have newer discoveries: Catherine Breillat, Zhang Yimou – I think *The Road Home* [1999] has a lot of connection with our Peruvian mountains – Béla Tarr, Carlos Reygadas.

*Actually,* Madeinusa *reminds me of Reygadas's work. In* Japón *there's the idea of the outsider who comes from the city and is at odds with the local community and its austere way of life. And* Battle in Heaven *deals with negative aspects of religion.**

I think we employ a different tone, but there is a connection thematically. I love his films, and *Japón* particularly. The way he tries to talk about the unconscious of the country, things that are difficult to voice, because they are so hard to accept. What Reygadas is saying is difficult to hear for Mexicans. And that's why I feel so attached to his work: he's putting himself on the line.

*\*Japón* (2002), *Batalla en el cielo* (*Battle in Heaven*, 2005).

*You are doing something similar: reminding Peruvians, in the cities at least, that there is another Peru they would rather ignore.*

It is a difficult movie for Peruvians, because they are used to Hollywood films. And they are not used to looking at themselves. They don't like it. The paternalism in Peru is very strong and conservative. You have to show what is real. They didn't like me inventing things. So a lot of people were saying, 'How come this film is the Peruvian nomination for the Oscars?' But there were also a lot of people who liked the originality, who thought it was an important film.

What was very interesting was that the distribution company said we were going to have success only in the A/B cinemas, because it was an art-house film. In fact, we did much better with theatres in the suburbs, and with lower-budget families. The theatres there were packed. It proves to me that these kinds of people are willing to see challenging films, with things maybe you don't want to hear, about religion and family life. But I think what really shocked them was Magaly Solier. She was the image of Cinderella: the poor Indian girl who is now an actress.

## Josué Méndez

*San Sebastián, 2008*

*What gave you the idea for* Days of Santiago?

The film is my reaction against the city. I studied in the US, came back to Lima, and I felt the city was so hostile to young people. That was in 1998, when the war with Ecuador had just finished, and I started seeing all the young war veterans returning, also, to Lima. Obviously we were different, but I felt completely related to them. All these kids my age, twenty, twenty-one, with nothing to do, they couldn't get jobs, the government did not care about them. Many of them were amputees.

I had already started to interview war veterans when I met Santiago, who was the brother of my old nanny. He was definitely fucked up. The psychology of the character is completely based on this guy. So the film tells the story of the war veteran, but it's also the story of all young people feeling bad in the city. The city is very oppressive in the film.

*Is society's inability to reintegrate these young soldiers still a problem?*

Yes. And it's really been a problem in the analysis. We had a commission of truth and reconciliation a few years ago. They reviewed the last twenty years of violence and they came up with numbers for everything: how many peasants were killed by the military, how many by the Shining Path, numbers for everyone except the war veterans. It is a void in our social sciences. At one point, between 1995 and 1998, the military were fighting against everybody: Ecuador, Shining Path, drug traffickers. So these kids were sent everywhere, to kill everybody. It was really tough. But they're forgotten.

*I like the street quality of the film. Santiago does a lot of walking, so we see the city from that perspective.*

I grew up in the terrorist time, in the eighties, and when I was a kid you couldn't really walk around downtown Lima. It was really dangerous, with bombs and whatever. When I came back from the States, Lima was peaceful. So my return was also a time of discovery for me, of my own city, which I never knew.

*And why did you return to Peru?*

When you go to the US, you think you are going to stay in the US, because that's where the industry is. But when I finished there, it was very clear to me the sort of films that I wanted to make at that moment. And it would be tough to make them

Portrait of a corrupted society: Josué Méndez's *Days of Santiago*

there. When you make independent films you have to be really honest with yourself, and really know what you're talking about. Personally, I don't understand the Americans, I don't know what they're thinking about. For me, they're completely crazy. But I understand Peruvians, that's my culture, what I think I can talk about.

Of course, it's not easy. There's no real industry in Peru. There are a lot of directors, but very few who make one film, fewer who make two. When applying for grants, you are competing against another forty projects. When I applied for *Days of Santiago*, they obviously didn't think it was a good idea to give a twenty-three-year-old $150,000. I managed to raise $20,000 and we shot the film just with that, with theatre actors.

Then we won Hubert Bals funding for post production. I had no money when I finished. When I went to the Rotterdam Film Festival, I didn't have a single dollar in the bank. Hubert Bals also gave us money to distribute the film in Peru, because in Peru there are no distributors who put their money into Peruvian films. It's all American distribution, and two small companies which distribute art films from Europe. You have to finance distribution yourself – the marketing, the prints, everything. And of

387

course there are problems with exhibitors. You have to beg them to keep your film in the cinemas.

*How many tickets did the film sell?*

We did fifty thousand, which is standard for a Peruvian film. That was in ten screens. You have to bear in mind that there are two hundred screens in Lima: if a Spiderman film came out, it would be in a hundred of those.

*Dioses is another social strand altogether. What kind of background are you from?*

My parents are engineers, but my father did pretty well I am an only child, and he was able to put me in a private school. My schoolfriends' families all own mines and banks. My father doesn't own anything, but that's the school I went to, so I know a lot of these kids. Whenever I went to a schoolfriend's birthday party it would be at the beach house. The idea's been in my head my whole life that I wanted to do something about them.

*The film is extremely critical of this class.*

They are my friends, but they are pampered, ignorant. They never talk about social issues. Whenever I've tried to discuss the government or whatever, they say, 'Come on, man, don't get too serious, drink up.' They have never been to downtown Lima. The shanty town I show in the film – I'm sure none of my schoolfriends has ever gone there.

*Nevertheless, you make their world incredibly seductive.*

The point for me was to show the very beautiful, clean facade of a world that is also sordid, fucked up. Everything works perfectly, everyone assumes a role – and it's all wrong. It's funny, when you interview the maids they all feel so fortunate to work in these places, even though they don't make much money at all, and often are not even allowed to go into the sea. They are happy, they have completely conformed.

*Do the lower classes go to the cinema in Peru?*

In Lima, yes. But the really poor are not in Lima, they are in the provinces, where fifty per cent of Peru's population live on less than a dollar a day.

*In both films, family life is not seen as positive.*

Well, drama always starts with the family: it's society under one roof. Both the families in my films reflect what I think about my society, which is that it's fucked up. It's a society where no one really listens to each other, everybody has his own agenda, we are ignorant of the person next to us.

*What next?*

There is something very interesting happening in Peru now. It feels like something is cooking in the country, beyond the Shining Path, beyond the other problems of the past. You see, Peru as a nation doesn't really exist. You have the Andean people, the Amazonian people, you have the people in Lima. But there's no Peruvian nation, it's like different nations, different countries really. Ours is very different to European society, where everything has already been kind of worked out. In Peru nothing has been worked out yet. García Márquez used to say that we're living in the Middle Ages here. But what's happening now in Lima is that everything is starting to mix up, culturally, in a way that has never happened before.

We call it *chica* culture. *Chica* is a beverage. But now everything that's *chica* is everything that's mixed. We have *chica* music that plays Andean rhythms on electric guitars – people of my background, who used to hate popular Andean music, now we embrace it. We have a *chica* culture in terms of clothing, arts.

And I think as a subject it's very interesting, maybe more than dictators, more than terrorism.

*Why is it happening now?*

Migration to Lima, definitely. Also, before, four or five families with money determined the taste, what was cool. That's changing. Now the masses in Lima, who have more money than before, are determining what's cool, what's nice, what's good, the music that you listen to on the radio, the TV shows you watch. For example, when I was growing up all the Peruvian soap operas were made with white actors. For the last five or six years they are done with *mestizo* casts. Recently, they made a soap opera with white actors, and nobody watched it. So now what's being portrayed as Peruvian – on the television, in ads, in music – is changing. I would like to address that, in some way. I'm fascinated by it.

# Cannes, 2008

Ten years after *Central Station* triumphed at the Berlin Film Festival, the 2008 Cannes festival was heralded as one in which the South Americans were showing in force. It was no longer the case that a lone Brazilian of an international bent, namely Salles, or a maverick Argentine such as Trapero would be making a solo appearance at a film festival. All in all there were twenty-one Latin American films in different selections on La Croisette, prompting Fernando Meirelles to tell *Variety*: 'I believe the wave is finally shaping up and showing its size.'

Salles and Meirelles, Trapero and Martel were all in the prestigious Official competition, with Meirelles' *Blindness* opening the festival; Lisandro Alonso was featured in the edgy Directors' Fortnight, as was the Chilean Pablo Larraín; while the still relatively unknown Argentine Pablo Fendrik was in the section aimed at first- and second-film directors, Critics' Week. As is likely with any collection of films, and predictably, given the hype and Cannes' infamous capriciousness, the ultimate responses were mixed. But that Martel got a roasting and none of them won the Palme d'Or was immaterial. More significant was the expectation: for what may have been an oddity in Berlin in 1998, or when *City of God* stormed La Croisette in 2002, now seemed like the casual appearance of a permanent force in world cinema.

Cannes offered an opportunity, then, to reflect on the South American cinema renaissance that now involved three generations of directors and, to differing degrees, virtually every country on the continent. Had the Brazilian big guns decamped to Hollywood? Had the freshness that had made *Mundo grúa* and *La niña santa* so exhilarating been replaced by rote? Had Lisandro Alonso made a romantic comedy?

The first thing that needs to be said about Salles and Meirelles is that they have shown themselves to be remarkably consistent: as directors, conducting careers that neatly bridge the local and the international; as producers, continuing to nurture Brazilian talent. It's tempting to regard Salles as the custodian of Brazil's film heritage, and both men as the unofficial ambassadors for their country's cinema.

Salles' *Linha de passe* is a return to the ongoing project (sometimes solo, sometimes, as here, with Daniela Thomas) of throwing light on the social problems that are prevalent for Brazilians. Following the trials and tribulations of four brothers struggling to survive, let alone realise their dreams, in São Paulo, the film is a sterling slice of social realism, imbued with a slow-burning, powerful poignancy. And by casting Vinícius de Oliveira, the young shoe-shine boy he discovered for *Central Station*, Salles reminds us that in the right hands adopting non-actors is anything but affectation.

Behind the scenes, he was operating on all fronts: producing his countryman Sérgio Machado's second film with his company VideoFilmes, and giving coveted first opportunities to others; co-producing his friend Trapero's Cannes entry, *Leonera*, thereby maintaining the fragile but imperative continental network that he has done so much to nurture; and looking to the next stage of his international career, his adaptation of *On the Road*. In essence, the new project, just as *The Motorcycle Diaries*, will represent everything that Salles is best at: it will be a road movie that investigates what makes a man, and a nation, tick.

Meirelles' dystopian satire, *Blindness*, has equally strong Latin credentials, despite the Hollywood stamp of stars Julianne Moore, Mark Ruffalo and Danny Glover: Meirelles shot the film in São Paulo, again used his Uruguayan cameraman César Charlone and Brazilian editor Daniel Rezende, and included in the cast the Mexican Gael García Bernal and the actress he introduced in *City of God*, Alice Braga. With him, as with Salles, the customary dynamic of a Third World director moving onto the international stage – of ideas and talent being merely appropriated by the studios – has to be revised. The exchange is not one-way: Meirelles is bringing business to South America and exporting his skilled collaborators to the mainstream.

Based on the novel by Portuguese writer José Saramago, this is a drama with a chilling premise: when an epidemic of blindness sweeps the world, the military locks the afflicted up, leaving them to cope, sightlessly, for themselves. Director and cameraman do a fabulously discomforting job of capturing the anarchy and degradation that ensues, playing with our own senses by flitting between near-darkness and the strangely milky blindness of those afflicted. Sadly, the gratingly sardonic script (by the Canadian Don McKellar) never quite engages with the allegory, or its audience. Nevertheless, if *Blindness* is Meirelles' least successfully realised film, it is an intriguing failure.

As he was completing *Blindness*, Meirelles the producer was juggling publicity for the last of his *favela* projects, *City of Men*. While he has stated the desire to move on from this particular sort of social-issue movie, his interests have not strayed from Brazil. In 2008, O2 Filmes had a heavy slate of projects directed by local film-makers, and the director himself swore me to secrecy over a project with a political nature which suggests that the last thing he plans to do is turn his back on his country.

Back on La Croisette, the answer was, of course, no: Alonso did not make a rom-com, or a musical, or anything in which a great deal would be expected to happen. *Liverpool* is the same again, triumphantly so – another journey home (a sailor hops ashore in southern Argentina's Tierra del Fuego, venturing into the snowy wilderness to see if his estranged mother is still alive), another loner's confrontation with nature and another exercise in prolonged non-communication. But in a scenario in which 'nothing happens' – we watch as the man eats, guzzles from an illicit bottle of spirits and trudges through the snow; when he finds his mother, and an unexpected daughter, he can barely say anything to either – so much loneliness and misery is conveyed

Trapero's *Lion's Den* competed for the coveted Palme d'Or

that surface banality seems the work of inspired genius. As the protagonist walks away from the camera and into the landscape, back the way he came, surprisingly leaving his story in other hands, the director had a packed graveyard screening gripped.

I eyed Trapero and his producer/star (and wife) Martina Gusman strolling happily along La Croisette, perhaps the most glamorous film couple the continent possesses, enjoying competition acclaim for *Leonera* (*Lion's Den*). The director's assured and original take on the prison drama – one that continues his predilection for strong stories informed by social issues – has an outstanding performance by Gusman as a woman accused of murder who gives birth in confinement, then fights for the right to have her child remain with her.

Two scenes show a hugely confident director at the top of his game: the introduction of the women's cell block – a majestic, waist-high tracking shot that presents not the usual array of gnarled jailbaits, but a roll call of babes in arms (and a few pregnant stomachs) – and the customary riot scene, which is not only transformed by the fact that the rioters are women, but lent a

Pablo Fendrik's *Blood Appears*

surreal quality by its framing and the strange undulation of the
action. I would love to see the Argentine follow Salles and
Meirelles for the occasional sojourn in Hollywood, not because
he needs a US studio, but because American cinema needs him.

Meanwhile, fellow Argentine Pablo Fendrik confirmed the
promise of his *opera prima*, *El asaltante*, with *La sangre brota*
(*Blood Appears*). This is an uncompromisingly ill-natured
thriller, in which there is no focal crime, no dry and dusted vil-
lain, only the enigmatic city wanderings of a fragmenting family
of misanthropes. The handling of narrative and actors (including, again, the supreme Arturo Goetz) is first-rate, leaving me to
wish someone would do the decent thing and distribute both of
Fendrik's films in Europe and the US.

Fendrik's rendition of family life as a nefarious pursuit ought
to appeal to his countrywoman Lucrecia Martel, whose *La
mujer sin cabeza* (*The Headless Woman*) includes within its
complex weave her own, particular doubts on the family unit.
Though underestimated in Cannes, *The Headless Woman* is
Martel's most challenging film to date and, I'm sure, will be

recognised as a great one. Moreover, the support here of producer Agustín Almodóvar (and, in spirit, of his brother Pedro), her
renowned champions, was apt. Martel is cut from the same cloth
as the Spanish director, and has everything it takes to emulate his
long career as one of the most stylish and provocative icono-
clasts of the international art house.

But along with Trapero's film and, for the hard core who gathered for it, Alonso's, the Latin movie that most excited here was
*Tony Manero*. Larraín's film is at once dazzling and disturbing.
It's a shame that the Pinochet-era drama is perhaps too dark for a
commercial release; nevertheless, its ingenuity and twisted
humour – its central conceit, of a John Travolta wannabe murdering to further his disco career while death squads roam the city, is
satirically brilliant – would succeed easily in an art-house run.

Elsewhere in Cannes, in the hotels and the marketplace of Le
Palais, South American cinema was making its presence felt,
from Rio's Conspiração Filmes pursuing negotiations on seventeen co-productions with companies across South America,
Europe and the US, to representatives from the Venezuelan film
agency being the very last to leave the market on its closing day,
to Argentina's film institute, INCAA, announcing its plans to
increase its own Espacio INCAA cinema circuit from seventeen
screens to a hundred in a bid to bolster the exhibition of home-
grown films.

That latter move underlines what is the continuing, perhaps
dominant struggle for these film-makers: the battle for their own
audiences. Argentina produces sixty or seventy films a year, yet
few break even. It's a problem that the Latin Americans of an
artistic bent share with their fellow film-makers all over the
world. In Cannes, of course, they can all take heart from the
French, who have successfully battled against American hegemony in cinemas. And what Cannes 2008 suggested was that the
producers and directors – aided by an extraordinary array of
actors, and increasingly supported by their state systems – are
determined to do battle. When I met with Juan Carlos Losada,

the president of Venezuela's state film funder, CNAC, he told me of the strict distribution and exhibition rules the country had established, including one that compelled the country's cinemas to show Venezuelan films for at least three weeks. The result, this year, was that of the top ten films at the box office, three were Venezuelan.

Cannes was not and would not be the only showcase of the year: *Elite Squad* won the Golden Bear in Berlin; Daniel Burman's new film, *El nido vacio* (*Empty Nest*), would win prizes in San Sebastián, as would the breezy romantic comedy *Amorosa soledad* (*Lovely Loneliness*), whose newcomers Martín Carranza and Victoria Galardi tapped a nice blend of Gallic flightiness and New York neurotic on a Buenos Aires shopping street; the same actress who essays Diane Keatonesque ditziness in that film, the startling Inés Efron, touched audiences all over the world as a transsexual in *XXY* (which proved to be one of the most popular foreign-language releases of the year in the UK); and in Thessaloniki Celina Murga won the best director prize for her second feature, the hugely impressive *Una semana solos*. An enviable year for Murga included selection by the Rolex Mentor and Protégé Arts Initiative* for a seven-week, personal masterclass in the company of Martin Scorsese.

When I was in Buenos Aires in 2007, a young film-festival programmer, quite possibly still at school when *Mundo grúa* was setting the inaugural BAFICI alight and a little baffled by the discussion about the 'future' of New Argentine Cinema, said to me, 'I'm glad we can just talk, now, about *Argentine cinema*. It doesn't have to be "new" any more.'

This was not a weary comment, rather a positive sentiment, one that is applicable to the whole continent. I, myself, think there is one more 'new wave' to come: I'm keen to see what

*Founded in 2002, the Rolex Mentor and Protégé Arts Initiative pairs talented young artists with renowned figures in their discipline for a year of collaboration. Other South American directors to have taken part have been Josué Méndez and Federico León.

Venezuela and Colombia will produce in the next few years. It is only a matter of time (and in Venezuela it's imminent) before the directors in those countries start to ally the powerful subject matter of their recent histories with original cinematic expression.

Then, with these countries throwing their weight behind Latin American co-productions and viable distribution agreements – helping to take the financial pressure off the auteurs of this prodigiously gifted continent of film-makers – we can dispense with the 'new', stop being surprised at every great film that emerges from South America, and eagerly anticipate the next.

Lisandro Alonso, on the set of *Liverpool*

# Postscript

At the turn of the decade, I can't help feeling that a tide is turning, away from Hollywood and towards international cinema. I'm not talking about a Richter-busting revolution in audience habits, more a reality check about where the genuine creative forces in cinema actually lie.

It was partly a question of quality – the best of 2009 film lists in newspapers and magazines had a notable dearth of US titles. But this was accompanied by the feeling, certainly amongst UK critics, that the hegemony of English language films in supposedly international awards ceremonies – with the rest of the world hemmed into the 'best foreign language' category – needed to be challenged. Writers were tired of championing films with the assumption that they would, however good, remain on the margins.

In this context, the acceptance of South American cinema in the top echelon of world cinema, which I argued for when I completed this book last year, seems timely. Incidentally, when *Sight & Sound* opened 2010 with its '30 Key Films of the Last Decade', that list included two Latin American films: the Mexican Carlos Reygadas's *Battle in Heaven*, and Lucrecia Martel's *The Holy Girl*.

The past twelve months have seen a continuation of the renaissance that I've described – not with another *City of God* assault, but quietly, and on different fronts.

In Berlin 2009, the Peruvian Claudia Llosa continued the Latin love-affair with that festival, by winning the Golden Bear for her second film, *La teta asustada* (*The Milk of Sorrow*). The film stars Llosa's discovery from *Madeinusa*, Magaly Solier, as another superstitious Andean girl, nurtured to be a shy loner by her mother, who bore the girl after being raped during the years of terrorism and 'transmitted her fear' – through her breast milk, no less – to her child.

It's as strange as *Madeinusa*, then, with the added dimension of the girl's attempt to interact in the more grounded world of the capital, Lima. And it proves that the impressive sensibility of the first film was no flash in the pan. For a young director, from a country with a tiny industry, to win one of the biggest film prizes in the world was a massive achievement.

It was good to see a rare Colombian film at the London Film Festival, and a good one at that. Ciro Guerra's *The Wind Journeys*, a fable about a legendary accordion player on the road, with a boy desperate to imbibe his magic, is handsomely shot and well-acted. It also features some stirring musical set pieces, which had a packed London audience on the edge of their seats.

One of my personal favourites of the year also has one of the best titles of any year: *Viajo porque preciso, volto porque te amo* (*I Travel Because I Have to, I Come Back Because I Love You*).

Directed by the Brazilians Karim Ainouz and Marcelo Gomes, the film brilliantly investigates that border between fiction and documentary, discussed so often in these pages. Ainouz and Gomes have performed a telling act of alchemy: taking hours of travelogue footage, they have used an invented narrative voice-over and expert editing to invest it with a fictional life; then, inversely, this fictional construct – a road trip in which a geologist contemplates his love–hate relationship with the north-east of the country – becomes the device by which a documentary eye is cast on Brazil and its people.

Indeed, one would be hard pushed to see a more vital document about the *sertão*. With its constant movement between the real and the imagined, the film echoes the seminal *Iracema* from the seventies. As such, it offers another fine example of Brazilian directors who touch base with their past, while striking a path into the future. Ainouz and Gomes rightly won the directing prize at the Rio festival.

Making waves wherever it played last year was *La nana* (*The Maid*), by Chilean Sebastián Silva. This fabulous film posits the idea that 'hell hath no fury' like a family maid who thinks she's being scorned – and who will do anything to see off the younger competition. Like a number of the film-makers featured here, Silva throws a light on the unfortunate prevalence of domestic service in Latin America; he has particular fun with the subject, though, steering a sly course between psycho-thriller, black comedy and sympathetic social drama. As the maid in question, Catalina Saavedra gives one of the most complex performances I've seen in a long time.

*The Maid* will have a UK release in 2010, when it will accompany three Argentine films into cinemas: Lucrecia Martel's *The Headless Woman*, which received five-star reviews and a record attendance for its London screenings; Trapero's *Lion's Den*; and *El secreto de sus ojos* (*The Secret in Their Eyes*), a mature, involving thriller by Juan José Campanella, which has been a box office hit at home and reminds one of the potential of the mainstream in that country.

When *The Secret in Their Eyes* opens here, it will be as an Oscar winner, Campanella's film having staved off stiff competition to win the award for best foreign language film. This year's contenders also included *The Milk of Sorrow* – South America, therefore, providing two of the five nominations. That is fantastic news. But one does wonder if being nominated, even winning as the best foreign language film is now enough.

I can't help thinking back to 2004, when *City of God* received four Oscar nominations – for directing, writing, cinematography and editing – yet, somehow, was not deemed worthy of a nod at the top of the card, for best film. Perhaps it's time for events that expect global television audiences to break down such barriers. For the resurgent South America cinema, such acknowledgement would be richly deserved.

London, March 2010

# Bibliography

## Books

Linda Badley, R. Barton Palmer and Steven Jay Schneider (eds.), *Traditions in World Cinema*, Edinburgh University Press, 2006

Alberto Elena and Marina Díaz López (eds.), *The Cinema of Latin America*, Wallflower Press, 2003

Tamara L. Falicov, *The Cinematic Tango: Contemporary Argentine Film*, Wallflower Press, 2007

Ernesto Guevara, *The Motorcycle Diaries: A Journey Around South America*, Verso, 1995

Stephen M. Hart, *A Companion to Latin American Film*, Tamesis Books, 2004

John King, *Magical Reels: A History of Cinema in Latin America*, Verso, 2000

Paulo Lins, *City of God*, Bloomsbury, 2006

Lúcia Nagib (ed.), *The New Brazilian Cinema*, I. B. Taurus, 2003

Lúcia Nagib, *Brazil on Screen: Cinema Novo, New Cinema, Utopia*, I. B. Taurus, 2007

Nikos Savvatis (ed.), *Cinema em Transe*, Thessaloniki International Film Festival, 2006

Deborah Shaw, *Contemporary Cinema of Latin America: Ten Key Films*, Continuum, 2003

Elsa R. P. Vieira (ed.), *City of God in Several Voices: Brazilian Social Cinema as Action*, Critical, Cultural and Communications Press, 2005

## Selected Articles

Marcelo Cajueiro, 'What's Cookin' on the Croisette', *Variety*, 16 May 2008

Mike Goodridge, 'Focus Latin America: Talking 'Bout a Revolution', *Screen International*, 17 September 2004

Quíntin, 'Uma experiência única', Indielisboa Film Festival programme, 2005

Peter Stephan Jungk, 'An Interview with Walter Salles', Projections 12, Faber and Faber, 2002

# Acknowledgments

I would like to thank all the featured interviewees of the book, whose collaboration extended way beyond our taped conversations; the supremely patient Walter Donohue and Kate Ward at Faber; Geoff Andrew, James Bell, Kieron Corless, Jason Wood, Adriana Rouanet, Sandra Tabares, Mariana Cunha, Anamaria Boschi, Don Ranvaud, Bianca Tal, Richard Kelly, Geoffrey Macnab, Oscar Cárdenas Navarro, Pablo Stoll, Fernando Epstein, Ana Luiza Beraba, Eloísa Solaas, Leandro Listorti, Ilse Hughan, Veronica Cura, Maria Nuñez, Maria Carlota Bruno, Agustina Llambi Campbell, Eduardo Leon, Natasha Slowik, Milena Guerini, Nelson Lafraia, Bárbara Francisco, Cecilia Sosa, Fernanda Giminez, Patricia Barbieri, Will Clarke, Anna Godas, Ed Orlebar, Fiona Ncill and Anne Dixey; the press office staff at the Cannes, Berlin, Thessaloniki, Rio de Janeiro and Bafici film festivals, and the festival team at Premier PR; Mar Diestro-Dópido and Emily Prince for some life-saving translations.

Special thanks to Eduardo Escorel, Ariel Rotter and Rodrigo de la Serna, whose conversations I wish I could have included in the book, and to the film-makers and industry administrators from Colombia and Venezuela, who gave me their time and their movies, and whose work I'm sure I will write about in the future.

Last, but not least, my enormous gratitude to Walter Salles and Maria Delgado, whose undimmed enthusiasm, inspiration and guidance kept me on the road.

## Images

The images in this book are reproduced courtesy of: VideoFilmes, O2 Filmes, Regina Filmes, Zazen Produções, Tata

Amaral, Gullane Filmes, Conspiração Filmes, Film4, Matanza Cine, BD Cine, Rizoma Films, Lita Stantic Producciones, K&S Films, Patagonik Film Group, Albertina Carri, Lucrecia Martel, AquaFilms, El Deseo, Slot Machine, Teodora Films, R&C Produzione, Celina Murga, Lisandro Alonso, Ariel Rotter, Magma Cine, Andrés Wood, Fabula Productions, La Ventura Producciones, Retaguardia Films, Claudia Llosa, Chullachaki Producciones.

# Index

Page numbers in **bold** refer to illustrations

407